YO-BRM-843

THE LAST HOURS OF JESUS

Fr. Ralph Gorman, C.P.

The LAST HOURS *of* JESUS

From Gethsemane to Golgotha

SOPHIA INSTITUTE PRESS
Manchester, New Hampshire

Copyright © 2017 by Sophia Institute Press

The Last Hours of Jesus was formerly published by Sheed and Ward, New York, in 1960. This 2017 edition by Sophia Institute Press includes minor editorial revisions.

Printed in the United States of America. All rights reserved.

Cover design by Coronation Media.

On the cover: *Altarretabel von San Zeno in Verona* (1459), by Andrea Mantegna; image courtesy of Wikimedia Commons.

Scripture citations are taken from the Confraternity Version of the Bible.

No part of this book may be reproduced, stored in a retrieval system, or transmitted in any form, or by any means, electronic, mechanical, photocopying, or otherwise, without the prior written permission of the publisher, except by a reviewer, who may quote brief passages in a review.

Nihil obstat: Richard Kugelman, C.P., S.T.L., S.S.L.
Imprimi potest: V. Rev. Canisius Hazlett, C.P.
Nihil obstat: John R. Ready, *Censor Librorum*, November 22, 1959
Imprimatur: Robert F. Joyce, Bishop of Burlington, November 23, 1959

Sophia Institute Press
Box 5284, Manchester, NH 03108
1-800-888-9344

www.SophiaInstitute.com

Sophia Institute Press® is a registered trademark of Sophia Institute.

Library of Congress Cataloging-in-Publication Data

Names: Gorman, Ralph, author.
Title: The last hours of Jesus : from Gethsemane to Golgotha / Fr. Ralph Gorman, C.P.
Description: Manchester, New Hampshire : Sophia Institute Press, 2018. Originally published: New York : Sheed & Ward, 1960. Includes bibliographical references.
Identifiers: LCCN 2017044646 ISBN 9781622824700 (pbk. : alk. paper)
Subjects: LCSH: Jesus Christ—Biography—Passion Week.
Classification: LCC BT431.3 .G67 2018 DDC 232.96—dc23 LC record available at https://lccn.loc.gov/2017044646

CONTENTS

AFTER CHRIST'S DEATH

PREFACE

I have not written this book for Scripture scholars, who have the same access as I have to sources of information on the Passion of Jesus Christ. I have directed it to nonspecialists who would like a fuller treatment of the Passion than is found in the great lives of Christ, such as those by Lagrange, Prat, Lebreton, Fillion, and Ricciotti. I have used their works, of course, as well as the best commentaries on the Gospels and various treatises on aspects of the Passion in English, Latin, French, German, and Italian. It has been my effort to tell the story of the last hours of Jesus accurately and in a manner interesting and intelligible to the ordinary reader. The description of some scenes may appear fictionized but is based on information concerning the period, places, and persons involved.

The four Gospels are the main source for the history of the Passion. New Testament quotations are from the Confraternity edition and are used with the permission of the Confraternity of Christian Doctrine. Background information is provided by the Mishnah and by early historians. For archeological data, I have used freely the lectures and writings of Père Vincent, greatest of all Palestinian archeologists and my former professor at the

École Biblique in Jerusalem, where it was my privilege to do postgraduate studies for three years.

I wish to express my gratitude to my friends and fellow religious, Fathers Richard Kugelman, C.P.; Hilary Sweeney, C.P.; and Barnabas Aherne, C.P., for valuable and constructive criticism. Special thanks are due Miss Claire Foy, editorial assistant of the *Sign*, for typing the manuscript and for many helpful suggestions.

THE LAST HOURS OF JESUS

PROLOGUE

Chapter 1

THE BACKGROUND

The story of Jesus' last hours properly begins at the Garden of Gethsemane. Here begins His Passion, in that frightful agony wherein the God-Man almost seemed to have been rejected by His Father even as He was neglected by His sleeping Apostles.

And here, too, strengthened at the end of His agony, Jesus confronts His enemies, the antagonists in the tragic yet soaring drama of His suffering and death: the religious leaders of His Chosen People and Judas Iscariot, one of his chosen Twelve, who had betrayed Him for a price.

How could such a thing come to pass? How could anyone harm a man who traveled around the country with a few poor disciples, teaching about the Kingdom of God, working wonders in healing the sick, proclaiming a doctrine of love of God and neighbor? How could such a man be betrayed by one of His closest followers, arrested like a thief in the night, condemned by the highest court of the Jews, condemned again and sentenced to death on the cross by the highest Roman authority?

That mystery needs some explanation. To understand how such a thing could happen, it is necessary to know something of the ideas and institutions of the Jews at the time of Christ, and especially to understand two Jewish sects, the Sadducees and the Pharisees. It is also necessary, against this background, to probe the psychology of Judas, that enigma of perfidy.

The military threat from their neighbors was not the only menace to the Jews during several centuries before the birth of Christ. Pagan Greek culture and philosophy threatened to destroy the monotheistic religion of the Chosen People. Hellenizing influences pressed in upon them from all sides. The Sadducees and Pharisees owed their origins in large measure to the varied reaction to this threat.

The Pharisees reacted strongly against the pagan influences and clung tenaciously to the Mosaic Law. As the name itself indicates in Aramaic, the language of Palestine at that time, the Pharisees were "separatists." This may have been a nickname given them by others. They called themselves "Haberim" (comrades), or "the pious." They were called "separatists" because they kept themselves apart from anything that might render them legally impure, even the "people of the land" who were "impure" because they found it impossible to observe all the legal purifications practiced by the Pharisees.

The Pharisees were probably the descendants of the Assideans, mentioned at the time of the Maccabees. They were a religious rather than a political party, and their religion was strongly nationalistic. We have little information on their organization, but it is likely that candidates passed through a period of trial before becoming full-fledged members.

At the very heart of the party were the Scribes, although it is a mistake to identify Scribes and Pharisees. There were Scribes who were Sadducees. For the most part, however, the Scribes were Pharisees trained in the knowledge of the Law and its application.

In fact, the most important characteristic of the Pharisees was their claim to know the Law better than anyone else, their rigor in practicing it, and their determination to impose it on others. They emphasized three points of the Law in particular: observance of the Sabbath, legal purifications, and the payment of tithes to Levites and priests.

By the time of Christ, the Pharisaical Scribes had developed an extremely complex and detailed oral law that, theoretically, expounded and applied the Torah. This mass of legal tradition was declared to be as binding as the Torah itself. Finally, a point was reached where it was considered more blameworthy to teach contrary to the precepts of the Scribes than contrary to the Law of Moses. The observance of the dictates of the Scribes became an end in itself, to which all other moral and religious considerations were secondary. Toward the close of the second century after Christ, the rabbis began to consign the teaching of the Scribes to writing, in works that developed into the Jerusalem and Babylonian Talmuds. A cursory reading of the Talmuds reveals the casuistic hair-splitting of the Scribes, as well as the complicated mesh of man-made traditions and observances in which they entangled their followers. Nevertheless, it was the knowledge and observance of these legal minutiae that constituted the perfection to which the Pharisees aspired.

It must be conceded, in favor of the Pharisees, that in spite of their legalistic excesses they represented orthodox Judaism and did much to save the Jews from pagan Greek influences. They professed belief in divine providence and free will, the resurrection and final retribution, and the existence of angels and spirits.

Like the Pharisees, the Sadducees appeared first in the second century B.C. They probably took their name from Saddok, high priest at the time of David and Solomon. At first, they were devoted, orthodox religious leaders recruited chiefly from the priestly families. Over the years, they became increasingly tolerant of Hellenizing influences and proportionately less devoted to their own religion. By the time of Christ, religious leadership had passed to the Pharisees, especially to the Scribes, who were doctors of the Law. This was so true that the Sadducees found it prudent, at least in public, to show deference for the teachings of the Scribes and to conform to their legal prescriptions. Most of the priests were Sadducees, although there is occasional mention of priests who were Pharisees. The Sadducean priests performed the rituals and sacrificial functions reserved exclusively to the priesthood, but otherwise the religious life of the people took its form and direction from the Pharisees.

An outstanding characteristic of the Sadducees was their complete rejection of the oral traditions of the Pharisees. Infected by Greek skepticism, many of them denied the providence of God, the existence of spirits, the immortality of the soul, the resurrection, and future retribution. This world and this life were enough for them, and their efforts were directed to providing a cushion of riches and honors against possible adversity. Their influence was derived from their priestly rank, their wealth, and their political power under the Romans.

The people to whom Christ addressed Himself in His public ministry looked to the Sadducees as high-ranking priests who represented them before God in the Temple and as the political leaders who administered civil and criminal law under the general direction of the Romans. They looked to the Scribes and the Pharisees for the teaching and example that would indicate what they were to believe and the way in which they were to walk. From what we know of the Sadducees on the one hand and the Scribes and the Pharisees on the other, it was almost a foregone conclusion that, in spite of their differences, they would close their ranks against Christ in a concerted effort to maintain their control over the people.

Another important religious group of the period were the Essenes, but we are not concerned with them here, as there is no record that they were directly involved in Christ's life and Passion. They are mentioned in contemporary writings but not in the pages of the Old or New Testament. They were a semimonastic organization living near the Dead Sea and rightly identified, we think, with the brotherhood revealed in the writings known as the Dead Sea Scrolls. It is highly probable that there were some contacts between this brotherhood and some of Jesus' first followers. St. John the Baptist lived in the same neighborhood near the Dead Sea, and some of his followers, such as Andrew, John, and Peter, became the first disciples of Jesus. The language of the Gospel of St. John shows certain resemblances to the Dead Sea Scrolls.

The Jewish rejection of Christ is difficult to understand without some knowledge of popular conceptions of the Messiah current at the time. The people formed their ideas on this subject from the teachings of the Scribes and the Pharisees rather than from the Sadducees, whose agnostic outlook on life and religion left no room for Messianic hopes. Fortunately, many writings have come down to us from this epoch in Jewish history, and scholars can describe with considerable accuracy the Jewish attitude toward the hoped-for Messiah.

In 63 B.C., Pompey, the Roman general, had taken Jerusalem; the Jews had become vassals of the Romans and Palestine a mere outpost on the eastern fringe of the vast empire. This state of affairs naturally revived Jewish preoccupation with the Messianic promises and renewed hopes for a great deliverer to come. When Christ appeared on the banks of the Jordan to be baptized by John and then went north into Galilee to begin His public ministry, a ferment of Messianic agitation stirred the people, a feeling that Israel was at the threshold of a new era that would soon dawn.

It is strange that in the popular imagination as it pictured the Messianic times, the Messiah himself had assumed a secondary place, while the restoration of the nation became the event on which all hopes centered. The distinguishing marks of the hoped-for period were the deliverance of Israel from its conquerors, the return of the Jews from exile abroad, and the dominion of God over the world—a dominion that was to be exercised through Israel. Various ideas were current as to how this redemption of Israel was to be effected. Some thought it would be accomplished by natural means, through the ordinary course of historical development; others thought that Israel would be miraculously transferred to a new land, marvelously fertile and transfigured; still others thought that the restoration would be accompanied by the resurrection of the dead and the beginning of eternal rewards and punishments.

The divine revelation of the Old Testament contained indications of the divinity of the Messiah. The teaching of the Scribes not only ignored these prophecies but progressively belittled his role and person. In their teaching, the Messiah was a mere man, whatever his gifts and office; his mission had nothing to do with supernatural benefits or the salvation of souls; his sole purpose, as far as they were concerned, was the delivery of Israel and the conquest of the Gentiles, who would then be forced to submit to the law, which the Scribes regarded as their private property and their instrument of subjection. The Messiah had become in popular imagination a source of national glorification, a person through whom the Pharisaical conception of legalistic perfection would be imposed on all men. No consideration was given to the repeated prophecies concerning a suffering Messiah.

Chapter 2

THE CONFLICT

Even before Christ appeared on the banks of the Jordan to be baptized by John and to begin His public ministry, there were rumblings of the conflict that was to break out later into open hostility. Seeing the Pharisees and Sadducees coming to His baptism, Christ's Precursor lashed out at them in public rebuke. "Ye brood of vipers," he cried, "who hath showed you to flee from the wrath to come?" (Matt. 3:7). This public denunciation must have hurt deeply the pride of men accustomed to every public mark of respect. From that moment, John and the One mightier than he, to whom he pointed, must have been the objects of suspicion and surveillance on the part of the political and religious leaders of the Jewish people.

Throughout the public ministry of Christ, there was an undercurrent of opposition, an ominous surcharge of suspicion and hatred that broke out occasionally like the lightning that precedes the storm. The Scribes and Pharisees were ever present, mingling with the crowd or hovering on its fringes, listening with cold hatred or suppressed fury to the teaching of this man who would lead the multitude away from them and their way of life. Long before the final Passover, they had made up their minds concerning Christ, and on many occasions they had sought to apprehend and kill Him (Matt. 12:14; John 7:1, 20, 30; 10:31; Luke 13:31).

The opposition of the Scribes and Pharisees derived from a variety of sources. One was undoubtedly professional jealousy. The Scribes, who were for the most part learned Pharisees, formed a closed circle, with their own schools, their own disciples, their own doctrines and teaching methods. They had built up a self-cult that almost passes belief. The Scribes demanded complete reverence and obedience from their pupils. The pupil was to show greater respect for his teacher than for his own father. If a man's father and his teacher were both carrying burdens, the pupil must first help the teacher. If a man's father and his teacher were in captivity, the pupil must ransom the teacher first. Everything was taught and learned by rote. The disciple had to conform not only to the content of the teacher's doctrine, but even to his words and expressions.

To the Scribes, Christ was a rank outsider, an upstart. He had not studied in their schools. He did not use their methods; He did not teach their doctrines. Far from bolstering His teaching by quoting the famous rabbis of the past, He appealed only to His own authority and that of the heavenly Father, in whose name He spoke. How radical was this departure from custom is evidenced by the surprise of the people: "The crowds were astonished at his teaching; for he was teaching them as one having authority, and not as their Scribes and Pharisees" (Matt. 7:29).

Christ's teachings differed greatly from those of the Scribes and Pharisees. Throughout His public ministry there was constant friction on a variety of subjects. One of the most frequent causes of dispute, and one that most quickly and most certainly aroused the ire of the doctors learned in the Law, was the question of Sabbath observance. Without going into great detail, the Law of Moses simply forbade work on the Sabbath. This was not enough for the Scribes, whose business it was to apply the Law. By the time of Christ, they had refined a simple prohibition to a point where their teaching on that subject alone had become one of the widest of all fields of knowledge.

Thus, Christ openly offended the Pharisees when He justified His disciples, who had plucked and eaten ears of grain on the Sabbath (Matt. 12:1–8). On this occasion, Christ went further and openly declared what must have sounded blasphemous to the startled Pharisees: "For the Son of Man is Lord even of the Sabbath." It seems strange to us that particularly violent objection was made to Christ's merciful healing on the Sabbath. After He had healed the man with a withered hand on the day of rest, "the Pharisees went out and took counsel against him, how they might do away with him" (Matt. 12:14). Christ met opposition and condemnation for the same reason when He cured the man born blind (John 9:1ff.) and healed an infirm woman (Luke 13:10ff.).

The Israelites in general avoided all contact with the Gentiles. The Pharisees went further and avoided all contact with non-Pharisees, because they considered them unclean and almost as low as the pagans. They were therefore angered and scandalized when Christ ate with publicans and sinners (Matt. 9:9–13) and when He ate without the ritual washing prescribed by the rabbinical tradition (Mark 7:1–23). Their national pride was cut deeply by Christ's clear references to the fact that Gentiles would be admitted to His Kingdom and some Jews excluded (Luke 13:23–30). But above all, the Scribes and Pharisees were aroused to fury against Christ by His patent assumption of divine prerogatives, as when He forgave sins (Luke 5:17–26), and particularly when, on the feast of the Dedication that preceded the final Passover, He openly declared in Solomon's Porch within the Temple area, "I and the Father are One" (John 10:30). So angered were Christ's adversaries that they took up stones to kill Him.

The story of the opposition to Christ on the part of the Sadducees is quite different from that of the Scribes and Pharisees. Christ must have appeared to the Sadducees as a sort of eccentric itinerant preacher, teaching a doctrine different from that accepted by the Scribes and Pharisees, but of no interest or importance to the rich, influential, and agnostic clergy. As a result, the Sadducees appear rarely in the Gospel narrative until the final fateful days in the life of Christ. The only time He cut squarely across their path was when He drove the merchants and money changers from the Temple, for the profit from this desecration of the sacred area fell in large measure to the Sadducees.

The event that precipitated final action against Jesus Christ was one of His greatest miracles and acts of mercy: the raising of Lazarus from the dead. After an absence of several months, Jesus appeared suddenly at Bethany, only two miles from Jerusalem, and, in view of a large assembly of mourners, called Lazarus forth from the tomb.

Word of the miracle must have caused widespread public commotion. Jesus' enemies decided to put aside their differences and take action. They called a council of the rulers, at which Caiaphas, the high priest, presided. One of those present stated the case briefly: "If we let him alone as he is, all will believe in him, and the Romans will come and take away both our place and our nation" (John 11:48). Wearied by the futile argument that followed, Caiaphas rose to his feet and declared: "You know nothing at all, nor do you reflect that it is expedient for us that one man die for the people, instead of the whole nation perishing" (John 11:50). That settled the matter. The assembly accepted Caiaphas' solution. St. John concludes, "So from that day forth their plan was to put him to death" (11:53).

Jesus knew the plans of his enemies and retired from the Jerusalem area until the Saturday before the final Passover.

On Sunday, Jesus entered Jerusalem in a triumphal procession as the crowds of pilgrims hailed him as the Messiah. When His enemies protested, Jesus said: "I tell you that if these keep silence, the stones will cry out" (Luke 19:39–40).

Early Monday morning, Jesus returned to Jerusalem and entered the Temple area. He immediately proceeded to drive out those who were buying and selling. He overturned the tables of the money changers and the seats of those who sold doves. He stopped those who were making the sacred place an avenue of traffic, as a shortcut from one part of the city to another, and then sternly rebuked those responsible for these desecrations of the Holy Place: "It is written," he said, "'My house shall be called a house of prayer,' but you have made it a den of thieves" (Matt. 21:13).

In the Gospel passages that follow, there is a climax in the conflict between Jesus and the leaders of the Jewish people. Jesus fearlessly denounces His enemies, while they employ every trick they can to catch Him in His words so that they can denounce Him to the people. Jesus narrates the parable of the two sons and applies the lesson to them in the biting words: "The publicans and harlots are entering the kingdom of God before you" (Matt. 21:31). He concludes the long parable of the wicked husbandman with the humiliating prophecy: "Therefore I say to you that the kingdom of God will be taken away from you and will be given to a people yielding its fruits" (Matt. 21:43).

Christ's patience has been exhausted, and His indignation is vented on these hard-hearted leaders of the people. His voice rings out through the silenced Temple area and echoes back from the surrounding walls and porticos: "Woe to you, Scribes and Pharisees, hypocrites! Because you shut the kingdom of heaven against men.... Woe to you, Scribes and Pharisees, hypocrites! Because you traverse sea and land to make one convert; and when he has become one, you make him twofold more a son of hell than yourselves.... Woe to you blind guides.... You blind fools!... Blind ones!" Again and again comes the biting refrain as the discourse moves on and gains momentum: "Woe to you, Scribes and Pharisees, hypocrites! because you clean the outside of the cup and the dish, but within they are full of robbery and uncleanness. You are like whited sepulchers.... You are full of hypocrisy and iniquity.... Serpents, brood of vipers, how are you to escape the judgment of hell?" (Matt. 23:13ff.).

The Evangelists do not inform us of the reaction of the Scribes and Pharisees to this public castigation on the very spot where they thought their power and influence most secure. They must have been aghast. No mere words could answer the awful outburst of vituperation. They were cut too deeply in their pride to attempt further argument. They probably walked off in silence, deeply resolved to make Christ pay soon and fully for this open affront to their persons and office. If they spoke at all, it was probably to assure one another that they would call an immediate meeting to take proper steps to deal with this insufferable upstart.

On Wednesday, Christ's enemies called another meeting. Chief priests, Scribes, and ancients, representatives of the three groups that made up the Sanhedrin, supreme council of the Jews, met in the palace of Caiaphas. After much discussion, they again concluded that Christ must be put to death, but that nothing could be done on the approaching feast lest there be a riot among the people. They therefore decided to lay hands on Jesus secretly.

Chapter 3

JUDAS ISCARIOT

It probably never entered the minds of Christ's enemies that they could find an ally among the twelve Apostles, one of the little group most closely associated with Him. And yet it is "one of the Twelve" who took the fateful and tragic step of going to these men to strike a bargain for the betrayal of Jesus Christ.

Who was this man who could betray his friend and master for a sum?

We know nothing about Judas except what is recorded in the Gospels and in the Acts of the Apostles. The legends concerning him in some of the apocryphal works are entirely without historical foundation, as are the purely fictitious interpretations of some moderns who would make a hero and patriot out of this "son of perdition" (John 17:12).

Judas was a common and honorable name among the Jews. In fact, another Apostle was also called Judas. When the Evangelists refer to this latter, they take particular care lest the reader confuse him with Judas Iscariot, and they refer to him as "Judas, not the Iscariot" (John 14:22) or as "Jude the brother of James" (Luke 6:16). The betrayer of Christ is referred to as

"Judas Iscariot," or as "Judas who betrayed him," or, occasionally, as "Judas, one of the Twelve." This last expression seems to indicate the Evangelists' feeling of horror that one so close to Christ could betray Him.

There is a variety of opinions concerning the meaning of the name Iscariot. The simplest and most probable is that it is derived from the Hebrew and means "man of Carioth." This would indicate that Judas, or at least his family, came from Carioth Hesron in Judea. If this is true, then he was the only Apostle who was not a Galilean. This fact would have more than academic interest, as it could explain a possible source of friction between Judas and the other Apostles. The people of Judea looked down upon the Galileans. Galilee was at a distance from Jerusalem, the religious center of the nation, and was separated from it by the heretical and racially impure province of Samaria. It was regarded as infected by the pagan ideas of the surrounding peoples, to such an extent that it was referred to as "Galilee of the nations" (Isa. 9:1). There was a difference in dialect also between Galilee and Judea, as St. Peter's manner of speaking in the court of the high priest was to betray immediately his Galilean origin (Matt. 26:73).

If Judas was from Judea and shared the Judean antipathy for Galileans, it must have been difficult for him to associate intimately with the other Apostles. It is evident from their quarrels over precedence that they were not free from personal ambition. In Judas' case, the feeling of frustration at not obtaining preferment would have been increased by his sense of superiority over his fellow Apostles. He may even have come to feel that the Kingdom preached by Christ was essentially a Galilean movement and, as such, a rebellion of sorts against the supreme spiritual authority of Jerusalem.

Judas Iscariot first enters the pages of history in the Evangelists' account of Christ's selection of the twelve Apostles. The Gospel story indicates that in Christ's mind this event was one of very special import. Leaving behind Him the crowds by the shores of the Sea of Galilee, Christ went up into a nearby hill and spent the night in prayer. As dawn broke the following morning, a crowd of disciples rejoined Him. From among these disciples, Jesus selected twelve Apostles, as He called them, "that they might be with him and that he might send them forth to preach. To them he gave power to cure sicknesses and to cast out devils" (Mark 3:14–15).

It would be impossible to describe fully the honor and privilege conferred on Judas by the call to the apostolate. He was chosen to be one of the closest associates of Jesus Christ, the Son of God, in His redemptive work here on earth and to be a cornerstone of the Church He would establish to continue human redemption until the end of time. Judas, with the other Apostles, was especially commissioned to preach the Kingdom of God and to work miracles. Christ Himself said to His chosen Twelve: "Amen I say to you that you ... shall also sit on twelve thrones, judging the twelve tribes of Israel" (Matt. 19:28).

So exalted was the dignity of the apostolate, so sacred the office, that one cannot help wondering whether Judas was evil at the time of his call or whether he fell from grace later. There can be no doubt that Jesus knew Judas' sentiments at the time and foresaw the ultimate fateful outcome. The Gospels throw no light on this subject, however, so we are left to draw our own conclusions from the circumstances.

Whatever doubt there can be concerning Judas' sincerity in following Christ could be traceable to his ideas of the Messiah. It is highly probable that Judas, like the other Apostles, originally followed Jesus because he believed him to be the Messiah (John 1:41, 46). Undoubtedly, he and the other Apostles shared the false ideas current at the time concerning the person of the Messiah and the kingdom he would inaugurate. The Apostles, for example, until after the death and resurrection of Christ, found it difficult, if not impossible, to accept the idea of a suffering Messiah. Judas, then, may have attached himself to Christ in the belief that He was the Messiah and that it was only a matter of time before He would show Himself in His role of king and conqueror. In this case, Judas must have become more and more disillusioned as time passed, for Christ not only failed to fulfill His expected role but fled from honors and even talked of His approaching Passion and death.

About a year passes before Judas is again mentioned by an Evangelist. Apparently he has conformed in externals to the life of an immediate follower of Christ, or he would have occasioned comment. To his fellow Apostles, he is still simply "one of the Twelve." But Jesus makes a sudden and apparently unprovoked remark that, like a lightning flash in the night, illumines momentarily the depravity into which Judas has sunk.

It was near the end of the first year of Christ's public ministry, and He was teaching at Capharnaum, on the northwest shore of the Sea of Galilee. Christ had spent so much of His time in this town that it was spoken of as His home. On this particular day, our Lord explained the doctrine of the Holy Eucharist. Christ's teaching was met at first with raised eyebrows and murmurs of incredulity: "The Jews therefore murmured about him because he had said: 'I am the bread that has come down from heaven'"

(John 6:41). As Jesus continued His discourse, emphasizing His teaching, those present began to argue with one another, asking, "How can this man give us his flesh to eat?" (6:53). Jesus not only did not withdraw His teaching, a cause of scandal to His listeners, but reiterated it and insisted on it: "Unless you eat the flesh of the Son of Man, and drink his blood, you shall not have life in you" (6:54). As Jesus continued in the same vein, even his disciples began murmuring among themselves, saying: "This is a hard saying. Who can listen to it?" (6:61). Jesus was well aware that many of his hearers would not pass this test of faith. As St. John writes: "Jesus knew from the beginning who they were who did not believe, and who it was who should betray him" (6:65). Jesus knew the unbelievers and the betrayer. Since the Evangelist makes a distinction between unbelievers and the betrayer, it would not be logical to conclude from this passage that Judas had already lost or was losing his faith. Nothing is said of his faith in the text.

It is evident from St. John's account that Jesus has reached a moment of crisis in His public ministry. Since the beginning of His preaching, He had spent most of His time in and near Capharnaum, and probably most of His disciples were from this area. By this time, they should have had sufficient faith in Jesus to believe Him for His own sake, even if they could not understand His teaching or accept it without difficulty. Yet when Jesus announced the doctrine of the Holy Eucharist, many of His disciples murmured and argued among themselves and they finally came to the conclusion that this teaching was too hard for them. St. John says: "From this time many of his disciples turned back and no longer went about with him" (6:67). The first part of Christ's ministry had apparently ended in almost complete failure.

St. John then relates Christ's question to the Twelve. If this question followed immediately on the departure of the disciples, it would seem that all of them deserted Christ and only the Apostles remained. It may be, however, that there was at least a little interval of time between the two events and that Christ waited to put his question to the Twelve when He was alone with them.

There is something tragic in this incident. Jesus must have watched sadly as He saw His disciples turn their backs on Him and go their way, probably still discussing in small and animated groups the impossibility and even absurdity of His teaching. An atmosphere of frustration and discouragement must have surrounded those who remained. We can imagine Christ watching for a few pensive moments before He turned to the silent group of Apostles still with Him and asked: "Do you also wish to go away?"

There was a moment of silence, a moment in which each Apostle searched his heart for his reply. The first to find and formulate his answer was St. Peter, and he spoke in words that have come ringing down the ages: "Lord, to whom shall we go? Thou hast the words of everlasting life, and we have come to believe and to know that thou art the Christ, the Son of God" (John 6:70).

In his simplicity and forthrightness, Peter thought he spoke for himself and all the others. Jesus calls attention to his mistake in words that must have been a shock to the little group: "Have I not chosen you, the Twelve? Yet one of you is a devil" (John 6:71). They had not become Apostles by their own choice; they had not merited this singular grace and honor; but Christ Himself had chosen them as members of a special group, "the Twelve." In spite of this, one of them is a devil. Christ's emphasis on the fact that He Himself had chosen them casts into greater relief the ingratitude and malice of the one who is a devil. The term *devil*, as Christ uses it here, does not indicate diabolical possession. It means simply that the one referred to was doing the work of a devil, was like a devil, or was as evil as a devil. Jesus does not foretell the betrayal, nor does He identify the one to whom He refers. His words were a warning, a grace proffered secretly to one who has already gone far on the road to destruction. St. John, in the light of later events, tells us that Christ referred to Judas Iscariot, "who was to betray him."

We have no record of the reaction of Judas or the other Apostles to Christ's words, but the course of subsequent events reveals that Judas did not heed Christ's warning. We do not know whether he or the others made a protestation similar to Peter's. It is probable that St. Peter's answer was accepted as the reply of all. Judas, by his silence, associated himself hypocritically with St. Peter's declaration of faith; his whole existence until his tragic death had now become a living lie.

For over a year, a veil of silence descends upon Judas in the Gospel narrative. He does not reappear until the supper at Bethany on the Saturday evening before the death of Christ. During this time, although he was "a devil," as Christ called him, he must have continued to live the life of an Apostle in all externals; up to the very end his companions had no suspicion of the evil locked in his heart.

At Bethany, it is again St. John who casts a clear light upon Judas and reveals an ugly facet of his character. At a supper in the home of Simon the leper, Mary Magdalen poured an extremely precious ointment over the head and feet of Jesus and wiped His feet with her hair. As so often in this life, vice comes quickly face-to-face with virtue, and niggardliness with generosity. Those present began to realize, and then to discuss, the great value of the ointment that Mary had used. They estimated that it was worth more than three hundred denarii, a laborer's pay for a year, more than enough, according to St. Philip's estimate, to supply food for five thousand men (see John 6:7). Such extraordinary prodigality they found shocking, and they did not hesitate to express their indignation to one another. Some of Christ's followers, probably the Apostles, joined in the remonstrances. Judas seems to have protested the loudest, as St. John, who was present, mentions him by name: "Judas Iscariot, he who was about to betray him, said: 'Why was this ointment not sold for three hundred denarii, and given to the poor?' Now he said this, not that he cared for the poor, but because he was a thief, and holding the purse, used to take what was put in it" (12:4–6). The other disciples were undoubtedly sincere, but St. John, with inspired knowledge, looked into the heart of Judas and revealed the hypocrisy in his pretended interest in the poor.

St. John thus clearly tells us that Judas was a thief who stole money that had been committed to his care. We have certainty from the words of St. John that Judas had been abusing the confidence Christ and the Apostles placed in him by stealing from the common purse.

There, etched by the pen of an inspired Evangelist, we have the portrait of a thief, a hypocrite, and an avaricious man, one who is on the verge of plunging into the depths of evil.

The events of the first two days of Holy Week could leave no doubt in Judas' mind that the day of final settlement between Jesus and His enemies was fast approaching, when he and the other Apostles would have to "stand and be counted," would have to declare themselves for Jesus or against him, for the leaders of the Jews or against them.

Judas decided, and his decision was one of monstrous perfidy. He would go over to the enemy and, in so doing, would betray his master into their hands for whatever price he could get from them. He would, by one act, free himself from the suspicion and danger now surrounding an Apostle of Jesus Christ; he would win favor with the chief priests and Pharisees by executing their order to report Jesus' whereabouts (John 11:56); and he would line his own pockets.

Judas left Jesus and the Apostles, probably at Bethany, and headed for Jerusalem. He mounted the western hill of the city toward the spot where tradition places the palace of the high priest. Once he had given some inkling of the purpose of his visit, he had no difficulty in gaining admission. It is likely that he was interviewed by some of the chief priests, those whose duty it would be to make the decisions and act in the matter. Also present were officers of the Temple police. It would be their duty to take the necessary steps to arrest Jesus under the guidance of Judas. As a matter of fact, we find them present later at the arrest of Jesus in the Garden of Gethsemane (Luke 22:52).

Judas went straight to his point, brutally and frankly. There were no evasions about losing faith in the Master, no protestations about fulfilling his duty as a true Israelite: "What are you willing to give me, and I will deliver him to you?" (Matt. 26:15).

How much haggling there was over the payment we do not know. The Evangelists tell us only that Judas and the chief priests reached an agreement on the sum to be paid. St. Matthew alone specifies that it was for 30 pieces of silver. This coin was worth 4 denarii. The 30 pieces of silver would therefore equal 120 denarii, and since the denarius was a day's pay for a soldier or laborer, the amount of money promised Judas was the equivalent of a laborer's pay for 120 days of work. St. Matthew probably mentions the exact amount because he recalled the fact that the law decreed 30 pieces of silver as the compensation for a slave killed by an ox (Exod. 21:32; see also Zach. 11:12). Judas agreed to the offer and from that moment determined to put into execution his part of the bargain.

With the insufficient data given us by the Gospels, it is difficult to analyze the character and motives of Judas Iscariot. He is, and will remain to the end of time, a mystery of evil. It is frightening to compare the pinnacle of greatness to which he was called with the abyss of wickedness to which he plunged. What could have led him to such depths of evil?

As we have seen, Judas was a thief as well as an opportunist who joined Christ because he believed that He was the Messiah and that, as one of his earliest followers, he would ensure himself an important place in His kingdom. On the one hand, Judas must have been deeply impressed by Christ's miracles but, on the other hand, repelled by His refusal to accept honors, by His teaching of humility, charity, and self-sacrifice, by His poverty and complete indifference to worldly goods and comforts, His revelation of a Messianic kingdom completely devoid of all that Judas imagined it should be, and, above all, His adoption of the role of a suffering and dying Messiah.

In any case, the day finally arrived when Judas no longer believed in Christ or loved Him. The latter period of Judas' life is a frightening illustration of the power of the human will to resist grace. Judas looked upon Christ day after day; he talked with Him and supped with Him; he slept alongside Him under the stars at night; he listened to Him teach the lessons of His Kingdom; he watched Him work miracles of compassion; he heard Him denounce the hypocrisy of the Scribes and Pharisees; he trudged wearily alongside Him as he climbed the steep hills of Judea to the holy city for the great feasts of the religious year; he enjoyed all the intimacies of a friend and confidant of Jesus Christ, the Son of God.

And yet, after more than two years of this, he refuses to open the doors of his soul to the rays of Christ's divine grace. The evil that Judas did was compounded a thousandfold by the fact that it was conceived and born in the very presence of Jesus Christ.

Chapter 4

THE LAST SUPPER

The Last Supper was one of the most important and significant events of Christ's life. A detailed treatment of this Supper, of the institution of the Holy Eucharist and of the beautiful discourse that followed it, belongs more properly to a life of Christ than to a book that treats specifically of His Passion. We shall confine our attention, therefore, to whatever pertains directly to the events that were to follow on that night and the next day.

The Passover was the greatest of all the Jewish feasts. It was the annual commemoration of the delivery of the Israelites from the bondage of Egypt. It was celebrated on the fifteenth of the month of Nisan (roughly, our April) but, since the Jewish day began at sunset, the feast really began at sunset of the fourteenth Nisan. The Passover meal constituted the main part of the celebration, and it was eaten on the evening of the fourteenth Nisan. For Christ and His Apostles, and undoubtedly for many others also, the Paschal meal was to be eaten that year on

The LAST HOURS *of* JESUS

Thursday evening.[1] The Apostles knew that He would want to eat the Paschal meal in Jerusalem, and yet they knew also that

[1] There is an apparent contradiction between the first three Gospels on the one hand and St. John on the other as to the time of the celebration of the Passover. It is not a question of law but of fact. According to law, the Paschal lamb was immolated on the fourteenth Nisan and eaten that evening after sundown. In the first three Gospels, the Passover supper took place on Thursday evening, which would therefore be the fourteenth Nisan (Matt. 26:17; Mark 14:12; Luke 22:7). Yet even in these Gospels there are indications that the next day was not the Passover, at least not for all: Joseph bought a linen shroud (Mark 15:46), the holy women prepared spices and ointments (Luke 23:56), both Jews and disciples carried arms (Mark 14:47), and Simon of Cyrene was returning from the fields, evidently from work (Luke 23:26). None of these activities was permitted on the great feast.

In St. John, the Jews ate the Passover meal on Friday and the Passover itself was on Saturday. On Friday morning, the leaders of the Jews refused to enter the courtyard of the praetorium of Pilate lest they be defiled and therefore unable to eat the Passover meal (John 18:28). But our Lord and His Apostles had already eaten it on the night before. There are other similar indications in St. John's Gospel.

We do not know the solution of this difficulty because we do not have the facts. Many explanations are possible. The best are based on the fact that all did not agree on just which day was the fifteenth Nisan.

The Dead Sea Scrolls prove that the Qumran sect followed a different calendar from other Jews. It was probably an ancient religious calendar. We do not know whether this sect had a wide following among other Jews, but that is not so important as the fact that there was disagreement at the time of Christ over the day on which the fifteenth Nisan fell. Some Catholic scholars are now of the opinion that Christ and His Apostles ate the Last Supper on Tuesday rather than Thursday evening.

The Pharisees postponed sacred times for various reasons. Sometimes they lengthened the preceding month, for instance, neither He nor they had an abode in the city. It would not be easy to find suitable quarters because of the crowds, and they were concerned that Jesus had taken no step toward making the necessary arrangements. Their uneasiness became so great that they finally approached Jesus with the question: "Where dost thou want us to prepare for thee to eat the Passover?" Christ selected Peter and John and directed them to go and make the necessary preparations. He told them how they were to get in touch with one who was evidently a friend or disciple and who would provide the necessary "guest chamber." The anonymous benefactor showed Peter and John "a large upper room furnished" which he placed at the disposal of Jesus and his Apostles (Mark 14:12–16).

The guest chamber was usually the whole or a part of the second story of the house. When it was a part, the rest was used as a balcony or a terrace, opening on an inner court and sheltered from the public gaze. The approach was by a staircase from the inner court. Here, guests were received, thus avoiding the first floor, where were located the stables, the kitchen, the lodgings of the servants, and the rooms for ordinary family living. The guestroom was furnished with low divans, cushions, and carpets.[2]

---

in order to prevent the Day of Atonement from falling on the day before or after the Sabbath.

The Jews did not have a calendar fixed by astronomical means. The new month began when the new moon was visible to the naked eye. Such a method could lead to doubts and disagreements. Something similar occurred in 1955 when Egyptians began Ramadan a day later than other Moslem countries because the religious authorities in Egypt were prevented by haze from seeing the new moon on the first night of its appearance.

[2] The place where our Lord ate the Last Supper and instituted the Holy Eucharist is known as the Cenacle, from the Latin word

The LAST HOURS of JESUS

Before the appointed hour, Peter and John had completed preparations for the Paschal meal, and Jesus and the ten Apostles arrived at the Upper Room. It was about six o'clock. All waited expectantly for the blast of silver trumpets blown by the priests at the Temple announcing the exact moment of sundown and the beginning of the meal.

The Law commanded that the first Passover be eaten hastily, with the loins girt, shoes on the feet, a staff in the hand. By the time of Christ, all this had been changed, and the Israelites, as a sign that they were free, ate the Passover reclining. In the middle of the room was a low table. Around this table were rugs and cushions on which the guests reclined on their left elbows, leaving their right hands free to reach food from the table. Sometimes the tables were round and surrounded by guests. At other times, the places for the guests formed three sides of a square, leaving one side open for the convenience of the servers.

Coenaculum, used by St. Jerome to translate the Greek word for "guestroom." The Evangelists do not give its location beyond stating that it was in the city. Christian tradition places it on the west hill of Jerusalem near the present south wall. An earlier tradition identifies the Cenacle as the place where our Lord appeared to the disciples on the Sunday of His Resurrection and also a week later, and where the Holy Spirit descended upon our Blessed Mother and the Apostles. The Cenacle thus became the earliest Christian center in Jerusalem and was called later the Mother of all Churches. This quarter was spared the destruction visited upon the rest of the city by Titus in the year 70. It was only natural that with peace the Christians should return to a spot hallowed by so many sacred memories. Through the intervening centuries down to our own days, this place has been venerated as one of the most sacred in all Christendom, although we must admit that the tradition is not sufficiently verified to impose complete certitude.

The Paschal supper began with a first cup of wine and a prayer calling down a blessing on the wine and on the feast. Then bitter herbs, unleavened bread, and a sauce in which to dip the herbs were brought in and placed on the table with the Paschal lamb. A second cup of wine was poured, and the leader of the group explained the meaning of the feast. The lamb was eaten along with the bitter herbs. The Jews were familiar with the use of forks, but for this meal they used their hands, dipping the herbs into the sauce and using pieces of the flat loaves of bread in their fingers to pick meat from the platter. A third and a fourth cup of wine were poured, accompanied by a benediction of the repast and the recitation of a group of psalms known as the Hallel.

As the Apostles started to take their places to begin the meal, a dispute broke out among them over precedence. Jesus quietly rebuked them and then gave them a lesson in true humility. He put aside His outer garments, girded Himself with a towel, poured water into a basin, and began to wash and dry their feet. After overcoming Peter's resistance, Jesus spoke rather cryptic words: "You are clean, but not all" (John 13:10). St. John tells us that Jesus referred to Judas. It is likely that our Lord spoke these words as He moved on from Peter to begin washing the feet of Judas, thus giving the traitor a broad hint that He was aware of his evil intention.

When they had reclined again around the table, Jesus insisted further on the lesson He had just taught. "If you know these things," He said, "blessed shall you be if you do them." Referring again to Judas, Jesus went on to say: "I do not speak of you all." And, lest the Apostles think that Christ had made a mistake in selecting the traitor to be an Apostle, he continued: "I know whom I have chosen," and then He explained that the choice was made that a prophecy concerning Himself might be realized: "that the Scripture may be fulfilled, 'He who eats bread with me has lifted up his heel against me'" (John 13:18). This quotation is taken from a psalm ascribed to King David (Ps. 40:10 [41:9]). While these words refer directly to David, they refer indirectly to Christ, as David was a prefiguring of the Messiah. Christ tells them in advance so that they will realize later that this prophecy refers to Him.

St. John, quick to note the sentiments of Jesus, tells us that "he was troubled in spirit" (John 13:21). It is obvious that Jesus was disturbed by the presence of Judas. He who had wept over the blindness of the people of Jerusalem was saddened now by the presence of a chosen one who resisted all His advances, persisting in His evil course. Again Jesus spoke of the betrayal, and this time in words that sound like the solemn deposition of a witness against an accused: "Amen I say to you, one of you will betray me — one who is eating with me" (Mark 14:18). Jesus reveals in these words the reason for His trouble of soul. He will be betrayed — and betrayed by one of those now eating at table with Him, one admitted to His friendship and intimacy, one of the Twelve.

The meaning of Jesus' words finally penetrated the incredulous minds of the Apostles. They realized from His troubled mood that He was not using figures of speech. The Apostles, in turn, became sad and troubled. They looked around at one another doubtfully, but their glances were shamefaced rather than suspicious. Each was conscious of his own good intentions yet feared that he might be the one to whom Jesus was referring. They began "to inquire among themselves which of them it might be that was about to do this" (Luke 22:23). Their inquiries led nowhere, so all turned to our Lord for an answer to the disturbing question, and each asked: "Is it I?"

Jesus' answer evidently interrupted the questioning, as Judas put his question later. Jesus still avoided designating the traitor and replied in general terms: "It is one of the Twelve, who dips with me in the dish" (Mark 14:20). It is likely that this expression is only a somewhat different way of saying: "One who is eating with me." Jesus then continued: "The Son of Man indeed goes his way, as it is written of him." Jesus was not deceived by a trap laid for him; He was not forced; He walked the way of the cross of His own free will in the manner foretold by the prophets of the Old Testament—betrayed by a friend. Yet the fact that the betrayal was the fulfillment of a prophecy offers no excuse to the betrayer, for Christ went on to say: "But woe to that man by whom the Son of Man is betrayed! It were better for that man if he had not been born" (Mark 14:21).

These are the most terrible words Jesus spoke during His life on earth. Their menace is inescapable: they are a direct threat of eternal damnation to Judas. Certainly, it would have been better for Judas to have been born if a time could ever come when he would enjoy the Beatific Vision in heaven, but this possibility seems clearly eliminated by Christ's statement.

It is likely that our Lord's words interrupted the Apostles' question: "Is it I, Lord?" Judas knew very well that Jesus referred to him, but he felt that in order to avert suspicion, he too must question him, so he said: "Is it I, Rabbi?" Christ's answer came quickly and unequivocally: "Thou hast said it" (Matt. 26:25). Evidently, the others did not hear Christ's reply, or there would have been an uproar. They were probably busy questioning one another. Then, too, it would appear from the incident that follows immediately that Judas reclined very close to Jesus. Only Judas heard and understood. He could have no doubt that Jesus saw through his hypocrisy and knew his evil intentions.

The next incident is another of those in which St. John shows himself so clearly an eyewitness of the events he narrates (John 13:23–30). To understand the scene, it is necessary to recall that the guests reclined at table on their left elbows and reached for the food with their right hands. When the ancients used the expression, "to recline at one's bosom," they referred to the place one occupied at table in relation to another, and not to one's posture. When St. John says that the beloved disciple "was reclining at Jesus' bosom," he meant simply that he was at Jesus' right. From what follows, it is clear that Judas reclined near Jesus, possibly at His left, and that Peter was at a little distance, no closer certainly than the right of John, the Beloved Disciple.

Peter made a sign to attract John's attention and then said in a low voice: "Who is it of whom he speaks?" Thereupon John leaned back until his head was directly over, or even touching, the breast of Jesus and whispered: "Lord, who is it?" Our Lord answered, "It is he for whom I shall dip the bread, and give it to him." Jesus then took a piece of bread, and with it in His fingers, picked a choice morsel of meat from the dish of lamb and offered it to Judas. This was a delicate mark of attention on the part of the host. As John watched Judas accept the morsel, he must have experienced a feeling of shock and loathing. There is no evidence from the Gospel whether he revealed to Peter the identity of the betrayer. It is highly unlikely that he did, or the volatile Peter might have been at Judas' throat.

At this moment, St. John again mentions the influence of Satan: "And after the morsel, Satan entered into him." It would seem that, in designating him as a traitor, Jesus excluded Judas from the Apostolic college. As Judas became more and more abandoned by God, Satan became freer to exercise his power over him. Each rejected grace, each rebuffed overture from Jesus weakened his will and reduced his power of resistance to Satanic suggestion.

The last hope for Judas had faded. Jesus could expect nothing from him now. His efforts to win him back had failed. He turned to him and said quietly: "What thou dost, do quickly." Jesus wanted to be relieved of the presence of the traitor so that He could spend the little time that was left with the faithful eleven. The others overheard Jesus' words and thought that He was directing Judas to make some purchase for the feast or to give alms to the poor.

One can well imagine St. John watching in stunned silence as Judas rose from his place after receiving the morsel from Jesus and started to leave. As he passed through the doorway, John caught a glimpse of the darkness that seemed to envelop Judas like a cloak. The outer darkness contrasted sharply with the light of the supper room. John is evidently struck by the contrast, because he adds: "It was night."

This brief sentence of John's makes a profound impression. It would seem that John saw in the darkness more than a mere physical phenomenon; the darkness into which Judas goes is a symbol. This is the hour of darkness which men prefer to the light (John 3:19); it is the hour of the power of darkness (Luke 22:53), which has taken possession of the soul of Judas; it is into this darkness that the light shines, and the darkness does not comprehend it (John 1:5).

After the supper, Jesus spoke earnestly to the eleven Apostles, warning them of what was about to take place. During his discourse, he made the stunning announcement: "You will all be scandalized this night because of me" (Matt. 26:31). Jesus makes no exceptions. All of them will be scandalized because of Him. The nature of the scandal is indicated by Christ's reference to a text of Zechariah that referred to Him: "I will smite the shepherd, and the sheep of the flock will be scattered" (13:7).[3] Events of that very night and the next day would indeed bring about the fulfillment of Our Lord's words. To the Apostles first, as to the Jews later (1 Cor. 1:23), the Passion of Christ was a stumbling block. In spite of all His forecasts and warnings, in spite of His efforts to prepare them in advance, the Apostles refused to face the facts, and the awful reality of Christ's sufferings and death swept over them with the suddenness and completeness of a tidal wave.

Again, Peter ignored what our Lord was saying and interrupted in order to return to the subject that was on his mind. He flatly contradicted Christ. Our Lord had said, "You will all be scandalized." Peter now declared loudly: "Even though all shall be scandalized, yet not I" (Mark 14:29). Peter was full of self-confidence. He was perfectly willing to admit that all the others would be scandalized, but he—never.

Peter's protestations had no effect on Christ. Our Lord's reply is incisive and definite. Every word adds clearness and emphasis to the prediction: "Amen I say to thee, today, this very night, before a cock crows twice, thou wilt deny me thrice" (Mark 14:30). The events of the night will bear out the truth of Christ's prophecy regarding both Peter and the other Apostles.

---

[3] In the original Hebrew, this text reads: "Sword ... strike the shepherd and the sheep will be scattered." Christ quotes the text according to its sense rather than word for word. If God orders the sword to strike, then it is God who strikes.

But Peter was not to be silenced. He brushed aside Christ's clear, formal, and definite statement and went on "speaking more vehemently." Instead of reflecting on Christ's superior knowledge, he looked into his own heart and saw only his own sentiments of loyalty and devotion. Completely overlooking his human frailty, he declared boastfully: "Even if I should have to die with thee, I will not deny thee." And, unwilling to be outdone by Peter, the other Apostles now joined in with similar declarations of fidelity.

Did Christ make any answer? If He did, the Evangelists have not recorded it. Probably He did not, as He knew that a series of events was already beginning to take shape in the shadows of the darkened city that would answer for Him.

Before leaving the supper room, Jesus and the Apostles sang the group of psalms known as the Hallel. This was part of the prescribed ritual for the Passover, as we have said. Then they descended to the street and started eastward toward the Garden of Gethsemane. It must have been between ten and eleven o'clock by this time, although we can only conjecture. The full Paschal moon had risen high over the Mountains of Moab to the east and shed a pale brilliance over the silent city. If tradition is correct, the group must have passed very near the palace of Caiaphas, where preparations were already afoot for the capture of Christ this very night.

Jesus and the Apostles descended into the valley and left the city through the Fountain Gate. Once outside the city walls, they walked northward on a path that followed the brook Cedron, which was dry at this time of year. At this point, the Cedron is a deep, dark gorge that separates the city on the west from the

Mount of Olives on the east. As they walked along the path at the bottom of the ravine, they were in darkness, but above them the moon lighted the towering walls of the city on the left and on the right shed a soft radiance on the olive trees that covered the slope of the mount. At a point just opposite the Temple, not far from the present bridge, they turned eastward and mounted toward the Garden of Gethsemane on the lower slopes of the hill. The journey from the Upper Room was over difficult terrain and probably required about a half hour.

THE PASSION

Chapter 5

GETHSEMANE

At Gethsemane we begin the story of the Passion of Jesus Christ. All that has gone before is as a prologue to this greatest of all dramas. The narrators are the four Evangelists. They all believed in Jesus Christ as a divine person, the true Son of God, and offered their lives in witness of this belief. And yet there is no change in their style as they narrate the awful events of Holy Thursday night and the following day. There is no attempt to remove what was a stumbling block and a scandal to Jews and Gentiles. Through their eyes we see Jesus overwhelmed with fear and sadness; betrayed into the hands of his enemies; hurried from one tribunal to another; mocked, spit upon, scourged, and crowned with thorns; condemned to the death of the cross and left to die, nailed to a gibbet, beyond a gate of the city, beside a highway where passersby could behold what they thought was the well-deserved punishment of the false prophet from Nazareth.

And the Evangelists tell this story simply, objectively, and without any effort to avoid or color the facts. Indeed, we might say that they tell the story coldly. They are historians, recording what happened without expressing sympathy for the suffering

Christ or antipathy for His enemies. Their very simplicity and candor and lack of special pleading give a tremendous and moving eloquence to these greatest pages of Holy Writ.

The Evangelists are sparing in details describing the places where events in our Lord's life occurred. The Gospels were written for the early Christians; information of this kind would not be understood by those living outside the Holy Land and would be unnecessary for the Palestinian faithful, who must have preserved a loving memory of the places sanctified by Christ's presence. Between the data of the Gospel and tradition, however, we are able to locate with a satisfying degree of accuracy the garden where our Lord's agony took place.

St. Matthew and St. Mark speak of it simply as "a country place called Gethsemane" (Matt. 26:36; Mark 14:32). St. Luke refers to it as a "place" on the Mount of Olives (22:39–40). St. John says it was "beyond the torrent of Cedron, where there was a garden" (18:1) and states further that "Judas ... also knew the place, since Jesus had often met there together with his disciples" (18:2). The expression used by St. Matthew and St. Mark indicates a rural domain, a small country or suburban estate. The word used by St. John and translated "garden" can also mean an olive grove, and this is very probably the sense in which it is used here, since the name by which this place was known was Gethsemane, which means "oil press."

From the data at hand and from what we know of similar rural establishments of the time, it is not too difficult to reconstruct the general appearance of Gethsemane. It was an olive grove enclosed by a stone wall or by a hedge. That there was some sort of enclosure is indicated by the fact that St. John says our Lord and His disciples "entered" the garden and later "went forth" to meet Judas. It is not surprising that there should have been an oil press, as a wine or oil press was practically standard equipment for such a country estate. Jerusalem was surrounded by a band of verdant growth, and this particular area must have been noted for its olive trees, as the hill above was known as the Mount of Olives. The olive press was of stone, similar to those still found in many parts of the Holy Land. We are not told whether there was a habitation of any sort, but there probably was a shelter for the guardian, or even a house where the owner could retire to enjoy the shade in summer.

St. Luke tells us that Jesus went to the Mount of Olives "according to his custom" (22:39), and St. John says that Jesus and His disciples often went to the garden. The Evangelists had already informed us that during Holy Week, our Lord left the city and spent the night on the Mount of Olives. It is likely that, when He did not want to go on as far as Bethany, further up the steep slopes of the Mount, He stayed here in the Garden of Gethsemane near the foot of the hill. The Evangelists do not satisfy our curiosity as to the owner of Gethsemane. He must have been a friend and disciple of Jesus, because here, as in the Upper Room, our Lord made Himself quite at home.

Christian tradition has held in veneration a particular spot identified as the Garden of Gethsemane and marked today, as in centuries past, both by a beautiful basilica and by a small grove of olive trees that are offshoots of the trees that witnessed our Lord's agony. It is east of the Cedron, a short distance up the slope of the Mount of Olives, about two hundred yards from the Temple enclosure. This location is a logical one, as it is the only place in this area where the Cedron Valley widens out enough to leave space for the rural estate mentioned in the Gospels. We know that, from the early part of the fourth century, at least, pilgrims have revered this spot as the place where our Lord underwent

His agony. A church commemorating this event was built here between 380 and 390.

About a hundred yards to the north of the spot identified with the agony of our Lord is a grotto hewn out of the rock. It is very irregular in shape but measures about ten by fifteen yards. The earliest tradition does not identify the grotto with the prayer and agony of Christ, but there is a later tradition that makes it the scene of the betrayal. We do not have sufficient evidence to determine with any degree of certainty whether any of the events of Holy Thursday night took place in or at the entrance to the grotto. If there were no habitation in the garden itself, it is possible that our Lord and the Apostles sought shelter occasionally in the grotto when the weather was cold or inclement. We have no evidence that any of the Apostles did so on this night. It would appear, however, that Judas expected Jesus and the Apostles to be asleep in the grotto, as he and his associates approached with lanterns and torches and without much effort at concealment. He would surely have been more careful if he thought his quarry was in the open garden.

In any case, the Gospel accounts indicate that Christ and the chosen three were not in the grotto. The temperature is variable at this time of year, and this night it must have been at least chilly, as St. Peter later sat at a fire with the servants of the high priest to warm himself (Mark 14:54; Luke 22:55). Accustomed as they were to a rough, outdoor life, however, it would have been nothing extraordinary for the Apostles to sleep under the stars at this time of year, with their mantles wrapped snugly around them. In the light of the above data, we can reconstruct in its general outlines what took place at Gethsemane. Jesus and His eleven Apostles crossed the bridge and started up the side of the Mount of Olives. At a short distance beyond the bridge, near the point where the highway branched into several roads, one leading directly over the mount and another around its side to Bethany and Jericho, the little group stopped at the gate of a garden. The owner had probably provided them with a key so that they could enter freely. Once inside the garden, our Lord turned to eight of the Apostles and said to them: "Sit down here, while I go over yonder and pray" (Matt. 26:36). Taking Peter and James and John with Him, He went a little farther into the interior of the garden. Already beginning to feel the first onslaughts of fear and sadness, He said to the favored three: "Wait here and watch with me" (Matt. 26:38).

There is much in the Gospel accounts of the life and teachings of Jesus that we understand without difficulty. We believe that Christ is God, but we believe also that He is man, so it does not shock us to read that He became tired, hungry, and thirsty; that He wept; that He felt the heat and the cold; that He became angry and lashed out at His enemies. Christ's birth in a poor stable at Bethlehem hardly gives us pause. Even most of the events of His Sacred Passion, while shocking, come into focus in our minds in the light of the dogma of Redemption.

But at Gethsemane we come face-to-face with what is perhaps the greatest mystery in the life of Jesus. Always before, there had been a transparent serenity of soul, a sureness of self, a close bond of unity with the Father, an utter fearlessness, a complete certainty and assurance in every word and act. But at Gethsemane there is a change. Christ's sadness and trouble of mind; His timidity and hesitation; His prayer, repeated over and over as He lay prostrate on the ground; the apparent contradiction between His will and that of His Father; His seeming cowardice in the face of death; His weakness and agony and bloody sweat—all these present us with problems that our finite minds can solve only in part because we cannot penetrate fully into the mystery of the union of the divine and human natures in one Person. Indeed, the events that took place in the Garden of Gethsemane are so hard to comprehend that some of the greatest Fathers of the Church, fearing that they detracted from the divinity of Christ, have done violence to the Gospel texts in interpreting these passages. We must accept the words of the Evangelists in their obvious sense, but we must in all humility acknowledge that at Gethsemane we are in the presence of one of the most profound mysteries of our Faith.

There are several reasons why Jesus chose Peter, James, and John to accompany Him. They had been the specially selected witnesses of the raising to life of the daughter of Jairus (Mark 5:37) as well as of the Transfiguration of Jesus (Mark 9:2). Because of this, they should now be better prepared not to be scandalized by Christ's sorrow and agony. Then, too, they were probably the Apostles Jesus loved most and from whose presence He hoped to receive the most comfort during His time of supreme trial. It is evident that the circumstances of the moment are extraordinary, as Jesus departed from his usual custom of praying entirely alone and even of seeking out complete solitude for prayer in a desert or mountainous region (Mark 1:35; 6:46). Our Lord had even instructed the Apostles to pray to the Father in secret (Matt. 6:6). Now He wanted His friends near Him not only for the comfort of their presence but also that they might be the witnesses of the agonies of mind as well as of body that He suffered in the work of our redemption.

While He was still with the three Apostles, before He left them to go on farther into the garden and begin His prayer, the floodgates of His soul opened and a wave of sorrow seemed to overwhelm Him. "He began to be saddened and exceedingly troubled" (Matt. 26:37). Both Evangelists use the expression "he began." It was the beginning, indeed, but the mental anguish came with the suddenness and force of a flash flood that sweeps all before it. Jesus felt already as if the very hand of death were upon Him, for He said to the three: "My soul is sad, even unto death" (Matt. 26:38; Mark 14:34). This was not the first time Jesus had declared His mental anguish. In the Temple area but a few days before, He had said: "Now my soul is troubled" (John 12:27). And he had added the prayer that He would repeat over and over this very night: "Father, save me from this hour" (John 12:27). But now the anguish that assailed Him was so acute that it was capable of causing His death, for it was, as He Himself said, a sadness "even unto death."

There is a tender and human touch in the fact that our Lord takes the three into His confidence, reveals to them the state of His soul, and seeks their company: "Wait here," He said, "and watch with me" (Matt. 26:38). In this critical moment, He wishes to associate the three with His prayer and watching. He did not say simply, "Wait here and watch"; He added the touching words, "with me." Yet it was by no means for Himself that He asked prayers, for He added: "Pray that you may not enter into temptation" (Luke 22:40). The terrible events that would put them to the test were even now taking shape in the darkness of the nearby city, and Jesus warned them to pray that they might have the strength to pass safely through the ordeal.

The words used by the Evangelist throw some light on the emotions that suddenly overwhelmed the soul of our Lord. Jesus feared. All His life, He had looked forward to His Passion without fear, even with eagerness. But now that the dread reality was upon Him, there was in it an element of terror. Present too was a feeling of sorrow, an emotion caused by an evil grasped by the mind as actually present. He was also "exceedingly troubled." The word used by the Evangelist in the original Greek usually refers to a confused, restless, distracted state of mind in which one feels utterly at a loss as to how to face up to something very difficult that must nevertheless be done.

After Jesus had confided His sorrow of soul to the three chosen Apostles and had warned them to watch and pray, He left them and went on a little farther into the garden, a "stone's throw," St. Luke says, a distance of about thirty paces (22:41).[4] The expression used by St. Luke in referring to our Lord's withdrawal from the Apostles implies that there was an element of compulsion. Jesus evidently felt an interior force drawing Him strongly aside to prayer. In the light of the full Paschal moon, the three Apostles could see Him clearly and also hear Him, as He undoubtedly followed the oriental custom of praying aloud. There is nothing to indicate that the three fell asleep immediately, so they had time to hear and observe what was taking place.

What they saw and heard must have shocked them. Jesus falls to His knees and then prostrates Himself on the ground. Clearly through the still night air comes the sound of His voice calling to His heavenly Father: "Father, if it is possible, let this cup pass away from me; yet not as I will, but as thou willest" (Matt. 26:39). The other two Evangelists who describe this scene use expressions slightly different but essentially the same. St. Mark, who derived his information from St. Peter, uses the Aramaic word *Abba* for

---

[4] St. Luke makes no mention of the chosen three, so that some think he means that our Lord was separated from the eight Apostles by "a stone's throw." It seems to us more in harmony with the other Evangelists to refer this expression of St. Luke to the three Apostles.

"Father," the very word our Lord used and which undoubtedly had remained engraved on Peter's mind. In his time of trial, it is to the Father that He turns.

On the mount of the Transfiguration, Jesus' divinity was so apparent that He appeared hardly human. Here in Gethsemane He was so human that He appeared not at all divine. Always before, He had spoken to the Father with a quiet calm and as to a loving equal. Now He sent up to the Father a cry from a soul flooded with anguish and tormented with fear.

And yet our Lord's prayer is hardly a prayer, at least of petition. It is rather a baring of his soul to the Father, a statement of His natural abhorrence of the awful fate that weighed upon Him. "If it is possible," our Lord said—if it were possible in accordance with the divine plan, He asked the Father to remove "the cup," "the hour" from him. Both these expressions refer to his impending Passion.[5]

Often before, Jesus had prayed to the Father. As God, He had no need to pray. Whatever He willed was accomplished. But He was also man, possessed of a human will and natural inclinations, and it was as man that He prayed here in Gethsemane; He addressed the Father and made a request. But He did not ask absolutely. He asked conditionally. He modified and completed His request by a reservation: "Not as I will but as thou willest" (Matt. 26:39). In the very breath in which He made known to the Father the extreme repugnance He felt toward accepting the cup of his Passion, our Lord disclosed His complete abandonment to the will of His Father. He showed in His resignation how to

---

[5] The expression "the cup" indicates a difficult trial (see Mark 10:38; John 18:11). "The hour" refers to the time of the Passion in the divine predestination.

practice what He had taught the disciples in the Lord's Prayer: "Thy will be done on earth as it is in heaven."

At first glance, there seems to be something strange and new in the words of our Lord's prayer in Gethsemane. Never before had He made a distinction between His will and the will of the Father. His life had always been so completely dependent on the will of the Father that He could truthfully say: "My food is to do the will of him who sent me" (John 4:34). Again and again he had spoken of the will of His Father. It was the light that guided His every step, the end toward which He directed His every action, the inspiration of His every word. But here in the shadows of the olive trees, now kneeling, now prostrate on the ground, Jesus used strange new words: "*I* will, *thou* wilt; not *my* will, but *thine*." Never before in His references to the Father's will had Jesus ever spoken of His own.

Here we are in the face of a mystery that has its origins in the substantial union of the human and divine natures in Christ. Our Faith throws light into the depths of this mystery, and we can safely follow the guidance of the Church's theologians, especially of the great St. Thomas Aquinas, in trying to understand something of what was taking place in the soul of Christ. In the light of their teaching, we shall see that the "contradiction" between Christ's will and that of His Father is not real but only apparent.

When Jesus Christ became man, He took to Himself a complete and perfect human nature. It was natural, therefore, for Christ to abhor suffering. He shrank instinctively from the scourges, the crown of thorns, the nails piercing His hands and feet. Like the rest of us, Jesus felt a natural inclination toward the pleasant and a natural aversion to the painful. All of this is evident from even a cursory reading of the Gospels.

Since Jesus took to Himself a complete human nature, He had a human as well as a divine will. It is to an act of this human will, as a natural sensitive inclination, that Christ referred in His prayer in the garden when He said, "I will," and, again, "My will." Although Christ had a single human will, that will had a twofold act or operation. These two acts are referred to as the natural will and the rational will.

St. Thomas explains these two terms quite simply. The act of the natural will is directed to something willed in itself, as, for instance, health. The act of the rational will is directed toward something that is a means to an end, such as taking medicine. It is to the natural will, which abhorred the sufferings of the Passion, that Christ referred when He said, "I will," and again, "My will." But the act of the rational will in Christ placed Him in complete and absolute conformity with the will of the Father.

When Jesus said, "Thy will be done," He accepted unequivocally and unconditionally the chalice of His Sacred Passion. His sufferings were the divinely ordained means of attaining our Redemption, so He willed them in order to secure that end. There was no contradiction whatever, therefore, between the human and divine wills in Christ.

Christ's prayer is a perfect example of what our prayer should be. He expresses Himself with filial confidence, using the term Father: "my Father." He explains the natural aversion, the extreme repugnance He experiences toward the awful sufferings that await Him; He asks to be delivered from them "if it is possible"; and He ends on a note of complete and absolute resignation to the will of the Father.

A person in the grip of mental anguish is agitated, restless. From the Gospel accounts of what took place at Gethsemane, it was evidently so with Jesus. At times He knelt, at times He cast

Himself on the ground, face downward. Probably, too, He prayed in the ordinary manner of the time, standing with outstretched arms. After a while, He broke off His prayer and returned to the Apostles. No doubt he felt the need of some consolation from speaking with His chosen three. Jesus was obviously disappointed to find them sound asleep. It is difficult for us to understand how they could have fallen asleep in view of what they had just seen and overheard.

They had watched and listened during the first part of Christ's prayer, but as Jesus continued to express the same thoughts in more or less the same words, they gradually wearied and fell asleep. We must remember that they never took our Lord's warnings sufficiently to heart, so great was their confidence in His miraculous powers. St. Luke offers an excuse for them when He says that they were "sleeping for sorrow" (22:45). Sorrow, caused by what they had seen and heard, undoubtedly contributed to their fatigue. Nevertheless, it is a little shocking that the three chosen Apostles should be stretched out in sleep while Jesus was prostrate in prayer and while His enemies were gathering their forces in the surrounding darkness in preparation for His arrest.

Jesus aroused the sleeping Apostles with words of gentle reproach addressed directly to Peter: "Simon, dost thou sleep? Couldst thou not watch one hour?" (Mark 14:37). There is a touch of irony in our Lord's words. He addressed him as Simon, the name by which he was known before his call, to indicate that he had not really changed, that he still had not become Peter, the rock. He questioned him: "Dost thou sleep?" as if such a thing was incredible; and then, to press the point still further, added, "Couldst thou not watch one hour?" But a short time before, Peter had led all the others in his boasting that he would follow Jesus "to prison and to death" (Luke 22:33). Now he could not watch one hour with Him. Jesus' words were a gentle rebuke, a reminder to Peter of his recent boast.

"Watch and pray," our Lord now said to them. This was no time for sleep; this was the time to watch lest they be taken unaware by the dangers that threatened. And they were not only to watch but also to pray that they might not fail but might pass safely through the dangerous times ahead. They were to watch and pray that they might not "enter into temptation." Trials and temptations there must be in life, but vigilance and prayer give assurance of victory. Christ referred to the storm that was about to break over their heads, but His words of admonition have a permanent value that the passage of time has not lessened.

Jesus went on to say: "The spirit indeed is willing, but the flesh is weak" (Mark 14:38). He was still thinking of their boastful protestations of a few hours before, but at the same time He offered an excuse for the weakness of the Apostles. Christ's words give a reason for the necessity of watching and praying. A man may be full of goodwill and good intentions, but these can be brought to nothing in a moment of trial through human weakness. How completely the truth of His words was to be realized in the conduct of the Apostles in the hours that followed.

After admonishing the Apostles, Jesus returned to His prayer. The subject of his prayer was still the same, but there is a slight difference noticeable in the words as related by the first Evangelist. In this prayer, our Lord said: "My Father, if this cup cannot pass away unless I drink it, thy will be done" (Matt. 26:42). No longer was there any mention of His own will. Now there was question only of the Father's will. If the Father did not wish that this cup should be removed from His lips, the human will of Jesus made an act of complete resignation and conformity.

Jesus was still restless; again He sought solace in the company of the three, and again He found them sleeping. How long Jesus' second prayer lasted we do not know, but it must have been some time, as it is probable that, after our Lord's rebuke, the three had made an effort to remain awake. Nevertheless, they had finally given way to slumber, for as Matthew and Mark both say: "their eyes were heavy." Our Lord must have awakened them, because as Mark tells us: "They did not know what answer to make to him" (14:40). They were too embarrassed to speak. It is easy to picture them. They had been lying on the ground in a sound sleep. When Jesus awakened them, they sat up, rubbing their eyes and looking at Him shamefacedly. These are the same three who had been with Jesus on Mount Tabor at the time of His Transfiguration. There they had been elated. There Peter had found his tongue quite easily and had known what to say. Now even Peter was too ashamed to speak.

Jesus left them again and went off a third time to pray. The Evangelists do not tell us whether He warned them again to watch and pray. It is likely that He did. This third prayer of Jesus is a repetition of the first and second. It is evident that the struggle continued in the soul of Jesus. His repeated acts of resignation to the will of the Father had not destroyed the opposition His human nature felt to humiliation, suffering, and death. Indeed, it is evident that the struggle in the soul of Jesus was mounting in intensity, for it was during this final prayer that an angel from heaven came to strengthen Him and that He suffered an agony and a bloody sweat.[6]

---

[6] St. Luke, who alone mentions the angel, the agony, and bloody sweat, mentions only one prayer. It is not clear, therefore, during which prayer these incidents took place. Some commentators

St. Luke tells us that "there appeared to him an angel from heaven to strengthen him" (22:43). It was an angel in human form, as the expression used by St. Luke indicates an apparition visible to bodily eyes. An angel announced Christ's coming into the world, a choir of angels proclaimed His birth, and, after the temptation in the desert, angels came to minister to Him. The angels who ministered to Jesus came to assist Him after the trial of the forty days' fast and the temptation. In Gethsemane an angel appeared in order to strengthen Him in advance for the awful climax of His mental anguish in the agony and bloody sweat. Jesus' sufferings were concentrated in His soul, but from the soul they overflowed to the body, distressing and weakening it. It is likely, therefore, that the angel brought Jesus strength for both soul and body.

How the angel did this is a mystery that God has not revealed to us. The explanations given are therefore conjectural. Some think that the angel spoke to our Lord, reminding Him of the great good that would be accomplished by His Passion and death. While the angel could not act directly on the soul of Jesus, He could act on His sensitive faculties by suggestions that would have their echo in His soul and assist Him to triumph in the terrible struggle that was even now reaching its climax. By His acceptance of help from an angel, Jesus manifested His humility, for as a member of the human race, He had taken to Himself a nature lower in rank than the angels. As the Sacred Scriptures put it: "Thou hast made him [man] a little lower than the angels" (Heb. 2:7; Ps. 8:5).

---

attach them to the first prayer of our Lord. We prefer to follow those who think they took place during the third prayer.

After telling of the angel, St. Luke goes on to say: "And falling into an agony he prayed the more earnestly" (22:43). The Greek word for "agony" does not mean the final spasms that often precede death. The ancients used the word in referring to a struggle such as the contests of the sports arena. Sometimes it was used of the emotional upset that athletes often suffered before a contest, or of any violent emotional disturbance. St. Luke uses the term here to express the supreme anguish that gripped the soul of Jesus in the struggle to submit His natural inclinations to the will of the Father and accept the awful shame and sufferings of His Passion. Even before He began His prayer, Jesus had said: "My soul is sad, even unto death" (Matt. 26:38; Mark 14:34). After He had expressed to His Father His submission and His acceptance of the cup of His Passion, His mental anguish did not subside but went on increasing until it reached a climax in the supreme moments of struggle that St. Luke calls an "agony." Everything indicated that this was indeed the culminating point in Christ's mental sufferings. Just before it, an angel had come from heaven to strengthen Him. Now His prayer increased in intensity—"He prayed the more earnestly"—and finally, as a result of this racking interior anguish, Jesus suffered a sweat of blood.

One might almost think that St. Luke was detached from the whole matter, so laconic is the sentence in which he describes the symptoms of Christ's awful interior struggle: "And his sweat became as drops of blood running down upon the ground" (22:44). The violence of the conflict taking place in Christ's soul manifested itself outwardly in a bloody sweat. Blood was forced from the blood vessels through the pores to the surface of the skin, where it mingled with the perspiration and then formed into thick, heavy drops and flowed to the ground. It is not necessary to seek a supernatural explanation of this unusual happening. Both ancients and moderns have recognized cases of bloody sweat (hematidrosis) caused by a great sudden onslaught of fear or sorrow. Some have thought that St. Luke meant only to make a comparison—"His sweat became as drops of blood"—and that there was no bloody sweat at all. There could be no grounds, however, for comparing sweat to blood unless both mingled on the surface of Christ's body in blood-tinted drops.

How long Jesus' third prayer lasted we do not know. So intense was it, and so violent the mental anguish that agitated our Lord's soul, that it is likely that it was the longest of the three prayers at Gethsemane. At its conclusion, peace reigned again in the heart of Jesus. He saw the path that lay immediately before Him, and it was the stony way of the cross. But He was ready now, and willing. The weakness of His human nature had been given full play, but it had not prevailed. When Jesus rose from His prayer to return to the Apostles, His garments were stained with the bloody sweat of His agony, but He walked with confidence and serenity, ready to follow in the way marked out for Him by His heavenly Father.

Chapter 6

THE MEANING OF GETHSEMANE

In the Garden of Gethsemane, Jesus feared. He feared the awful sufferings He foresaw would come to Him in the following hours. He prayed to His heavenly Father a repeated and earnest prayer to remove this cup of suffering from Him if it was possible. During His prayer, He knelt; He prostrated Himself on the ground; He struggled so hard to reconcile His natural inclinations to the divine will that He fell into an agony and bloody sweat.

From earliest Christian times to the present, this event in the life of Jesus has been a scandal to unbelievers. As early as the second century, the pagan Celsus wrote: "If things took place as he wished, if he was struck obeying his Father, it is clear that nothing could be hard or painful to him, because it was God who willed all that. Why then does he lament, why does he moan, why does he seek to avoid the death he dreads, saying: 'Oh Father, if it is possible, let this cup pass from me'?"[7] Even some of the greatest Fathers of the Church, while admitting the authenticity of these passages in the Gospels, have strained their natural sense

---

[7] See Origen, *Contra Celsus* 2, 9.

beyond the breaking point to avoid admitting that Jesus feared. The references to the angel, the agony, and the bloody sweat were evidently particularly hard for some of the earliest Christians to accept, as we find the passages relating these incidents missing in many of the earliest manuscripts of the Gospel of St. Luke. One can for this reason be doubly sure of their authenticity, however, as it is easy to understand why they were omitted, but one would be completely at a loss to explain their addition to the Gospel.

Fear in the face of death was even more scandalous to the ancients than it is to moderns. The ancient world had widely accepted the philosophy of the Stoics, who cultivated indifference, whether to pain or to pleasure. It admired strength, power, and force. The ideal man had few of the lovable virtues taught by Christ. Even St. Augustine, great soul that he was, felt the need to be apologetic that he had wept at the death of his mother, St. Monica.

An added difficulty is the apparent contrast between Jesus' fear and the courage of the martyrs faced with death. St. Polycarp welcomed the soldiers come to arrest him, gave them to eat, and asked only that he be allowed a little time for prayer. Having prayed for all, he went off joyfully to his death. St. Ignatius of Antioch feared lest well-intentioned friends prevent him from dying for Christ. In his *Epistle to the Romans*, he said, "I shall willingly die for God unless you hinder me.... I am the wheat of God, and let me be ground by the teeth of the wild beasts that I may be found the pure bread of Christ."

This has been the story of the martyrs up to our own times. St. Thomas More could joke even at the last hour. In his weakened condition, he had difficulty mounting the scaffold, so he turned to one of the officials and said, "See me safe up, and, as for my coming down, let me shift for myself." After encouraging the executioner, who seemed more distressed than himself, he asked him not to strike with the axe until he had shifted his beard, for, he said, "It has never offended His Highness."

We must make a clear distinction between fear and cowardice. A coward is not one who fears but one who allows fear to overcome him. In Gethsemane Christ feared, but in a terrible interior struggle, He completely conquered fear. He asked that the cup of His Passion be removed from Him "if possible," but He proclaimed unequivocally His acceptance of the will of His Father. He had several hours at least in which to escape if He wished, but He not only remained at Gethsemane where He knew He would be apprehended; He also went forth calmly to meet His captors. With complete and detailed foreknowledge of what awaited Him, He walked deliberately the road to Calvary.

Christ was God as well as man. No suffering, interior or exterior, could touch Him unless He permitted it. Whatever He suffered in Gethsemane, He suffered because He Himself, by a deliberate act of His will, allowed Himself to suffer. He opened the floodgates of His soul and gave entry to the torrent of fear and disgust and sorrow that beat upon Him.

Nothing could have made Jesus more like us, more lovable, more our Brother, than the agony in the garden. Suffering inflicted on Jesus by others had the appearance at least of being involuntary. The sufferings of Gethsemane, deep in His soul, could touch Him only because He Himself willed it, and He willed it to show us how human He really is, to give us courage in our fears, to set us an example, to merit for us the grace needed in our interior conflicts. If the martyrs suffered courageously and even joyously, they were borne up and inspired by the thought of Jesus Christ suffering and agonizing; they were strengthened by the graces merited for them by His agony and His bloody sweat. Jesus' struggle to overcome His natural fear is our model and inspiration in time of interior trials. His agony teaches us better than any words that God does not despise or condemn the weakness of our human nature, that Christian virtue does not consist in callousness or stoical indifference but in dominating and controlling our human emotions. Fear and sorrow and weariness there must be in every life. Virtue consists not in an effort to bypass or ignore them but in conquering them, even though the struggle may mean for us, too, a Gethsemane.

Fear was not the only emotion that afflicted the soul of Jesus during His prayer in the Garden of Gethsemane. The Gospels mention also feelings of sorrow, of weariness, and of disgust. Jesus had accepted the role of Redeemer of the human race. He had taken it upon Himself to pay the penalty for sin. He had become man to redeem men, a sinless member of the sinful human family to save sinners. He had clothed Himself with flesh to conquer the flesh in its own domain; He had taken upon Himself our infirmities and our miseries in order to be the ideal pontiff opening to us the gates of heaven. Centuries before, the prophet Isaiah had foretold Christ's redemptive role in a moving passage in which He has Christ's Passion before his eyes:

> Surely he hath borne our infirmities and carried our sorrows; and we have thought him as it were a leper, and as one struck by God and afflicted. But he was wounded for our iniquities: he was bruised for our sins. The chastisement of our peace was upon him: and by his bruises we are healed. All we like sheep have gone astray, every one

hath turned aside into his own way: and the Lord hath laid on him the iniquity of us all (53:4–6).

In the Garden of Gethsemane, Jesus knew perfectly just what it was for which He was to pay the penalty. He was to pay the penalty for sin—for all the sins of mankind, from the first to the last. Isaiah the prophet had cried out: "Woe is me, because I have held my peace; because I am a man of unclean lips, and ... I have seen with my eyes the King, the Lord of Hosts" (6:5). Infinitely more than Isaiah, Jesus knew the utter purity of the Divine Majesty, His own complete innocence, and the awful malice of sin. Jesus loved His Father with an infinite love, and He loved the sinner. Jesus grieved over the offense sin gave to His Father and the harm it wrought in human souls. He grieved particularly as head of the human family, because it was in a very real sense His own family that gave offense to the Divine Majesty.

In the other scenes of our Lord's Sacred Passion, many are present. In the prayer in the garden, Jesus appears to be alone with His Father, except for the brief presence of the comforting angel. Although the Evangelists do not mention it, there is reason to believe that Satan also was present. At the beginning of our Lord's public life, after the forty days' fast, the devil tempted him, and the temptation was directed to Jesus in His role of Messiah. After this trial of strength, the devil left our Lord, but, as St. Luke says significantly, his departure was temporary: "He departed from him for a while" (4:13). Now, at the time of the Passion, the devil returns with all his cunning and power. St. John records that Satan entered into Judas after Christ had given him a morsel at the

Last Supper (13:27). A few minutes later, Jesus Himself declared: "The prince of the world is coming, and in me he has nothing" (John 14:30). On the same occasion, Jesus warned the Apostles that Satan would soon make an assault upon them, would sift them as the harvester sifts the grain in the sieve (Luke 22:31). As Jesus kneels and prays in the Garden of Gethsemane, Satan knows that the showdown is at hand in the struggle between Jesus and His enemies, and now he marshals all his forces to make a grand final assault.

The Gospel account of Christ's temptation at the beginning of His public life reveals that He could be and was tempted by external suggestion.[8] As St. Paul says in his epistle to the Hebrews: "For in that he himself has suffered and has been tempted, he is able to help those who are tempted" (2:18). In the Garden of Gethsemane, Satan again tempts Christ as Messiah. Again he pictures for him the easy and glorious role of a Messiah according to the popular ideas of the time. How easy it could be! How often the crowds following Jesus had tried to take Him by force and make Him King! On the preceding Sunday, they had given Him a glorious reception into the city of Jerusalem, strewing their garments in His path and proclaiming Him the Son of David, the Messiah. The path He had followed on that triumphal day lay just outside the gate of the garden where Jesus now prayed, and the hosannas of the people seemed still to echo through the valley and from the walls of the Temple on the hill opposite. One word from Jesus, and He could march from triumph to triumph. He could substitute the crown for the cross; He could save Himself and His people.

---

[8] On the temptation of Christ, see St. Thomas Aquinas, *Summa Theologica*, III, Q. 41, art. 1ff.

And the alternative? Jesus knew it well. It was the lot of the suffering Servant of Yahweh pictured in the somber prophecies of Isaiah (53). It was the betrayal, the condemnation by His own people and by the Roman tribunal; it was the scourging, the crowning with thorns, the carrying of the cross, the three long hours of suffering on that shameful gibbet, ending in death.

Jesus' answer to the diabolical temptation is contained in his oft-repeated act of resignation addressed to His Father: "Not my will, but thine be done." The words were simple and few, but they were difficult words to say. They were costly words. They cost Jesus hours of agonizing prayer. They cost Him His life.

It is impossible to place exact limits to the scope of Satan's temptation of Jesus in the Garden of Gethsemane. Jesus must have undergone a severe trial, too, from His own foresight of the consequences of His Passion and the utter ingratitude of those who should have benefited by it. To the great Apostle Paul, it was incredible that anyone could be so evil as to cause Christ to die in vain. "O foolish Galatians," he wrote, "who has bewitched you, before whose eyes Jesus Christ has been depicted crucified?" (Gal. 3:1). And yet, when Jesus was still a child, the holy Simeon had told His Mother, Mary: "Behold, this child is destined for the fall and for the rise of many in Israel, and for a sign that shall be contradicted" (Luke 2:34). That was part of the awful tragedy of Christ's Passion. In spite of its cost in blood and tears, many would not profit by it. For many, Jesus would die in vain. Worse still, their damnation would be deeper, their culpability greater, for the very reason that He had come to offer them their hard-bought redemption. This thought was surely in Jesus' mind. But a few hours earlier that evening, He had said: "If I had not come and spoken to them, they would have no sin. But now they have no excuse for their sin" (John 15:22).

The LAST HOURS *of* JESUS

The bitterest part of this suffering was undoubtedly the fact that His own people would be the first to reject Him and His saving mission. We cannot doubt that Jesus loved His people with a great and special love. The Apostle Paul later wrote in His epistle to the Romans:

> I speak the truth in Christ, I do not lie, my conscience bearing me witness in the Holy Spirit, that I have great sadness and continuous sorrow in my heart. For I could wish to be anathema myself from Christ for the sake of my brethren, who are my kinsmen according to the flesh; who are Israelites, who have the adoption as sons, and the glory and the covenants and the legislation and the worship and the promises; who have the fathers, and from whom is the Christ according to the flesh, who is over all things, God blessed forever, amen. (9:1–5)

Paul would not only willingly die for his people, but if it were possible, he would even accept an immeasurably greater suffering—he would become anathema from Christ in order to reconcile them to Christ. Jesus' love for His people was infinitely greater than Paul's. But a few days before, He had looked down on Jerusalem from a point a little above the Garden of Gethsemane, and He had wept at the thought of the punishment that would overtake this city for its awful sin of deicide. "If thou hadst known," he said, "in this thy day, even thou, the things that are for thy peace! But now they are hidden from thy eyes" (Luke 19:42). And again He had cried out: "Jerusalem, Jerusalem! thou who killest the prophets, and stonest those who are sent to thee! How often would I have gathered thy children together, as a hen gathers her young under her wings, but thou wouldst not!" (Matt. 23:37).

These people He loved so much and longed so ardently to save would reject Him. Already He could hear the cry that would go up but a few hours hence from the crowd gathered against Him before the tribunal of the Roman procurator: "Away with him! Away with him! Crucify him!" (John 19:15). And He could hear also that awful curse they would call down upon themselves instead of the blessings He would give them: "His blood be on us and on our children" (Matt. 27:25). His condemnation was difficult for Him to accept, but it was rendered more difficult by the thought that His condemnation was also the condemnation of those He loved so dearly.

And even among those nearest to Him, His twelve Apostles, there was one who would betray Him, one for whom He would die in vain, one for whom His death would be a cause of deeper damnation. Jesus loved Judas and strove to bring him to his senses before it was too late. His efforts were of no avail. Even now Judas was approaching to consummate the deed that would lead him to death and damnation.

The other Apostles would profit by Jesus' death, but they too were a source of sorrow to Him. He had tried unsuccessfully to prepare them for the awful storm that even now was ready to break over their heads. Instead of praying, they slept. Soon they would desert Him, and Peter would even deny that he knew Him. He was fully aware that they would return to Him, but He foresaw too the terrible trials that awaited them because they were His disciples. How truly He had told them: "They will expel you from the synagogues. Yes, the hour is coming for everyone who kills you to think that he is offering worship to God.... You shall weep and lament, but the world shall rejoice" (John 16:2, 20). And finally, they would be called upon to offer their lives as martyrs to their faith in Him.

Jesus foresaw too the fate that awaited His Church, the persecution and bloodlettings to which it would be subjected down through the centuries. Its history would be in a sense a prolongation of that way of the cross that He would soon tread. He was the Head of the Church. He suffered in its members. That is why he could truly say to the persecutor, Saul: "Saul, Saul, why dost thou persecute me?" (Acts 9:4). Jesus foresaw, too, those vast multitudes to the end of time who would reject Him and His saving grace, those for whom He would die in vain.

A feeling of futility must have been one of the major causes of the interior sufferings of our Lord in the Garden of Gethsemane. On the one hand was the terrible price He would pay for our redemption; on the other, indifference, ingratitude, neglect, and rejection. That Christ should accept the sufferings of His Passion to redeem even the saints was an act of divine prodigality; that He should accept the role for all of us was an act of generosity beyond all comprehension.

Chapter 7

THE BETRAYAL

When Jesus returned to the three Apostles from His third prayer, He was completely Himself again. Doubt, hesitation, fear, and conflict were gone. Wan, and undoubtedly somewhat weak, from the awful ordeal through which He had passed, He nevertheless manifested once again that complete serenity of soul and mastery of Himself and His surroundings that had characterized His entire life.

The three Apostles, still stretched out on the ground, were evidently not asleep, as Jesus immediately spoke to them: "Sleep on now, and take your rest! It is enough; the hour has come. Behold, the Son of Man is betrayed into the hands of sinners. Rise, let us go. Behold, he who will betray me is at hand" (Mark 14:41–42; cf. Matt. 26:45–46). This passage is not altogether clear. It is difficult to determine exactly what took place. St. Augustine, and many who follow him, think that Jesus permitted the three to go off to sleep for a while, and when He saw the betrayer approaching roused them with the words, "It is enough," and so forth. It seems more in conformity with the text of the Evangelists, however, not to introduce an interval of time during which the Apostles slept, but to consider that our Lord spoke all these words at one time. Jesus addressed the Apostles in a tone of gentle irony. In a sense, He says to them, "Go ahead and sleep if you can; I won't be the one to wake you. The time for prayer and watching is over. Now is the time for action."

If the three were still drowsy, they should have been aroused from their torpor by Jesus' words: "The hour has come." They had heard Jesus refer to "the hour" before (see Mark 14:35; Luke 13:32; 22:53; John 7:30; 8:20; 12:27; 13:1). It is the hour of His Passion, the hour that cannot be advanced or delayed, the hour of His enemies and of the powers of darkness. Now it is here. "The Son of Man is betrayed into the hands of sinners" (Matt. 26:45). Our Lord speaks in the present. Probably He already hears the footsteps of His enemies and sees the reflection of their torches on the leaves of the olive trees that line the road from the valley below. As on so many other solemn occasions, He refers to Himself in those words of prophecy, "Son of Man." The sinners Jesus refers to are the evil men into whose hands He is being betrayed.

Although thoroughly awakened by this time, the three were still sprawled on the ground. "Rise," Jesus now said to them, "let us go. He who will betray me is at hand." There is no thought of flight, of fear, of hesitancy; Jesus does not even wait for the danger. He goes to meet it.

The three scrambled to their feet, and Jesus led them toward the gate of the garden where He had left the eight Apostles. He quickly roused them and then went before them through the garden gate, out onto the open road beyond. There, with the straggly little group around Him, He waited.

The last that Jesus and the Apostles had seen of Judas, he was slipping quietly from the lighted Upper Room of the Last Supper into the darkness of the night. He had resisted our Lord's final appeals and had been dismissed by Jesus from His presence and from the apostolate. "What thou dost," our Lord had said, "do quickly."

The Gospels do not recount the actions of Judas after his departure, but from what followed, it is not difficult to trace his steps. In the darkness outside the Upper Room, Judas must have stood for a while, rapt in thought. He had to make a decision as to his course of action, and he had to make it immediately. The day had been a crucial one. Its events had brought matters to a head. He may have been suspicious when Jesus had appointed Peter and John to make the preparations for the Paschal supper. During the meal, his suspicions had become a certainty that Jesus knew what was afoot. Our Lord intimated to Judas that He knew what was taking place, and then He asked him to rid the little group of his presence.

What would Jesus do next? Would he reveal Judas' treachery to the other Apostles? If He did, what would be their reaction, especially that of the headstrong and devoted Peter? Anyway, the whole situation had changed. No longer could he remain with Jesus in the guise of a friend and disciple. No longer could he take his place in the ranks of the chosen Twelve.

Judas realized that he must act now or give up forever hope of success in his scheme. After the Passover, Jesus would return to Galilee without him; as a discredited disciple, he would no longer be of any value to the enemies of Jesus. The bargain he had made with them would be null and void.

Judas was faced with the choice of immediate action or abandonment of his design. He chose immediate action.

Once the choice was made, it was a matter of only a few moments to determine exactly what was to be done. The course of action was so obvious that a plan formed in his mind even as he made the decision to act. He knew that all he had to do was to present his scheme to the enemies of Jesus, and they would jump at the opportunity to put it into effect.

Judas walked quickly along the narrow streets leading to the nearby palace of the high priest. In spite of the lateness of the hour, he easily obtained admittance and soon found himself again in the presence of the chief priests with whom he had concluded a bargain but a day earlier for the betrayal of Jesus.

Judas explained to them the sudden change in the situation. Jesus knew what was afoot. Even by now He might have told His Apostles. It was tonight or never. Jesus would still be near the holy city, as the law governing the Passover required that the night be spent in Jerusalem or its immediate environs. Furthermore, the law of the Sabbath rest, which prevailed on the feast, forbade a journey of any length. Judas had been with Jesus on the preceding nights at Bethany and on the Mount of Olives. Bethany was beyond a Sabbath day's journey, so surely Jesus would spend the night on the Mount of Olives, and Judas knew the exact spot because he had frequently been there with Him. Everything was perfect for the capture of Jesus if immediate steps were taken.

We do not know whether there was hesitation on the part of the enemies of Jesus. If there was, it undoubtedly arose from fear of the reaction of the Galilean pilgrims who filled the city and dotted the surrounding hills and valleys with their makeshift abodes. They were a brave, even a violent people, and for the most part they accepted Jesus as a prophet. They could cause trouble.

On the other hand, it was night, and the capture of Jesus could be made under the cover of darkness. By the time the news of what had taken place got abroad the next day, Jesus would be not only a prisoner but a condemned criminal. After all, the Galileans were peasants, fishermen, people in large part from the lower strata of society. They had the countryman's regard for the big city and for its imposing Temple. They had the yokel's respect for the great men who formed the aristocracy of the religious capital—the chief priests, the Scribes, the Pharisees, and the ancients. It would not be too difficult to persuade them that Jesus was an impostor, but not a good enough impostor to impose on these great and learned men in whose hands lay the destiny of God's chosen people.

The decision was made to accept Judas' offer and to prepare immediately to capture Jesus this very night.

Soon there was a quiet hum of activity running through the palace. Messengers hurried in and out of the great gate that led from the courtyard onto the city street. We do not know just how the enemies of Christ went about organizing the band that was sent to arrest Him, but the Gospel accounts of the betrayal tell us the composition of the group that took Christ captive at Gethsemane.

One part of the group was made up of Temple police. This force had the responsibility for preserving order in the Temple area. Its officers were priests, and the commanding officer ranked high in the sacerdotal caste. Officers of this force had been present when Judas bargained with the chief priests over the betrayal of Christ, so it was only natural that they should be called upon now to execute the agreement that had been reached.

Although the Gospels state that the arrest of Jesus was ordered by the Sanhedrin, made up of chief priests, Scribes, and ancients, only one Gospel states that some of the chief priests, captains of the Temple police, and ancients were present at the arrest (Luke 22:52). A few chief priests and ancients came, motivated by curiosity or by zeal, to see that official orders were carried out promptly and properly. All but John mention that there was a crowd. This expression refers to the entire band, which included a certain number of servants and retainers, pressed into service at the last moment.

St. John alone mentions the presence of Roman soldiers at the arrest of Jesus. He refers to a cohort and its commanding officer, a tribune (18:3, 12). The ordinary garrison of the Castle Antonia, the fortress that guarded the Temple area, was a cohort, or six hundred soldiers. The expression used here by St. John often refers to a maniple, or two hundred men. It is probable that the Evangelist uses the term in a broad sense for a small detachment of soldiers from the cohort. The enemies of Jesus feared that His followers might resort to forceful resistance, which the Temple police might find difficult to overcome. Anyway, an armed disturbance, especially during the celebration of a feast, could bring down on their heads the wrath of the procurator, the Roman ruler of the Province of Judea, who was in Jerusalem during the Paschal celebration for no other purpose than to preserve order. The chief priests probably sent a messenger to the tribune, or possibly even to Pontius Pilate, the procurator, explaining the situation and requesting help. It would seem from the Gospel account that the Roman troops acted simply as a reinforcement and took no active part in the actual arrest. Their presence was a show of force intended primarily to intimidate the one to be arrested. Their role was similar to that of state militia called in to back up the local police in case a situation gets out of hand.[9]

---

[9] Some critics deny the authenticity of St. John's account. Here are some of their reasons and an answer. (1) The first three Evangelists

The first three Evangelists say that the crowd was armed with swords and clubs. Undoubtedly the Temple police as well as the Roman soldiers carried swords. The clubs were probably carried by the servants and retainers. Some of the group had lanterns and torches, standard night equipment for a police or military force. Although there was a full moon, it would be quite dark in the deep recesses of the Cedron Valley, as well as in the olive groves of Gethsemane.

Although the Evangelists give us no information on the subject, we can be sure that the point of assembly for the entire group was the Castle Antonia, which dominated the Temple area from the northwest and was connected with it by flights of stairs. Once the group was formed and orders given, they proceeded northward until outside the city, then turned eastward along the north wall. Beyond the northeast corner of the city wall they descended the

---

do not mention the cohort. Answer: St. John deliberately supplements their account. Furthermore, their silence is due to the inactive role of the Roman soldiers. (2) There would be no need of a cohort, the entire garrison of the Castle Antonia. Answer: The word used by St. John doesn't necessarily mean an entire cohort, although this is its technical sense. It is often used for part of a cohort. (3) Pontius Pilate shows no knowledge at the trial of Jesus that he had already heard of the case. Answer: Even if he had heard of it, he would not have given any indication but would have started the proceedings with a clean slate. He probably knew something about it, though the tribune, ordinarily the highest Roman officer in Jerusalem, had wide discretionary powers (see Acts 21:31). (4) If a tribune and Roman soldiers were present, Jesus would have been taken to the Roman rather than to the Jewish authorities. Answer: This would be true if the Romans had initiated the arrest or had been in charge of its execution. Neither was true. They were present simply as a reinforcement in case of need.

steep slope of the Cedron Valley and then mounted again on the east until they approached the Garden of Gethsemane.

At this point Judas moved forward to take over as guide. He immediately called for a consultation to assure the smooth operation of their plan. They were prepared for possible resistance. Now only a case of mistaken identity could rob them of their quarry. The Roman soldiers certainly would not know Jesus. Many of the others had undoubtedly seen Him on occasion teaching in the Temple, but most of His public life had been spent in Galilee. In the flickering, uncertain light of torches and lanterns, they might fail to recognize Him. Judas had a ready solution for this difficulty: "Whomever I kiss," he said to them, "that is he; lay hold of him, and lead him safely away" (Mark 14:44).

In itself there was nothing extraordinary in the sign selected by Judas. A kiss was a conventional manifestation of respect by the disciple to the master. The other Apostles would not suspect anything unusual or sinister in Judas' greeting. Jesus had revealed Judas' perfidy to only one of the Apostles. Taken by surprise, the others probably did not quickly associate him with those who were with him and may even have thought that he was just returning from the errand on which Jesus had sent him when he had said: "What thou dost, do quickly."

Conventional or not, the kiss was a sign of respect and affection. That Judas should select it as a means of betrayal gives a deeper insight into his calloused soul. And then he went on to reveal a further depth of evil within him. Instead of wavering at this critical moment, instead of being harassed by second and better thoughts, he directed the others to fulfill their part well: "Lay hold on him and lead him safely away." Judas had received a promise but not payment. He did not want his reward to slip through his fingers through the carelessness of others. He urged his accomplices to grasp Jesus firmly and to take precautions, lest He escape.

By this time, Jesus and the eleven Apostles were outside the gate of the garden, not far from the grotto a little to the north. His enemies now approached, led by Judas, "one of the Twelve," as the Evangelists record with what seems almost incredulity. In the wavering light of the lanterns and torches, two figures stood out—Jesus and Judas—each slightly in advance of his group. Whether because he wanted to get the deed done or because he feared Jesus might yet escape him, Judas strode quickly up to Christ and kissed him: "He went straight up to him," St. Mark says, "and said, 'Rabbi' and kissed him" (14:45). Judas was a careful man. He was taking no chances. Lest the kiss be not enough, he addressed Jesus aloud as Rabbi to make his identity doubly certain to his enemies. And the word used by St. Matthew and St. Mark indicates a tender or prolonged kiss. Judas kept his arms about our Lord's neck for an extra moment or two in order to make certain His enemies would recognize Him.

No words can describe the awful malice of Judas' deed or plumb the depths of his moral depravity. The dignity of Jesus' person, the close relationship between Him and this disciple whom He had called to the incomparable dignity of the apostolate and admitted to His friendship, the sordidness of Judas' bargain in selling Christ at a price, the kiss by which the betrayal was effected: all unite to make this deed unique in the history of human malice. So despicable was Judas' act that St. John, who revealed that Judas was a thief, passes over in silence the kiss of betrayal. He seems unable to bring himself to mention it. St. Luke, who describes the scene, seems unwilling to state that Judas actually kissed Jesus. He says simply that "Judas drew near to Jesus to kiss him," without stating whether he accomplished his purpose.

As Judas relaxed his embrace and stepped back a pace, Jesus spoke to him. They were the last words He would ever address to him, at least on this earth. Jesus must have looked at Judas with a little chagrin and perhaps hesitated a brief moment before He spoke. "Judas," He said, "dost thou betray the Son of Man with a kiss?" (Luke 22:48). There is a sharp and forceful contrast in those few simple words: Judas and the Son of Man, a betrayal and a kiss. They are a reproach aimed at Judas. Yet they seem more of an expression of disbelief on the part of our Lord, as if He could not bring Himself to comprehend the reality of what was taking place. That Judas should betray his friend and master was a great evil; that he should use a kiss, a sign of friendship and respect, to send Jesus to His death almost passes belief. Judas left Christ's divine embrace irremediably hardened, the type forever of all that is hypocritical and deceitful in human nature.[10]

---

[10] St. Matthew also records words of Jesus addressed to Judas (26:50). The passage is rather difficult and has been translated variously. We shall confine our remarks to two of the more probable interpretations. According to some, our Lord said to Judas: "Friend, for what purpose hast thou come?" The sense would be, "Friend, for what are you come? Did you not come to betray me? Why then this kiss?" The difficulty is that the relative clause was not used at the time as an interrogative.

Another translation of this text reads: "Friend, with that for which thou art come." What is taking place at the moment, the traitorous kiss, is understood but not expressed in the text. The sense is, "Friend, a kiss, with what thou art come to do." In this case, the meaning of Christ's words in St. Matthew and St. Luke is the same.

The Greek word used by Matthew for "friend" does not signify affection. It is rather "associate" or "comrade" and was often used to address a complete stranger.

Chapter 8

JESUS AND HIS CAPTORS

After the kiss of betrayal, Judas slunk back into the group that had come to capture Jesus. His work was done. Now all he had to do was to watch anxiously in the hope that Jesus' captors would fulfill their part of the bargain and not allow Him to slip away as He had so often in the past. Jesus had no such intention. Instead of waiting for His enemies to act, He spoke to them: "Whom do you seek?" It was probably the officers of the Temple guard who replied, "Jesus of Nazareth." Our Lord identified Himself: "I am he." In spite of the sign Judas had given them, Christ's enemies seemed confused. They suspected that this man who had come boldly forward to meet them could not be the one they had come to arrest.

At this point, there is an interruption in the narrative of St. John. Here, as on many other occasions, this Evangelist shows himself an eyewitness of the events he narrates. Writing his Gospel many years later, St. John can still see the scene with the vividness of a landscape illuminated by a lightning flash. He says simply, "Now Judas, who betrayed him, was also standing with them" (18:5). In his memory, John still sees the two groups facing

each other: Jesus and His little band of Apostles, and Jesus' enemies—the Roman soldiers, the Temple guards, the Sanhedrists,
and the retainers of the high priest. Burned into his memory is
the picture of Judas, not with the Apostles around Jesus, but in
the group of His enemies. This is the last time St. John mentions
Judas in his Gospel.

St. John tells us that when Jesus spoke the words, "I am he,"
His enemies "drew back and fell to the ground." While a natural
explanation of this fall is possible, there is no doubt that St. John
considered it a miraculous manifestation of our Lord's power.
It is not likely that the whole group fell; probably it was only
those in the front rank, the officers of the Temple guard who had
addressed Jesus. Our Lord permitted something of His divine
power and majesty to shine forth in His words and looks, and His
enemies recoiled quickly, falling over those immediately behind
them. This was not the first time that Jesus had overawed His
enemies by the majesty of His presence (see John 7:44; 10:39).
Now He will let them have their way because it is the will of His
Father, but not before showing them that He is acting freely. He
will fulfill the prophecy of Isaiah: "He shall be led as a sheep to
the slaughter, and shall be dumb as a lamb before his shearer"
(53:7). But He will do it not from weakness but by choice.

Those who had fallen quickly regained their feet. Jesus again
put to them the same question: "Whom do you seek?" and again
they replied, "Jesus of Nazareth." They replied this time with a
little less boldness. By now Jesus was surrounded by His Apostles,
who were gradually becoming aware of the import of what was
taking place. If Jesus was wanted, so were they; if Jesus was a
criminal, they could hardly be judged innocent. But they really
had nothing to fear at the moment. In spite of the apparently
superior power of His enemies, Jesus controlled the situation and

even directed what was to be done. "I have told you that I am he," He said. "If, therefore, you seek me, let these go their way" (John 18:8). In this moment of grave danger, Jesus identified Himself, gave Himself up to His enemies, and let His Apostles walk away free. Knowing their danger, He did not compromise them by identifying them as disciples. He simply referred to them as "these." St. John sees in this a fulfillment of what Christ had said in a prayer to the Father: "Of those whom thou hast given me, I have not lost one" (John 18:9; cf. 17:12).[11]

The enemies of Christ quickly appraised the situation. Christ was giving Himself up without resistance and dismissing His disciples. Since there was to be no conflict there was no danger, so some of the band, eager now to show their zeal and courage, stepped forward quickly and seized Jesus. Judas kept enough of his love and respect for the Master to prevent him from laying hands on Him. He let others do it. The Apostles were stunned at this turn of events. Never before had they seen Jesus subjected to such an indignity. On other occasions when His enemies had sought to take Him, He had walked quietly away. Now they saw Him held firmly in their grasp.

Yet, even in this emergency, the Apostles turned to our Lord for directions: "Lord, shall we strike with the sword?" Two of them were armed with swords. Earlier in the evening, misunderstanding our Lord's recommendation: "Let him who has no sword

---

[11] Here St. John gives the sense of Christ's words as found in 17:12. Some critics object that in this verse Christ referred to preservation from a moral fall, not from a physical danger. The explanation is that St. John simply applies Christ's words to an analogous situation. It is also possible that if Christ had not preserved the Apostles from physical danger at this time, they might have suffered a moral fall.

sell his tunic and buy one," they had replied to Jesus, "Behold, here are two swords" (Luke 22:36, 38). They may have thought that this was the emergency to which our Lord referred. Their valor was greater than their prudence. Armed with two swords, the few of them were ready, at Christ's word, to throw themselves onto a much larger armed group backed up by a detachment of Roman soldiers.

At this point, the action was rapid, as Christ had no time to reply to their question. The impetuous Peter was beside himself at the sight of his beloved Master in the hands of His enemies. He did not wait for Jesus to reply. He stepped forward quickly and swung his sword lustily at the head of Malchus, the servant of the high priest, who was evidently one of those holding our Lord. Either Peter's aim was poor or Malchus dodged quickly, as the blow only grazed his head and cut off his right ear.[12]

Even as Peter struck, our Lord spoke, perhaps in answer to the question of the Apostles whether they should strike with the sword. "Bear with them thus far," He said. The meaning of these words is doubtful. Perhaps Jesus meant simply, "Let be, no more violence," or else, "Let things take their course; permit them to arrest me." In the scuffle, Malchus must have loosed his hold on Christ, who took advantage of this freedom to touch Malchus' wounded ear and heal it. Peter might have fared very poorly later that evening in the courtyard of the high priest if it had not been for Christ's miracle of healing.

---

[12] The first three Evangelists do not identify the servant of the high priest or the Apostle who struck him. This silence was undoubtedly suggested by prudence. Peter's resistance to armed authority would not be regarded lightly by the Romans. St. John, who wrote after the death of St. Peter, had no need to keep silent on this point.

Jesus was still in command of the situation. Turning now to Peter, He told him: "Put back thy sword into its place; for all those who take the sword will perish by the sword" (Matt. 26:52). Jesus would have no part in a violent defense. The reason He gave in this verse is proverbial in form, probably an expression current among His contemporaries. Violence engenders violence, the spilling of blood brings on the spilling of more blood. Recourse to the sword must have the sanction of the civil power, or it will bring upon one the punishment of the sword. Furthermore, Jesus had no need of their help. "Dost thou suppose that I cannot entreat my Father, and he will even now furnish me with more than twelve legions of angels?" (26:53). A legion consisted of six thousand men. Instead of twelve weak Apostles to defend Him, He could call upon the Father for twelve times six thousand angels to aid Him. And then, according to St. John, who does not mention the agony in the garden, our Lord refers to it: "Shall I not drink the cup that the Father has given me?" (18:11). Jesus had just suffered a bloody sweat in the effort to conform His will to the will of the Father. He will not be deterred now from the course marked out for Him, for, as He adds: "How then are the Scriptures to be fulfilled, that thus it must happen?" (Matt. 26:54).

After addressing Peter, Jesus turned to the motley group that had come out to arrest Him. Although He spoke to all, He directed His remarks particularly to the leaders, who bore the responsibility for what was taking place — the chief priests, the captains of the Temple, and the ancients. "As against a robber have you come out," Jesus said to them, "with swords and clubs. When I was daily with you in the temple, you did not stretch forth your hands against me" (Luke 22:52–53).

Jesus did not make objection to the arrest but to the manner and time and place. They had proceeded against Him as if He were a brigand, the leader of a band of armed robbers, an outlaw who must be captured by a combination of stealth and armed force. If there was a question of doctrinal differences, they knew very well that they would find Him teaching in the Temple area. They could have arrested Him in broad daylight and brought Him before the Sanhedrin. Jesus knew why they had not—and they knew too. They understood the tone of accusation in Jesus' words. They feared the people because of the malice in their motives and the patent injustice of the whole proceeding.

Yet there is a deeper significance in what was taking place. These men were evil and the executors of an evil design. Nevertheless their actions were a fulfillment of a prophecy, for Christ went on to say: "It is so that the Scriptures may be fulfilled" (Mark 14:49). What they were doing was being used by God and fitted into the great plan of our redemption.

For the moment, however, Christ's enemies appeared to have everything their own way. "But this is your hour, and the power of darkness," Jesus said (Luke 22:53). They had tried many times to lay hands on Him and could not because His hour had not yet come. Now they were free to act. Satan, the prince of darkness, had entered into Judas, the instigator of the plot that was now coming to a successful conclusion. The hour of Christ's enemies and the hour of the power of darkness were the same, because these men were acting as the allies and tools of Satan.

After addressing His enemies, Jesus fell silent. The Evangelists do not tell us whether there was a discussion among the Apostles as to what they should do; nor was there much time for talk, in any case. The Gospels simply tell us what the Apostles did: "Then all his disciples left him and fled" (Matt. 26:56).

Their flight was a shameful act. They deserted Jesus at the first approach of real danger and left Him in the hands of

His enemies. Nevertheless, we should not find it difficult to temper the severity of our condemnation. Jesus had in effect dismissed them when He said, "If therefore you seek me, let these go their way." He had rejected their appeal to the sword, and on the other hand He showed no sign of flight. They had to decide quickly what to do, while the attention of the band was still centered on Jesus, and they decided to take the path of personal safety. When they saw Jesus held firmly by His captors and making no effort to overcome them or to escape, they slunk back into the shadows and fled into the darkness of the olive trees. Here was fulfilled the prophecy that Christ had recalled early in the evening: "I will smite the shepherd, and the sheep of the flock will be scattered" (Matt. 26:31). St. John in his flight must have looked back over his shoulder, for he alone adds the pathetic detail: they "seized Jesus and bound him" (18:12).

Once Jesus was securely bound and surrounded by armed guards, the group formed in marching order for the return to the city. St. John tells us that "they brought him to Annas first, for he was the father-in-law of Caiaphas, who was the high priest that year" (18:13). Ancient tradition places the palace of Annas—probably the same as that of Caiaphas—on the west hill of the city, only about two hundred feet from the Upper Room, where Jesus had eaten the Passover a few hours earlier.

It is quite likely that the group returned by the same route that Jesus and the Apostles had taken in going to Gethsemane. They turned westward and descended the slope of the Mount of Olives until they reached the path along the bed of the brook

Cedron. They then turned southward on this narrow road. On their right rose the steep slope of the east hill of the city, the most ancient Jerusalem, that of the Jebusites, of David, and of Solomon. On the crest of this hill, the walls of the Temple area and those of the city itself rose high above them. Ordinarily it would be quite dark in this deep ravine, but it was now past midnight and the full moon was almost directly overhead. Whenever the road widened a little, they passed the tents and makeshift shelters of pilgrims who were encamped in the open near the holy city. After about fifteen or twenty minutes, the group turned sharply to the right toward the city wall and entered through the Fountain Gate. Their pace was slow now because the ascent was steep. Going northward along the valley that cut the city in two from north to south, they passed the Pool of Siloe and then, turning sharply westward, ascended narrow streets so steep that parts were cut into steps in the solid rock.

It was the dead of night, and the city and its environs were silent in sleep. The only signs of life were the watchmen on the walls and at the Fountain Gate. There was one exception, however, and St. Mark alone among the Evangelists records it. After stating that the Apostles deserted Jesus and fled, St. Mark adds: "A certain young man was following him, having a linen cloth wrapped about his naked body, and they seized him. But leaving the linen cloth behind, he fled away from them naked" (14:51–52).

A study of the original text of St. Mark adds a little to our knowledge of this incident. The one who followed Jesus was quite young — in fact, still in his teens. He did not follow at a distance, but mingled with the group. This would indicate that he was not inspired by curiosity but by a real interest in the case and was therefore a disciple of Jesus. That he slept in a special linen garment is evidence that he was well off, as the ordinary peasant or worker had no special night clothes.

He could not have been with the group very long before someone noticed that he was an intruder and called attention to him. They quickly seized him, but he slipped out of his linen garment, leaving it in their hands, and fled naked.

Who was this young man? From early times, efforts have been made to identify him, but they amount to little more than conjecture. Many think it was St. Mark himself, since he alone thought the incident worth recounting.

The Gospel narrative does not tell us at what point in the march from Gethsemane to the palace of Annas this event occurred. It is usually placed immediately after the departure. It is possible that the young man was the son of the owner of the villa of Gethsemane and was awakened from sleep by the noise of the arrest. The possibility cannot be ruled out that he lived in a house along the route taken by the cortege and was awakened as it passed. There is an early tradition that the mother of St. Mark owned the house in which the Last Supper took place. If tradition is correct in the localization of the Cenacle and of the palace of Annas, the group with their prisoner passed near the Cenacle. The house of the mother of Mark was one of the first meeting places of the earliest Christians. It was there St. Peter went after his miraculous release from prison (Acts 12:12).

The evidence is not conclusive, but what little there is indicates that the young man was St. Mark. If it was St. Mark, we can well imagine that the event remained vividly impressed on his memory the rest of his life. If the other Evangelists knew of it, they passed it over as of no particular significance. To St. Mark it was like a seal with which he signed his Gospel, just as St. John refers to himself in his Gospel as the "disciple whom Jesus loved."

Chapter 9

ANNAS

Once Jesus had been delivered bound into the hands of the Jewish authorities, immediate steps were taken to bring Him to trial before the highest court of the nation. To understand the trial of Christ, it is essential to know something of the political situation of Palestine at the time.

During the second century B.C., the Jewish people gave promise for a while of renewing the ancient splendors of their golden era. Under the leadership of the family of the Maccabees, they rose in revolt against the Syrian oppressors, defeated them, and renewed their national and religious life. But the glorious period of the Maccabees was of short duration. Under constant pressure from without, the Jewish nation was also split within by religious conflicts and by the ambitious rivalries of the descendants of the Maccabees.

The beginning of the end came at the death of Queen Alexandra, who left two sons, Hyrcanus II and Aristobulus II, both contending for the throne. To add to the confusion and difficulties, the Sadducees and the Pharisees took sides, the Sadducees favoring Aristobulus and the Pharisees, Hyrcanus.

Onto the scene at this critical juncture stepped the ominous figure of the man who was to become the founder of the dynasty of the Herods. He was Antipater, the governor of Idumea, a region south of Judea, which had been forcibly converted to Judaism. Antipater sided with Hyrcanus and exerted all his energies to place him on the throne, with the intention of using him as a figurehead and ruling through him. During this civil conflict, word came that Pompey, the Roman general, had arrived in Syria after defeating Mithridates. Both sides made the fatal mistake of appealing to Pompey, who marched into Judea, laid siege to Jerusalem, and captured it in the year 63 B.C. That event marked the death of Jewish independence. The struggle between the two brothers continued for some time with neither prevailing. In the meantime, Antipater sedulously curried the favor of the Romans, and Caesar appointed him governor of Judea in 47 B.C. After his death, his son Herod, known as the Great, got himself appointed king at Rome in 40 B.C. and became king in reality by conquest of the territory in 37 B.C.[13]

Before his death in 4 B.C., Herod made a will dividing his territory among three of his sons. To Archelaus, the eldest, he left Judea and also Samaria, immediately to the north, a country of mixed religion and population. To Philip he left the northeastern districts. To Antipas, who appears as Herod during the public

---

[13] Herod the Great was still living at the time of the birth of Christ, as it was this monster who ordered the slaughter of the Holy Innocents. Since Herod died in the year 4 B.C., it is evident that Christ was born prior to this date and that therefore a mistake was made in computing the beginning of the Christian era. Herod Antipas, who played a part in the trial of Christ, was a son of Herod the Great.

life and trial of Jesus, he left Galilee, which lay to the north of Samaria, as well as Perea, which was beyond the Jordan. The Romans approved Herod's will but eliminated the title of king and granted Antipas the title of tetrarch.[14] In the year A.D. 6, Archelaus was deposed and exiled by the Romans, who then placed the territories of Judea and Samaria under the direct rule of a Roman governor with the title of procurator. This was the political situation at the time of the trial of Christ and must be known, at least in its broad outlines, in order to understand that momentous event.

The Roman procurator took up his residence in Herod's palace in the city of Caesarea on the Mediterranean coast, about fifty miles to the northwest of Jerusalem. This city became the center of administration for both Judea and Samaria. On the occasion of the great feasts of the Jewish religious year, the procurator went up to Jerusalem accompanied by reinforcements and took up temporary residence in the city in order to quell any attempted uprisings.

The procurator was a military commander as well as a civil governor. In the Roman army of the time there were two distinct types of troops, the legion and the auxiliaries. The legion, made up of Roman citizens and numbering from five thousand to six thousand men, was the core of the army. The auxiliary troops were not of the same caliber or status as the legion. They were men from the provinces of the empire and were formed into cohorts whose strength varied from five hundred to a thousand but was usually six hundred men.

---

[14] In popular speech both Archelaus and Antipas, perhaps Philip too, were referred to as kings (Matt. 2:22; 14:9; Mark 6:14; Josephus, *Antiquities*, 18, 4, 3).

The governor of nearby Syria had four legions under his command, but the procurator of Judea had only auxiliary troops. These soldiers were all Gentiles, as the Jews had been exempted from military service. They were recruited from the non-Jewish residents of the land, from coastal towns, from cities on the borders of Palestine, which were largely Gentile, and especially from Samaria. The soldiers who played a part in the tragedy of Christ's Sacred Passion were not Romans, therefore, in the sense that they came from Rome or even from Italy. Garrisons of auxiliary troops were stationed in the main cities. A cohort was quartered in the Antonia.

The procurator held supreme judicial authority in his territory. In Judea, this authority was exercised only in extraordinary cases, as the ordinary administration of justice, both in criminal and civil affairs, was left in the hands of the local courts. The procurator alone, however, could decide matters of life and death, except that a Roman citizen had the right of appeal to the emperor.

The Jewish religion was not only tolerated but protected by the Romans. It was not unusual for Romans to present gifts to the Temple in Jerusalem and to have sacrifices offered there. The Roman authorities made no demand on the Jews to worship the emperor but required only that twice a day a sacrifice be offered in the Temple for Caesar and the Roman people. In general, the Romans avoided offending the religious sensibilities of the people, especially in the matter of the public exhibition of graven images.

Jesus and His captors stood for a few moments before a great gate leading into an impressive mansion on the upper slopes of the west hill of the city. Slowly the heavy gate swung open, and Jesus, still bound, was led into the great interior court of the residence of Annas and Caiaphas.

From the Gospel stories, especially from a comparison of the accounts of St. Peter's denials in the Synoptists and in St. John, it appears that Annas and Caiaphas resided in different parts of the same building. This was not unusual in the ancient East. In this arrangement, the apartments of several families opened into a common courtyard in the center, which, in turn, opened through a corridor and gate onto the public street. The dwelling rooms of the family were on the ground floor, while the guest and reception rooms were on the second floor. Stairs led directly from the courtyard to the second floor.

The small group with Jesus in their midst stood quietly in the courtyard as the commanding officer sent a messenger to Annas to announce their arrival. In a few minutes, the messenger returned with orders to conduct the prisoner into the presence of Annas. They mounted the steps to the second floor and entered the great reception room.

From what we know of Annas and other high priests of this period, we can reconstruct the scene without stretching our imaginations. The reception room was certainly furnished in royal style. As Jesus entered, He could probably feel His feet sink into the rich rugs that covered the floor. The walls were hung with bright tapestries, dimly visible now in the flickering light of the oil lamps hanging in brackets on the pillars. At the far end of the room, half-reclining on a divan, as was the custom of the time, was Annas, surrounded by servants, officials, and a few of the more prominent chief priests.

Annas was at that time a man of about sixty. The fact that Jesus was brought to him first, rather than to Caiaphas, the reigning high priest, is an indication that the father-in-law, Annas, was the power behind the scenes, directing the proceedings against our Lord.

It is unlikely that he had ever before seen Jesus, and now that Jesus approached to stand before him, he looked at Him sharply, trying to determine from His external appearance what sort of man this could be who had caused so much trouble and had even become a threat to the security of the nation. He had heard a great deal about Him. His spies had made detailed reports.

It is quite likely that Jesus had seen Annas before, exercising his priestly functions at the Temple during one of the great festivals. Annas was considered the greatest Jewish figure of his time. He was well known, not only throughout the Holy Land, but wherever Jews congregated in their tightly knit little groups in every country of the civilized world. Annas is known to history, too, as his record has come down to us in the New Testament, in the writings of the Jewish historian Josephus, and in the Talmud.

Annas was looked upon as one of the most fortunate of men. He had held the office of high priest from A.D. 6 to 15. But this was not all. He had the great happiness of seeing five of his sons raised to the same dignity. The high priest reigning at this very time was his son-in-law, Caiaphas. The Romans changed the high priest at will, but the Jews considered the tenure of office to be for life. There can be no doubt, therefore, that many pious people of the time looked up to Annas as the true high priest in the sight of God and that his influence was paramount in Jewish affairs.[15]

What sort of man was Annas?

Like most of the priests of high rank at this time, Annas was a Sadducee. As a priest, he was undoubtedly punctilious in the external performance of his functions. As a Sadducee, he was a skeptic whose vision was limited to the good things of this world, an agnostic for whom the Temple rites in which he played so important a part were mere formalities. His priesthood was dedicated to the service of himself, his family, and his class rather than to the service of God. His character is undoubtedly reflected in that of his son of the same name who was high priest in the year A.D. 62. Writing of him, the historian Josephus says he "was a bold man in his temper and very insolent; he was also of the sect of the Sadducees, who are very rigid in judging offenders, above all the rest of the Jews."[16] And of one of the successors of Annas, a typical high priest of the time, the same contemporary author says: "He was a great hoarder-up of money; he therefore cultivated the friendship of Albinus (the Roman procurator of the time) and of the high priest by making them presents. He also had servants who were wicked, who ... went to the threshing floors and took away the tithes of the priests by violence, and did not refrain from beating such as would not give the tithes to them."[17]

Later Jewish writings include the family of Annas in the woes pronounced on the evil priests whom the Temple itself

---

[15] Note that in Acts 4:6 Annas is referred to as high priest, although Caiaphas actually held the office at that time.

[16] *Antiquities*, 20, 9, 1.

[17] Ibid., 20, 9, 2.

bids depart from its sacred precincts. The house of Annas is specifically accused of whispering, or hissing like vipers, which probably refers to the part it took in the corruption of judges.

There is no question that Annas and his family were wealthy. In fact, they were probably the wealthiest family in the country. The Romans had the power to appoint high priests, and they sold the office to the highest bidder and deposed high priests frequently in order to open the bids again as soon as possible. A goodly sum of money must have changed hands to secure the office of high priest for Annas, his five sons, and his son-in-law. We have information on the source of this vast priestly wealth. At the time of Christ, the sacred area around the Temple had become a banking center and marketplace. Every adult Jew was under the obligation of contributing a half shekel annually toward the support of the Temple. There can be no doubt that the wealthy contributed much larger sums. A great variety of money was current in the Holy Land itself, and then too, many pious pilgrims journeyed from far countries to visit the Temple. It was necessary for them to convert their money into a local currency appropriate for the offering for the sanctuary. To facilitate this, the money changers had set up their booths and tables in the very shadow of the Temple. They charged a fee for their services and took advantage of the strangers' ignorance of local currency to defraud them.

Besides the money changers, there were the merchants who sold the various birds and animals for the sacrifices: the oxen and sheep and doves, and at this time of year the lambs that each family needed for the Passover supper. Then too, there was the oil and salt and wine required for various rituals.

It was big business, and it was profitable. But it was also sacrilegious. Not only was it largely dishonest, but it desecrated a sacred place. The Temple and the Temple area were holy, and they were dedicated entirely to the worship of God. Avaricious men had changed the holy ground into an oriental bazaar in which money changers and merchants called out their wares, tugged at the sleeves of customers to attract them into their stalls, haggled and quarreled over the business at hand, cheated when they could, and screamed their outrage when customers left them to do business elsewhere. Much of the business was what today would be called a racket. The big racketeers, the ones who really ran the show and took the major part of the profits, were the higher members of the priesthood, and especially the family of the high priest. That Annas and his family were the kingpins in this business is evidenced not only by their wealth but by the fact that the rabbis who wrote the Talmud more than two hundred years later referred to the Temple Market as the "bazaars of the Sons of Annas."

Only a few days before, probably on the preceding Monday, Jesus had made a public and frontal attack on this priestly desecration of His Father's house. The near approach of the Passover had greatly increased the business of the money changers and of the merchants. The noise of their trafficking, the sounds of the birds and animals, the shouts and greetings of people using the sacred area as a shortcut from one part of the city to another, all rose in a distracting clamor from a place dedicated to prayer and worship.

As Jesus entered through one of the eastern gates from the direction of the Mount of Olives and looked about Him, He was filled with disgust and anger at what He heard and saw. Putting together a makeshift scourge of leather thongs, He strode toward the money changers and, as He passed, overturned their tables, spilling the coins over the great flagstones. He went on toward the merchants, releasing the birds from their cages and lashing the animals in herds toward the gates of the Temple. The money changers and merchants stood back, aghast at this open assault on their long-established business. As soon as they could find tongue, we may be sure that they appealed for help to the Temple police who patrolled the area, but the police dared not intervene for fear of the people, who but a day before had welcomed Jesus into the city as the long-awaited Messiah. Jesus looked quietly at His frustrated enemies and said to them: "It is written, 'My house is a house of prayer,' but you have made it a den of thieves" (Luke 19:46).

This act was a direct threat to the authority, and to the pocketbooks, of the high priests. Jesus probably had a sympathetic audience, not only among His disciples but among the many devout Jews who had long been scandalized by the open violation of the sacred character of the Temple place. It made the chief priests realize still more the urgency of action against Jesus, and it helped to bind more closely together the Sadducees and Pharisees in the plot against His life. We have little doubt that Annas was not only the spokesman for the Sadducees but the man who was now directing, step by step, the proceedings against Christ. That is why Jesus was brought directly to him for an unofficial interrogatory, so that Annas could make necessary preparations for the formal trial before the High Council of the Jews, presided over by his son-in-law, Caiaphas.

There was silence for a few moments as Jesus stood before Annas. Annas looked intently at Him, and there was more than curiosity in his dark eyes. There was hatred and determination: hatred of

Jesus as the man who had become the idol of large sections of the people, hailed as the Messiah and therefore a threat to the established order that had been so good to him and his family; and determination to take advantage of the present situation to bring about the condemnation and death of Jesus.

After a few moments of silence, Annas spoke. He began by questioning Jesus concerning His disciples and His teaching. The arrest of Jesus secretly and in the dead of night, His arraignment as a prisoner before the former high priest, and now the questions asked Him all implied that He was a conspirator, the chief of an outlaw band, a man who avoided the light of day and the surveillance of the proper authorities. At Gethsemane, Jesus had protested against the methods of His captors. Now, looking straight at Annas, He firmly and directly rejected the whole procedure: "I have spoken openly to the world," He declared. "I have always taught in the synagogue and in the temple, where all the Jews gather, and in secret I have said nothing. Why dost thou question me? Question those who have heard what I spoke to them; behold, these know what I have said" (John 18:20–21).

In His reply, Jesus made no mention of His disciples. He had protected them at the moment of His arrest and had demanded that they be permitted "to go their way." He stood alone now before His accusers and refused to implicate His followers. Anyway, His answer concerning His teachings showed the innocence of His disciples. In effect, Jesus declared to Annas that anyone interested in His teachings could quite easily have listened to Him in the public places in which He had addressed the public. He had indeed spoken confidentially to His disciples, but on subjects He had taught openly before all the world. In fact, Jesus had gathered disciples for the very purpose of spreading His teaching. He had told them: "What I tell you in darkness, speak it in the light; and what you hear whispered, preach it on the housetops" (Matt. 10:27).

The second part of Jesus' answer was a sharp and well-merited rebuke to Annas. If Jesus had done evil, proper procedure demanded the calling of witnesses. Annas was looking for judicial shortcuts. He was trying to make Jesus bear witness against Himself. Jesus rebuffed Him, and in no uncertain terms. Go get the witnesses, He said in effect, and listen to what they have to say. A tense silence followed Jesus' words. Annas had expected an attitude of submissiveness, diffidence, humility, obsequiousness, and fear. We know from Josephus that these were the attitudes expected in one accused before the High Council.[18]

Here was an accused who was different. He administered a public and well-deserved rebuke to the great Annas, and He did it without fear or hesitation.

Annas was startled. He was humiliated before the group around him. He had expected to show how quickly he would have this upstart begging for mercy. Instead, he was given a lecture on correct legal procedure in a few well-chosen words.

Annas did not know how to reply. The embarrassed silence became more embarrassing. There was really no answer to Jesus' words. As happens so often when the ignorant are faced with a dilemma, one of the attendants[19] of Annas, probably the guard standing beside Jesus, now resorted to violence. His betters could

[18] Ibid., 14, 9, 4.
[19] The Greek word used refers to an "attendant," "retainer," or "official." At times he has been identified with the Malchus whose ear Peter cut off (John 18:10). This identification is incorrect. Malchus is referred to in the Greek text as a "servant" or "slave."

not find an answer, so he would provide one and win the goodwill of his master. Turning to Jesus, he struck Him a blow with his hand, saying: "Is that the way thou dost answer the high priest?" (John 18:22).

This outcome of the inquiry before Annas is shocking—doubly shocking to the Christian, who believes that the One struck is the Incarnate Son of God. Violent hands had been laid on Jesus for the first time shortly before, when He was bound at the Garden of Gethsemane. Now, for the first time, He was struck violently by a human hand. Since it was our Lord's speech that caused the offense, it is likely that the attendant struck Him with his fist or open hand across the mouth.

For a moment Jesus looked steadily at Annas to give him an opportunity to reprove so evil an act. It was base and cowardly to strike a bound man; it was unjust to treat an accused as if he were a convicted criminal. But Jesus waited in vain. Annas felt relieved that attention had been diverted from his embarrassment. So Jesus turned to the man who had struck him and said with quiet dignity: "If I have spoken ill, bear witness to the evil; but if well, why dost thou strike me?" (John 18:23).

Jesus' reaction to the injury inflicted on Him is a model of meekness and patience.[20] The calm logic of His words is a rebuke not only to the attendant who struck Him but to Annas, who permitted it and let it go unreproved. Again, Annas felt embarrassed by the words of this man, who patently had no fear of

---

[20] St. Paul the Apostle was a great saint, but in similar circumstances he turned on his tormenter with angry words: "God will strike thee, thou whitewashed wall. Dost thou sit there to try me by the law and in violation of the law order me to be struck?" (Acts 23:3).

him. Realizing that his inquiry was getting nowhere, he made a quick decision to stop the proceedings. He gave orders that Jesus, still bound, was to be led away to his son-in-law, Caiaphas, the reigning high priest.[21]

[21] Some scholars believe that John 18:24 ("And Annas sent him bound to Caiphas the high priest") belongs immediately after John 18:13 ("And they led him away to Annas first, for he was father-in-law to Caiphas, who was the high priest of that year"). This would mean that the incident just described as taking place before Annas really took place before the ruling high priest, Caiaphas. The ancient manuscripts of the New Testament are very heavily in favor of the order we have followed.

Chapter 10

CAIAPHAS AND THE SANHEDRIN

As Annas watched Jesus turn to leave, he reflected ruefully that the interrogation had been a failure. He had hoped that he would obtain enough information from the prisoner to outline the case against him and to determine the mode of procedure in order to speed up the trial. All he had learned had been learned to his regret—that this man was no ordinary prisoner cringing in the presence of the great. He would be difficult to handle. Nothing could be taken for granted.

At least, Annas consoled himself, nothing had been lost. While he was questioning Jesus, messengers had been delivering summonses to members of the Sanhedrin, instructing them to appear immediately at the palace of the high priest. They were not taken unawares, as they had undoubtedly been informed of the steps that had been taken to arrest Jesus and bring Him to trial this very night. It would not take them long to assemble, as they probably lived near the high priest in the elegant section of the city on the west hill.

Jesus was led from the hall of Annas onto the balcony that overlooked the interior court of the palace. A fire had been built on the flagstones in the middle of the courtyard. Let us imagine the scene: the retainers who were huddled around the fire for warmth cast ghostly shadows against the walls; a few tardy Sanhedrists hurried across the courtyards and quickly entered the apartments of the high priest Caiaphas, opposite those of Annas. Preparations were now complete to bring Jesus Christ to trial for His life before the highest court of the nation.

At the time of Christ, the Sanhedrin was the supreme legislative, judicial, and executive body of the Jews in both civil and religious matters. We have only hazy indications of its origin and history. It was probably about 200 B.C. that it developed into the form in which we find it at the time of Christ. It consisted of seventy members, presided over by the high priest, bringing the total to seventy-one.

The Sanhedrin was a strictly aristocratic, rather than a democratic, body. We have no sure information on how its members were recruited, but we know that they did not receive their offices through popular election. They represented the wealth, the learning, the political power, and the religious influences that dominated the nation.

Three main groups made up the Sanhedrin: the chief priests, the Scribes, and the ancients. The chief priests were the most prominent members of the priestly caste: the high priest in office and former high priests, as well as members of the privileged families from which high priests were selected. The chief priests outranked all others in dignity, but since most of them were Sadducees, they lacked wide, popular support and were obliged to defer to the Pharisees, who were almost universally accepted as the true exponents of the Jewish religion.

The Scribes were Pharisees trained as lawyers in the Mosaic Law and in the traditions supposedly based on it. They had greater influence with the people than any other group in the nation. There is not sufficient evidence to determine with exactness the identity of the ancients (or elders, as they are also called), who made up a part of the Sanhedrin. It is probable that they were men who were neither chief priests nor Scribes but who merited the high office of Sanhedrist because of wealth or nobility or because of political or religious influence.

While the authority of the Roman procurator extended over both Judea and Samaria, the civil authority of the Sanhedrin was limited to the former. Neither the procurator, Pontius Pilate, nor the Sanhedrin could exercise jurisdiction over Jesus Christ while He was in Galilee or in Perea, the land across the Jordan, as these territories were subject to Herod Antipas. There can be no doubt, however, that Jews all over the world looked upon the Romans as usurpers to whom obedience was due only because no other course was open. In religious matters, particularly, Jews considered the Sanhedrin the supreme authority under God. It was as president of the Sanhedrin that the high priest authorized Paul to go to Damascus, far from Judea, to arrest and bring back in chains Jewish Christians (see Acts 9:2; 22:5; 26:12).

Within the confines of Judea, the Sanhedrin was authorized to handle all matters that the Romans had not specifically reserved to themselves. There was nothing extraordinary in this arrangement, as it was the common practice of the Romans to permit subject peoples to continue to administer ordinary affairs in their own way. The pages of the New Testament abound in evidence that the Sanhedrin exercised not only civil but criminal jurisdiction. It even had its own police force and made arrests on its own authority.

The power of the Sanhedrin was limited in several respects by the Roman authorities. It had no jurisdiction over a Roman citizen, except in one case: special permission had been granted the Jews to try and to execute non-Jewish Roman citizens who dared to pass the barrier of the Temple area beyond which only Jews were allowed.[22] At the time of Christ, the Sanhedrin had been deprived of the power over life and death. This is clear from the Gospels, particularly the Gospel of St. John, which records that the Jewish leaders reminded Pilate that "it is not lawful for us to put anyone to death" (John 18:31). Other sources confirm this statement of St. John.[23] At the time of Christ the Sanhedrin had the right to try capital cases but had no right to execute the death sentence. If a death sentence was passed, the Roman procurator had power to permit execution of the sentence or to retry the case before his own tribunal. There was also a general limitation on the power of the Sanhedrin in the fact that the Romans could interfere at will in any case, or in any manner that pleased them.[24]

---

[22] Josephus, *Wars*, 6, 2, 4. An inscription in Greek proclaiming this warning to strangers in the Temple has been discovered.

[23] Cf. Josephus; the Talmud. The stoning of St. Stephen, recorded in the Acts of the Apostles (7:54ff.), was not the result of judicial action by the Sanhedrin but of mob violence. This is also true of other such incidents quoted from the New Testament.

[24] In treating of the trial of Christ, we must keep in mind that we have very little detailed information outside the Gospels on the legal situation in Palestine in this period or on the conduct of trials. We do not possess the original Senate decree setting up the province and defining the legal status of Romans and Jews.

Information contained in the Mishnah should be used with the gravest caution. The data of the Mishnah concerning criminal trials was not codified until about A.D. 200, when the situation of the Jews was completely different, and therefore it has little validity for the period prior to A.D. 70. The Sanhedrin of the Mishnah is in reality the Beth Din of Jamnia, which was no

As Jesus walked across the courtyard toward the apartments of Caiaphas, He may have glanced toward Peter, hovering in the shadows at a little distance from the revealing light of the fire. Peter, man of sudden impulses, had recovered somewhat from his fright at the arrest of Jesus, had followed him at a safe distance, and, through the influence of a friend, had been admitted into the courtyard of the palace. But again he had run into difficulties. Only a few moments before, he had denied that he knew Christ. Now he could see Jesus clearly as He crossed the courtyard and mounted the steps leading to the great upper room.[25]

It is not difficult to reconstruct the scene that met Christ's eyes as He entered the upper room of the palace of Caiaphas. It was undoubtedly very large and richly furnished, suitable for large meetings and worthy of the dignity and wealth of the high priest Caiaphas and of the family into which he had married. The last of the Sanhedrists were taking their places as Jesus entered the room. They sat in a semicircle facing one another. Before

---

more than a scholastic group headed by a rabbi and devoted to theological and legalistic discussions.

Although accepted by some authors at face value, we must relegate to the realm of Pharisaical theorizing such prescriptions of the Mishnah as the following: prohibition of trial by night; the requirement that a death sentence be passed only a day after the trial; that a capital case could not be tried on the vigil of a Sabbath or feast; that a unanimous vote of condemnation left the accused free, etc., etc. These and like prescriptions were born in the imagination of rabbis who lived 130 years and more after the Sanhedrin had ceased to function. It is probable, of course, that the Mishnah contains some authentic information. The difficulty is to distinguish the true from the false.

[25] In order not to interrupt the narrative, we shall return to St. Peter and his denials later.

them to the right and left stood two clerks whose duty it was to record the proceedings and the decision of the court. In the middle of the semicircular row of judges sat the high priest, who was president of the Sanhedrin. Jesus was pushed forward till He stood before the high priest, facing the judges.

Who were these men who sat looking intently at Jesus Christ, standing before them for judgment as an accused criminal? The Gospels are explicit in stating that representatives of all three groups that made up the Sanhedrin were there: chief priests, Scribes, and ancients. It is not at all likely that the full membership was present, nor was it necessary. Twenty-three constituted a quorum. Everything leads us to believe that only those members were present who were actively hostile to Jesus Christ and who had already committed themselves to do what they could to be rid of Him. Their problem was to do it while preserving all the external forms of legality. They could have killed Jesus secretly, but that would have made a martyr of Him. Better far to present Him to the public as a man who had been tried fairly and with all the external trappings of legality and who had been found guilty of a crime worthy of death by the highest tribunal of the Jewish people, presided over by the high priest in person.[26]

---

[26] Some books on the Passion make a point of listing the illegalities in the trial of Jesus. These are based on data from the Mishnah, which, as we have said, is not an authentic source for a trial at the time of Christ. We are of the opinion that the trial of Christ was a formal trial before the Sanhedrin, that the external forms of legality were preserved, and that the verdict was a sentence of death that could not be carried out without an appeal to the Roman procurator. Even though they could not execute the sentence of death, it was of the utmost importance to the Jewish authorities to pronounce it themselves, as only the sentence of the Sanhedrin would have any influence with the people. Then,

The Gospels mention only one of the Sanhedrists by name, Caiaphas the high priest.[27] We have already met him at the meeting called by the chief priests and Pharisees after Christ had raised Lazarus from the dead. At that meeting, there had been doubt and hesitation as to how they could meet the threat of this new prophet who was gaining such influence with the people. Caiaphas had formulated the decision in his own rude words—but words which God used as a prophecy: "You know nothing at all; nor do you reflect that it is expedient for us that one man die for the people, instead of the whole nation perishing" (John 11:50). Those words reveal, too, how little of justice there was in the trial that Christ was now undergoing before the Sanhedrin. A caucus of some of its chief members had already

---

too, they kept in their own hands as much power as possible, and so proceeded with the trial even though the sentence required ratification.

The ordinary meeting place of the Sanhedrin was a council house situated to the west of the Temple near the Xystos, at a point where the wall from the upper city met the west wall of the Temple area (Josephus, *Wars*, 5, 4, 2; 6, 6, 3; 2, 16, 3). The *Lishkath Hagazith* referred to in the Mishnah as the meeting place of the Sanhedrin is apparently the same place, although this source places it within the Temple enclosure. There is no direct evidence as to why the trial of Christ was held in the palace of Caiaphas rather than in the official meeting place. It may be that the latter was closed for the night or that the Sanhedrists wished to conduct the trial as quietly as possible in order to avoid trouble with followers of Jesus. It is likely that they were making an effort to conceal the proceedings even from members of the Sanhedrin such as Gamaliel, who would be swayed by justice rather than expedience, as well as from those who were disciples of Jesus, as, for instance, Joseph of Arimathea and Nicodemus.

[27] Caiaphas was his surname. He is referred to in Josephus as Joseph. *Antiquities*, 18, 2, 2; 18, 4, 3.

declared through the presiding officer that Christ must be put to death.

Few facts are known about Caiaphas, but these few are revealing. That he married a daughter of the great Annas is proof that he was a member of one of the highest-ranking priestly families. To be acceptable to his father-in-law, he must have given indications that he had abilities of the kind that would be appreciated by the wily and powerful Annas.

Caiaphas was remarkable for the record length of time he held the office of high priest — from A.D. 18 to 36. There were twenty-eight high priests in the 107 years from the beginning of Herod's reign to the destruction of the Temple, so that the average term of office was slightly less than four years. The two who preceded Caiaphas had lasted but one year each, in spite of the fact that one of them, Eleazar, was a son of Annas. Caiaphas was high priest, therefore, during the entire public life of Christ and during the entire time Pontius Pilate was procurator. The length of his term in office is evidence that Caiaphas was cunning, cowardly, rich, and venal. At a time when others could manage to maintain themselves in office for only a year or two, he held on for eighteen years. To do this he must have pleased and bribed the Roman authorities, and he must have done both very well. During this period, the Romans infringed the rights of the people in many respects: the procurator brought images of Caesar into the holy city, robbed the Temple treasury, and even massacred the people. And yet history records no protest on the part of Caiaphas, the leader and representative of his people. He was interested only in his own power and position.

Caiaphas was deposed from office by the Syrian legate Vitellius in the year 36, the same year in which Pontius Pilate was recalled. History records nothing further concerning him. At least Annas retained his influence, as two of his sons succeeded Caiaphas in the high priesthood for very brief terms.

We are left to conjecture to identify other members of the Sanhedrin present that fateful night at the trial of Jesus. Certainly Annas must have been there. So too his five sons: Eleazar, Jonathan, Theophilos, Matthias, and Annas II. Patently it was a packed court. These judges had long before made up their minds as to what they would do. Their present problem was simply to give their sentence an appearance of justice and legality.

As Jesus stood facing his judges, witnesses were brought in. In the courts of the time there were no prosecutors; witnesses acted in this role. The witnesses had been carefully selected and prepared during the preceding days. Now each stepped forward in turn and, after showing proper marks of deference to the court and casting a covert glance at Jesus, recited his prepared speech of accusation.

The Gospels are not detailed at this point and tell us only in general terms that "the chief priests and all the Sanhedrin were seeking false witness against Jesus, that they might put him to death, but they found none, though many false witnesses came forward" (Matt. 26:59–60). Something had gone wrong. Perhaps the witnesses suffered stage fright in the presence of this highest assembly of the great of the land. Or perhaps they were merely unlettered people who found it difficult to memorize their lines. Anyway, their testimony against Jesus, whatever it was, was in open disagreement. This was fatal to the real purpose of the Sanhedrists, which, as we have said, was not to try Jesus justly but to give the trial the appearance of legality. No law was better known or more binding in criminal procedures than the Mosaic Law, which demanded that witnesses agree (Deut. 19:15). If the witnesses could not be brought into agreement, there was danger that the trial might fail in its only real purpose.

The Evangelists give us no information as to the nature of the accusations brought against Jesus. Which of His words and deeds did they attempt to twist into the appearance of a capital offense against the law? We can be pretty sure, however, as we know what had most aroused Christ's enemies against Him: the breaking of the Sabbath, the cleansing of the Temple, the triumphal entry into Jerusalem on the preceding Sunday, and, above all, Christ's claims to be the Messiah and a divine Person. In fact, there were so many possible accusations that their very number and variety may have confused the witnesses into presenting contradictory accounts.

It would be foolish, however, to underestimate the intelligence and determination of the enemies of Christ. There must have been a few moments of embarrassment in the tense room, followed by whispered consultations among the judges. As the crestfallen witnesses left the room, a court official escorted two others into the presence of the Sanhedrists. The Evangelists Matthew and Mark give us briefly the gist of their accusations against Jesus. "We ourselves," they said, "have heard him say, 'I will destroy this temple built by hands, and after three days I will build another, not built by hands'" (Mark 14:58).

This was a serious matter. Among the ancients, any profanation of a temple was an extremely grave offense. When the prophet Jeremiah foretold the destruction of the Temple and of the holy city, the people and their leaders cried out against him, demanding his death (Jer. 26:1–19).

The Gospels are not complete records, so we cannot be sure of the exact words of Jesus to which reference was made. Probably it was to the statement recorded by St. John: "Destroy this temple, and in three days I will raise it up" (2:19). As the Evangelist tells us, Jesus "was speaking of the temple of his body" and was prophesying His resurrection from the dead. Anyway, He made no threat that He would destroy the Temple. This accusation evidently made a considerable impression on the judges and bystanders, as the enemies of Christ later stood beneath His cross on Calvary and taunted Him with the charge that He had claimed the power to destroy the Temple and rebuild it in three days and yet could not now help Himself by coming down from the cross (Matt. 27:40).

In spite of the impression this accusation made, there was still the grave difficulty that the witnesses did not agree. What were the discrepancies? Unfortunately, the sacred writers do not give us any information on this. We can be sure that it must have been a rather glaring verbal as well as real difference, or the death-seeking judges would not have ruled out the testimony. It is altogether possible that here, as elsewhere, the Evangelist edits his material for the sake of brevity and presents the testimony of both witnesses in one sentence. If this explanation is correct, one witness declared that Jesus had said, "I will destroy this temple built by hands," and the other, "I will build another temple not made by hands."

In any case, it was now evident that the trial of Jesus had reached an impasse. It was all important that external legal forms should be observed, but the bumbling witnesses had made that impossible. Annas and Caiaphas must have experienced a feeling of regret that they had rushed the arrest and trial of Jesus so much that the witnesses had not been properly prepared. It is easy to imagine them in whispered conversation at this critical moment, glancing up occasionally at Christ, the cause of their chagrin.

Annas and Caiaphas now decided to adopt a completely different tactic. There was no justification in law for a condemnation based on a confession elicited from the accused, but they were resolved to make Christ's confession the very crime for which He would be convicted.

There was silence in the room. Jesus was calm. His obvious indifference to the conflicting testimony of His accusers annoyed His judges. All looked toward Caiaphas, from whom, as the presiding officer, the next move must come. Caiaphas rose in his place and stood facing Jesus.

Caiaphas began with words of pretended concern for our Lord. "Dost thou make no answer? What are the things these men prefer against thee?" (Mark 14:60).[28]

Caiaphas was indeed clever, but he greatly underrated the man who stood before him if he thought Jesus naïve enough to trust him or foolish enough to enter into a discussion of testimony that was patently contradictory. Jesus completely ignored him and his questions.

Caiaphas knew now that there was nothing for him to do but to come straight to the heart of the matter and provoke the accused into a declaration that could seal his fate. Addressing Jesus, he said: "If thou art the Christ, tell us" (Luke 22:66). Jesus was silent for a moment as Caiaphas looked to the right and left at the other judges, and then they too joined in the questioning, urging Jesus to tell them if He really was the Christ, the Messiah.

This time Jesus deigns to give an answer. "If I tell you," He said quietly, "you will not believe me; and if I question you, you

---

[28] The double question is better authenticated, although the Vulgate and some of the manuscripts unite the two questions into one.

will not answer me, or let me go" (Luke 22:67–68). Jesus tells them in effect that they are not seriously in search of information. They have no more intention of believing Him now than they had when He taught publicly. Neither would they now answer His questions concerning the true role and nature of the Messiah, since but a few days before they had refused to answer His inquiries (Matt. 22:42).

Caiaphas still was not through. He would stake all on one final effort to draw from Jesus an admission that would be a cause for condemnation. He knew that Jesus had been hailed as the Messiah. A confession that He was the Messiah would lay the groundwork for a trial and death sentence for treason before the Romans. He knew that Jesus had claimed to be the Son of God in a very real and special sense, as His enemies had only recently threatened to stone Him "because," as they said, "thou being a man, makest thyself God" (John 10:33). A confession that He was the Son of God would be a cause for His condemnation by the Sanhedrin as a blasphemer.

Drawing himself up to his full height and fixing his eyes on Jesus, Caiaphas asked in a voice that was like a solemn intonation: "I adjure thee by the Living God that thou tell us whether thou art the Christ, the Son of God" (Matt. 26:63). It was indeed a solemn moment. Jesus Christ is "adjured," asked to swear in the name of God, whether He is truly the Messiah and Son of God, and He is addressed by the high priest, presiding over the Great Council of the Chosen People.

The moment was tense. Caiaphas had played his last card. Beyond this there was nothing that could be done with any certainty of success. If Jesus answered no, He would have to be dismissed as innocent, or the whole weary process of bringing in and instructing witnesses would have to be started all over again. And there was great need for haste so that the case could be finished before the great feast and before Pilate left Jerusalem for his ordinary residence at Caesarea.

Jesus could not be silent now in the face of this challenge to His person and mission by the official representatives of His people. He would give them a clear and unequivocal answer that could leave no doubt about His teaching concerning His person and His mission. "Thou hast said it," He replied to Caiaphas.[29] "Nevertheless, I say to you, hereafter you shall see the Son of Man sitting at the right hand of the Power and coming upon the clouds of heaven" (Matt. 26:64).

These words of Jesus are among the most solemn and significant ever pronounced. Jesus Christ declares under oath, before the high priest and the supreme court of the land, that He is the Messiah and in a strict and unique sense the Son of God.

In His reply, Jesus applies to Himself and completes two prophecies that the Jews of the time referred to the Messiah. One is from a Messianic prophecy of Daniel (7:13), who describes a vision in which "one like the son of man came with the clouds of heaven. And he came even to the Ancient of days: and they presented him before him." The other reference is to a psalm of David (109:1 [110:1]) which all regarded as Messianic: "The Lord said to my Lord, 'Sit thou at my right hand: until I make thy enemies thy footstool.'" Only a few days before, Jesus had used this verse to prove to the Pharisees that while the Messiah would be the son of David, He would be a great deal more, since David himself was inspired to call Him Lord.

---

[29] There can be no doubt that this expression is a simple affirmative. This is evident from the context and from the parallel passage in Mark 14:62.

The term "son of man" was an expression used in prophecy to designate the Messiah, and Christ had often applied it to Himself. Now He combines the two prophecies to picture Himself, the Son of Man, seated on a throne at the right hand of God. He participates in the divine power; He shares the divinity of the Godhead; He is equally God with the Father. His judges now see Him as an ignominious and humiliated pretender, an accused before their tribunal of justice. The day will come when their roles will be reversed and Jesus will appear in all His glory, not only as Messiah but as the Son of God.

The Sanhedrists must have gasped at Jesus' words. That this Galilean upstart should claim to be the Messiah was bad enough. But that He should claim also to be the equal of God was the rankest blasphemy to these formalists who avoided even pronouncing the name of God. There must have been an outcry of shocked indignation followed by a murmur of satisfaction when they realized that they now had what they wanted. Jesus had been induced to commit a capital offense before their very eyes. To express and dramatize his verdict, Caiaphas clasped his cloak in both hands and rent it in a sign of horror at the blasphemy.[30]

Looking to both sides of him at his fellow judges, Caiaphas cried out: "He has blasphemed; what further need have we of witnesses? Behold, now you have heard the blasphemy. What do you think?" As if there could be any doubt as to what they

---

[30] Rending of garments as a sign of sorrow was a common practice of biblical times (Gen. 37:34; Acts 14:14). It was particularly used as a protest against blasphemy. It is not to be supposed that Caiaphas rent the special vestments of his high-priestly office, which at this time were kept under guard in the Castle Antonia by the Romans and brought out and delivered to the high priest only for the major feasts.

thought! As one man, they declared Him guilty. "He is liable to death" was their verdict (Matt. 26:65). For the sake of legal appearances, it is probable that the judges were then polled individually, but that would make no change in the sentence of death they had just passed on Christ by acclamation.

The Gospel narratives leave no doubt that Jesus Christ was condemned to death by the Sanhedrin for blasphemy. What, exactly, constituted the blasphemy? It could not have been Jesus' claim to be the Messiah. There is no evidence whatsoever in Jewish writings that a false claim to being the Messiah constituted blasphemy. No pretenders to this office were ever prosecuted for blasphemy.

The objection is raised that when Caiaphas asked Jesus if He was "the Christ, the Son of God," the two terms are in apposition, and therefore all that Caiaphas asked Jesus was whether He was the Messiah. A close study of the Gospels indicates, however, that here, as elsewhere, Matthew and Mark have edited their text for brevity and simplicity and have run together phrases that are really separate. The Gospel of Luke shows a certain progression in the questioning. Caiaphas asks our Lord if He is the Christ (Messiah); Jesus answers by a reference to His divine power. This leads Caiaphas to ask Jesus if He is the Son of God, and Jesus answers affirmatively.

The order followed in the Gospel of St. Luke helps also to answer the objection that since the Jews did not expect a divine Messiah, Caiaphas could hardly have asked Jesus if He was the Son of God in the strict sense of the term. Caiaphas was led into asking by Jesus' reply, which indicated His divinity. Furthermore, it is absurd to state that Caiaphas did not know by this time about Jesus' claims and about the disturbances they had caused among the people. Indeed, it was for these claims that He now stood before His judges. It was for them that His enemies had on many occasions sought to put Him to death (Mark 2:7; John 5:18; 8:59; 10:33). Christ's enemies had their spies everywhere. It would be incredible if they had not brought back information on Christ's claims to divine Sonship, for which even some of the people had threatened to stone Him.

The so-called blasphemy for which a sentence of death was passed upon Jesus Christ was His public and solemn testimony that He was in a literal and unique sense the Son of God and therefore a divine Person.

This verdict of death was a historic moment for Israel and the world. Jesus had come to "his own" and had presented His credentials as Messiah and Son of God by His teaching, His life, and His miracles. A few had received Him and believed in Him. But now His own Chosen People, through their highest and most authoritative council, not only reject Him but condemn Him to death. God's ways are indeed mysterious, for that death was to become the source of life to all who would accept and follow Him.

When the sentence of death had been passed on Jesus Christ, the members of the Sanhedrin had accomplished all that could be done at the moment. Their success evidently did not relieve the pent-up hatred in their hearts. For a long time they had waited for this day. They had planned and plotted and schemed in vain. They had borne as best they could the whiplash of Christ's tongue denouncing them in the Temple area and in the public places as hypocrites, whited sepulchers, and leaders of the blind. Now their hatred overflowed all bounds of decency and self-respect. They rose to leave, and as they passed Jesus, bound before them, they spat on Him.

Spitting is a rather universal sign of contempt, especially among the Semitic peoples of the Near East. To spit into one's face was to the Jews the sign of supreme contempt (Num. 12:14; Deut. 25:9). Perhaps only a few began this disgusting action, but the Gospels leave no doubt that they were joined by other members of this august assembly of chief priests, Scribes, and ancients. No doubt they were egged on by a gnawing doubt that even yet their prey might be snatched from their hands. They had condemned Jesus to death, but they knew they could do nothing to execute their sentence. The Roman procurator alone held absolute power over life and death, so it was necessary that the case pass through his hands.

Not content with spitting on Jesus, some began to strike Him. The example of their betters soon had an effect on the officers and retainers into whose hands Jesus had been committed as a prisoner. From all sides they rained blows on Him. They slapped Him in the face, they struck Him with the backs of their hands and with their fists. Then someone called to the others that he had an idea that was suited to the occasion. Jesus had made Himself out to be a prophet and more than a prophet. Had He not even foretold the destruction of the Temple? Then, give Him a chance to show what He could do. Bind His eyes and strike Him, and then let Him tell them who had struck Him.

The idea was applauded. It took but a moment to get a cloth and to bind it closely over the eyes of Jesus. Then the cruel affair started again. Jesus' tormenters took turns approaching Him and striking Him with their open hands and closed fists, and, as they did, each called out: "Prophesy to us, O Christ, who is it that struck thee?" (Matt. 26:68). As they struck Him they must have enlarged on this vulgar theme: "If you are a prophet, if you are the Messiah, if you are the Son of God, surely you can do something so simple as to tell the name of the one who is striking you." They must have taunted Jesus with other questions and accusations, for St. Luke says: "And many other things they kept saying against him, reviling him" (22:65).

There is no record that Jesus made any answer whatever. He accepted the insults, the slaps, and the blows in silence, as He later accepted the taunts of His enemies asking Him to come down from the cross. He had known what was coming. In one of His prophecies of the Passion, He had foretold that His enemies would mock Him and spit upon Him (Mark 10:34). Indeed, centuries before, speaking of Him in prophecy, Isaiah had said: "I have given my body to the strikers, and my cheeks to them that plucked them; I have not turned away my face from them that rebuke me and spit upon me" (50:6).

How long this shameful affair lasted we do not know. Probably only when Jesus' tormenters wearied of their cruel sport did they depart one by one and in small groups, leaving Him in the hands of the police officers who were to be His guard during the rest of the night. We do not know where Jesus was imprisoned, but it is likely that the palace of the high priest was equipped with cellars or dungeons that would suit the purpose. Jesus now finds Himself a prisoner under police guard, awaiting the dawn of what would be a momentous day in the history of the world.

Chapter 11

PETER'S DENIALS

All four Evangelists devote a large portion of their Gospels to the Passion of our Lord, and all four give what appears to be a disproportionate amount of space to the story of St. Peter's denials of Jesus Christ. Peter's importance, as the rock on which Christ built His Church, is undoubtedly one reason for this. So too the moral lessons of his fall and rise. We suspect that in later years the remorseful Peter told and retold the story to assuage in some manner the sorrow he felt for his shameful cowardice. Few incidents are better authenticated in the early Christian tradition, as the Evangelist St. Mark was a disciple of St. Peter, and St. John a close friend and an eyewitness of the event.

St. Peter was an ordinary workman, a fisherman born and bred on the shores of the Sea of Galilee. His education must have been limited, but he undoubtedly could read and write and had a fair knowledge of his religion. He was a pious man, as he and his brother Andrew were followers of St. John the Baptist. Both Peter and Andrew became disciples of Jesus and later were chosen Apostles.

Peter's character shines through many incidents in the Gospel narrative. He boldly asks Christ to bid him walk on the waters. At Christ's command he does, but almost immediately he loses courage, doubts the power that sustains him, and begins to sink (Matt. 14:28–32). At the sad moment when Jesus' disciples leave Him and He asks the chosen Twelve if they too are deserting, it is Peter who rises to the occasion and speaks for all in those immortal words: "Lord, to whom shall we go? Thou hast the words of everlasting life, and we have come to believe and to know that thou art the Christ, the Son of God" (John 6:69–70).

And when Christ asks His Apostles, "Who do you say that I am?" it is Peter again who is spokesman. "Thou art the Christ, the son of the living God." Christ forthwith makes Peter the foundation stone of His Church and delivers to Him the keys of the kingdom of heaven (Matt. 16:16–20). Jesus chose twelve Apostles, and from the twelve He chose three—Peter, James, and John—to be His most intimate friends. They alone witnessed the raising of the daughter of Jairus (Luke 8:51), the transfiguration on the Mount (Matt. 17:1), and the agony in the garden (Matt. 26:37). When Jesus foretold His Passion, Peter had the effrontery to take Him aside and chide Him about it, telling Him that all this would never be. Peter was put in his place—and quickly. "Get behind me, Satan," Jesus said to him, "thou art a scandal to me" (Matt. 16:23).

But Our Lord could not long be angry with Peter. Soon after, He singles him out for a special favor by paying the tax for Himself and Peter (Matt 17:23–26). Jesus sends him and his friend John to prepare the Paschal meal, at which Peter refuses to allow Jesus to wash his feet. When Jesus rebukes him, Peter goes all out, as usual, by telling our Lord to wash not only his feet but his hands and his head (John 13:9). During that Last Supper, our

Lord gives him an assurance that he will need, and will heed, later on: "Simon, Simon," Jesus says, "behold, Satan has desired to have you that he may sift you as wheat. But I have prayed for thee that thy faith may not fail" (Luke 22:31–32). But Peter feels no need of help. He is quite confident of his own powers and loyalty. "Lord," he says, "with thee I am ready to go both to prison and to death" (Luke 22:33). And when Jesus foretells that all of them will be scandalized in Him this very night, it is boastful, self-confident Peter who declares, "Even though all shall be scandalized, yet not I" (Mark 14:29).

Then it is that Jesus gives him a solemn warning of what is to come. "I tell thee, Peter," Jesus says, "a cock will not crow this day, until thou hast thrice denied that thou knowest me" (Luke 22:34). Peter hears but does not heed. He leads the others in loud boasts that he would die with Jesus rather than deny Him. And the boasts continue until Jesus changes the subject.

Peter's troubles began at the Garden of Gethsemane. When Jesus was arrested, he and all the other Apostles fled, as our Lord had predicted. But it was not long before Peter and another Apostle recovered their courage and followed after the detachment that was leading Jesus a prisoner to the palace of the high priest. St. John tells us that "Simon Peter was following Jesus, and so was another disciple. Now that disciple was known to the high priest, and he entered with Jesus into the courtyard of the high priest" (John 18:15).

Who was this other disciple? We must confess that we do not have a certain answer to that question. From earliest times, however, it has been thought that it was St. John himself. John seems to be giving an indication that he knew what happened because he was there. As we have said, he often referred to himself as the "disciple whom Jesus loved." Here he leaves out the words "whom Jesus loved" because they are not relevant to the events. Furthermore, the close friendship between Peter and John suggests their association in this incident (see John 20:3; Luke 5:10; 8:51; 22:8; Acts 3:1; 8:14). One might wonder, of course, how John, a humble fisherman of Galilee, could be known to the high priest. It is possible that he was—either directly or through a relative. Social distinctions were not quite as sharply drawn in those days as at present. We don't think it necessary, however, to assume a personal relationship between John and the high priest. The Evangelist probably means simply that he was known to the household of the high priest. He may even have had a relative among the servants of Annas or Caiaphas.

As the procession, with Jesus in the middle, marched through the great gate into the courtyard of the palace, St. John joined the last few stragglers and entered with them. No doubt the officers of the guard were relaxed and careless, now that they had Jesus securely in their possession, and without trouble from His followers. John had no intention of abandoning Peter, but he thought it prudent to enter and have a look around before bringing him in. He had to be particularly careful because, at Gethsemane, Peter had struck and injured a servant of the high priest.

Assuring himself that there was no immediate danger, and probably fearing that if he did not get Peter into the courtyard, he would do something rash, John returned to the entrance and spoke to the portress. It is likely that the great gate had been closed and barred and that the portress watched the street from a window near a small door that she opened to admit those who had a right to enter. The portress evidently knew John, because she made no difficulty about admitting Peter, who had been standing in the street outside.

The record of what happened then is somewhat confusing and has given scholars considerable difficulty. The most casual reading of the four Gospels reveals many differences of detail. The most natural explanation of these differences is to consider the three denials of Peter as the separate circumstances in which he denied Christ several times rather than as three isolated questions and answers. It is perfectly natural to assume that on each of the occasions that Peter was accosted, several of the bystanders got into the act and plied him with questions, which he answered with repeated denials. The Gospel narratives supplement rather than contradict one another.[31]

---

[31] The Evangelists seem to differ also as to the time at which the denials took place. Matthew and Mark, who omit the trial of Christ before Annas, speak of the denials of Peter as taking place after the night trial and the mocking of Jesus. Luke does not mention a night trial and speaks of the denials as taking place before the mockery of Jesus. Luke, who does not mention the Sanhedrists as taking part in the outrages against Christ and refers only to the subalterns who held Jesus, relates probably only the mockeries that took place after the Sanhedrists had departed and while Christ was on His way to the place where He was to be held prisoner till morning, and while He was detained there. His account would thus agree perfectly with that of Matthew and Mark. St. John places the first denial during the trial before Annas, while the Synoptists speak of it as if it had taken place during the trial before Caiaphas. This apparent discrepancy is easily accounted for. The Synoptists, not wishing to mention the trial before Annas, as it was of no great importance, grouped together the denials of Peter as if all had taken place during the trial before Caiaphas. This grouping of details is a common and well-known literary procedure of the Evangelists. Although John places the denial before Annas, and the Synoptists place it before Caiaphas, they are evidently speaking of the same place, as in both accounts those present are seated around a fire.

The LAST HOURS of JESUS

Peter slipped quietly through the arched vestibule into the open courtyard and looked about him. In the middle of the courtyard a group of servants and retainers huddled around a fire. In April, the days are usually warm, but the nights can be quite chilly, especially in the hilly country around Jerusalem. Peter evidently thought that his best course was to assume an air of nonchalance and to mingle with the servants as if he were one of them. He crouched over the fire and warmed himself. Mark, whose information came directly from Peter, mentions twice that Peter warmed himself, as if to insinuate that he was just a little too thoughtful of his own comfort at such a time.

Peter had not been quite as successful in avoiding attention as he had thought and hoped. The portress could not see him very clearly in the shadows of the entrance, but what she saw aroused her suspicions. She left the door in the care of another, approached the fire, and looked closely at Peter, whose features and garb were now clearly revealed in the light of the glowing embers. What she saw strengthened her suspicions, and going directly up to Peter, she said: "Art thou also one of this man's disciples?" Peter replied quickly and nervously, "I am not" (John 18:17). But the servant girl was not to be placated. She could see without difficulty that he was a Galilean and in all probability a fisherman, and so a likely disciple of Jesus. Instead of questioning Peter, she accused him directly this time: "Thou also wast with Jesus of Nazareth." Now he tried to give an evasive answer. He pleaded ignorance: "I neither know nor understand what thou art saying" (Mark 14:67–68). Peter knew and understood, but he lacked the courage to stand up to the maidservant and declare openly that he was a disciple of Jesus. He was guilty of a lack of moral courage. If the servants of the high priest had attacked him, he probably would have given a good account of himself.

But he went down to defeat before the verbal onslaught of a servant girl. He who had boasted that he would go with Christ to prison and to death, that he would be true to Him even if all others failed Him, and who had drawn a sword in His defense at Gethsemane, now denied that he had ever heard of Him. This was Peter's first denial.

There was a lapse of time between Peter's first and second denials; St. John narrates the story of Christ's appearance before Annas between the two. Peter had a little time to reflect. He felt uneasy. Perhaps he had made a mistake by his bravado in joining the group around the fire. As quietly and unobtrusively as possible, he went out to the vaulted vestibule leading to the outer gate. He felt that he could pass unnoticed here in the shadows and at a little distance from both the entrance gate and the group around the fire. As he took up his new position, the sound of an early cockcrow could be heard clearly. But it meant nothing to Peter at the moment. It was only afterward that he recalled it. Now he was too occupied with his own predicament, keeping a careful watch for any threat to himself.

The threat was not long in materializing, and again it took the shape of a maidservant. As likely as not, the portress was dissatisfied with Peter's answers and had acquainted other servants with her suspicions of this man whom she had admitted. Seeing him nearby, several approached Peter, and one of the maids said to the others: "This is one of them" (Mark 14:69).

Some of the men who had joined the group made the same accusation, but Peter repeated his denials. Somewhat frightened now, he retreated toward the fire in the middle of the courtyard, denying with increasing emphasis that he was a disciple of Jesus, or that he even knew Him. For a second time, Peter went down before a verbal attack.

The LAST HOURS *of* JESUS

For some reason, Peter was given about one hour's respite after his second denial. It would seem that attention was concentrated elsewhere during this period, probably on the trial of Christ before Caiaphas and the Sanhedrin. Peter had undoubtedly been torn between a desire to escape and a desire to see the fate that awaited his Master. His anxiety about Jesus overcame his fear, and he stayed on, as St. Matthew says, "to see the end" (26:58).

With the conclusion of the trial, some of the servants and retainers gathered around the fire again to warm themselves. To Peter's chagrin, one of them was a relative of Malchus, the servant of the high priest whose ear he had cut off in the scuffle in the garden. Some of the other servants again asked Peter if he were not a disciple of Jesus, and he denied it. The relative of Malchus looked closely at Peter now and said ominously: "Did I not see thee in the garden with him?" (John 18:26). Peter was shaken, and had good reason to be. Already in trouble as a possible disciple of Jesus, he was now recognized as one of those present at His arrest, possibly as the one who had attacked a servant of the high priest. Peter now multiplied his denials, and in his confusion and fear he probably spoke with an even broader Galilean accent than usual. Evidently the Jerusalem Jews identified Christ's followers as Galileans, because Peter was now accused of being a disciple for this reason. Peter felt cornered, surrounded by a hostile group pressing him with their accusations. A simple denial did not seem to be enough, so Peter began, as Mark says, "to curse and to swear, 'I do not know this man you are talking about'" (14:71). This is an awful climax to Peter's denials. He calls down a curse on himself if he is not telling the truth; he calls God to witness that he is telling the truth. And the "truth" in this case is that he, Peter, favored Apostle and friend of Jesus

Christ, is not a disciple of Jesus and, in fact, does not even know "this man." Yet, even in the depths of his abasement and in the vehemence of his denials, Peter seems unable to mention his Master's name. He can only speak of him as "this man."

Peter's recovery was as sudden as his downfall. Even as the words of denial were passing from his lips, a cock crowed. This time the sound got through to Peter's mind. He lapsed silent in a moment of reflection. He recalled Christ's prophecy: "Before a cock crows, thou wilt deny me thrice" (John 13:38; Luke 22:34). Almost simultaneously occurred one of the most beautiful incidents related in the Gospel narratives. Just at this moment, Jesus was being led across the courtyard to prison. As St. Luke says simply, "The Lord turned and looked upon Peter" (22:61). That look must have been one of compassionate reproach. Peter realized the full malice of what he had done and was overwhelmed with shame and sorrow. He could no longer trust himself to remain "to see the end." Anyway, the tears he could not restrain would betray him. The last we hear of St. Peter in the Gospel accounts of the Passion of our Lord is that "Peter went out and wept bitterly" (Luke 22:62).

St. Peter is one of the most human and lovable characters portrayed in the pages of sacred history. He was a man of ardor, impetuosity, and enthusiasm. He was candid, loyal, warm-hearted, and generous. He was outgoing, rough-spoken, friendly, and eager to be popular. But there were times when Peter was talkative, timid, vacillating, weak, and presumptuous. When he appears again in the Gospels, after the resurrection of Christ, and in the Acts of the Apostles, there is a notable change for the better in his character. Yet, even much later, the old Peter showed through on occasion. At Antioch, St. Paul withstood him to his face for his failure to act according to his principles. Out of human respect and fear of the Jewish element in the Church, Peter had stopped eating with Gentile Christians, to the scandal of many (Gal. 2:11–14). Whatever St. Peter's faults, they were more than offset by his intense personal love of Jesus Christ and by his long and fruitful apostolic ministry as the Vicar of Christ on earth. And all this was climaxed on that day in A.D. 67 when, on the Vatican Hill in Rome, he bore witness to his Divine Master by being crucified, head downward, at his own request, because in his humility he felt unworthy to die exactly as Christ had died on Calvary.

Chapter 12

THE DEATH OF JUDAS

The Gospel of St. Matthew is the only one that relates the story of the remorse and death of Judas (27:3–10). There is also a reference to this in the Acts of the Apostles (1:15–20). The tragic story of Judas was so well known to the early Christians and so deeply impressed on their minds that the sacred writers felt little or no need of recording it.

It would be satisfying to our curiosity to know what Judas did and said and thought after he had betrayed Christ into the hands of His enemies. Once Jesus was securely bound and led away, we can be sure that Judas' first thought was to collect the thirty pieces of silver that had been promised to him. It is possible that he remained behind and was paid on the spot in the darkness of the olive grove of Gethsemane. It is rather chilling to think that these silver pieces, the price of the blood of Jesus, probably mingled with the small coins that admiring followers of our Lord had given to help Him and His Apostles.

We do not know from just what point of vantage Judas followed the proceedings of that fateful night. But follow them he did, urged on by a gradually increasing uneasiness over what was taking place and over the part he had played in it. It is likely that he picked himself a dark spot in the street outside the entrance of the palace of the high priest. By this time, the full moon had passed its zenith and was descending toward the west, and the shadows of the buildings darkened the street. Judas could observe those who entered and left the palace and even gain an occasional momentary glance into the interior. In his mounting anxiety over the course of events, he may even have worked up enough courage to question some of those departing from the palace.

Judas spent several hours awaiting impatiently the outcome of what was taking place beyond the cold stone walls. His first uneasiness had become a chilling anxiety, which, in turn, developed into a desperate hope that his fears would not be realized. He must have been almost petrified when the great gate of the palace swung open and the line of marchers filed out into the street with Jesus bound. We do not know how close Jesus and Judas were at that moment. We do not know whether Jesus looked on Judas with compassion, as He had on Peter but a short time before. We do know that a sudden and crushing realization of what he had done overwhelmed Judas, for St. Matthew says: "Then Judas, who betrayed him, when he saw that he was condemned, repented" (27:3).

Judas had no doubt that Jesus was already a condemned man. So great was his regard for the authority of the Sanhedrin that, in his mind, it was a foregone conclusion that the Roman procurator would confirm its judgment.[32]

---

[32] In this we follow the order of St. Matthew. It is possible that the despair of Judas took place after the condemnation by Pilate, even after the death of Jesus.

It may seem strange that Judas became so disturbed at the sight of Jesus led away a condemned criminal. Had he not foreseen and intended exactly this outcome? There can be no doubt that he had. He knew exactly the sentiments and intentions of the enemies of Christ. He had dealt with them intimately. But like many criminals, Judas did not have a full realization of the horror of his deed until after its accomplishment. As he looked at Jesus and felt the weight of the silver coins in his wallet, he realized the awful nature of his crime and was overwhelmed with remorse. He had sold his Friend and Master for thirty miserable pieces of silver. Yet even Judas' remorse was not true repentance. It lacked hope, and there can be no true repentance without hope. Unlike Peter, who went out and wept bitter tears of compunction but never abandoned hope, Judas gave way to despair. Probably he had already lost faith in Jesus, the faith that would have inspired him to seek and obtain a full pardon of his heinous crime.

Judas had only one thought now. It would ease his mind to get rid of the coins. The procession had moved toward the east, then turned north up the valley toward the Antonia. As the procession turned north, Judas looked toward the east at the imposing wall of the Temple area. An idea struck him. He would give back the money to those from whom he had received it. Even in his disturbed state of mind, he had no thought that returning the money to Christ's enemies would deter them from their evil course. He sought only one thing: to rid himself of those coins that accused him ceaselessly by their very sound and touch and weight.

Judas entered the Temple area through one of the western gates. He was on familiar ground, and he probably went directly to the Hall of Hewn Stones, the ordinary meeting place of the Sanhedrin. Here he found some Sanhedrists gathered, perhaps even some of those with whom he had concluded his infamous bargain to betray Christ. Going up to them, he held out the wallet of silver coins and cried out: "I have sinned in betraying innocent blood" (Matt 27:4). Judas confessed his crime and retracted the implicit accusation he had made against Christ by delivering Him into the hands of His enemies. But even his confession was not complete and showed that he had lost faith in Jesus. He confessed only that he had betrayed "innocent blood," not that he had betrayed the Messiah and Son of God.

Judas' confession that his act was a crime was in itself an accusation against the Sanhedrists, his partners in the same evil transaction. They reacted with anger and contempt. Brushing aside the proffered coins, they said: "What is that to us? See to it thyself" (Matt. 27:4). If Judas was weak enough to have scruples over what had been done, they were not. If Judas thought he was guilty, let the guilt be upon his own head. They would have no part of it, nor would they take back the money he had earned by his base betrayal. They had no further use for him. They now had what they wanted, and they could afford to cast him aside as a useless tool.

Judas was enraged at their contempt and callousness. He determined that they would take the money, like it or not. He rushed out into the open toward the Temple. As he approached it, he grasped the wallet of coins and threw it toward the Temple with all his strength.

By this time, Judas was beside himself with anger, remorse, and despair. There seemed nowhere for him to turn. He had deserted and betrayed Jesus Christ. He had been brushed aside contemptuously by the chief priests, who had received him with smiling welcome just a few days before. He pushed his way through the throngs that were already beginning to gather at the Temple and left the enclosure by one of the west gates. Out in the streets again, he walked, not knowing where he was going. As he walked, despair took complete possession of him. In his distraught state of mind, death seemed better than life.

As he walked, Judas turned over a plan in his mind and determined just when and how he would die. At the southwest extremity of the city, to the west of the Fountain Gate, was the Pottery Gate. It got its name from the fact that beyond it were fields of clay deposits used by potters for making household vessels. Nearby too there was a cemetery. Between the gate and the cliff opposite was a deep valley known as the valley of the Sons of Hinnom. This region had an evil reputation dating back hundreds of years. It was here that some of the evil kings of Juda had worshipped Moloch. A hearth had been erected on which devotees burned children as an offering to the god. Perhaps because of its evil association, this area had become a city dump, and the name by which it was known, Gehenna, had become a symbol of hell because of the constant fire and smoke from its stinking refuse.

This was the place Judas selected for his death. With the Passover at hand, it would be deserted. There would be no one to interfere with his act of self-destruction. Going out through the Pottery Gate, Judas descended into the deep valley that ran eastward till it joined the Cedron a short distance away. On the other side of the valley was a steep, rugged cliff, bare except for a few stunted trees. This was the ideal spot for the work at hand, and Judas lost no time in climbing to the top of the cliff. He selected a tree whose branches overhung the valley below. Taking his girdle from his waist, he tied it around his neck, attached it to a limb of the tree, and leaped out into space. We do not know whether it happened while he was still alive, but it is evident, from the Acts of the Apostles, that either his girdle or the limb broke, and Judas went hurtling into the valley, striking against the jagged rocks strewn over this area. St. Luke tells us that "falling forward, he burst asunder in the midst, and all his bowels gushed out" (Acts 1:18, Greek text). An awful end indeed for the man who sold his Divine Master for thirty pieces of silver; an awful beginning for one about whom a merciful Lord could say: "It were better for that man if he had not been born" (Matt. 26:24).

In the meantime, Judas had precipitated a casuistic debate among the chief priests. Evidently they had lost no time in picking up the money. Now they engaged in a discussion on the niceties of the law. Speaking of the coins, they said, "It is not lawful to put them into the treasury, seeing that it is the price of blood" (Matt. 27:6). They gave no thought to the fact that they themselves were the source of the contamination of the coins. After much discussion, they came up with an altruistic, public-spirited solution; they would use the money to buy "the potter's field as a burial place for strangers" (Matt. 27:7). It was at the potter's field that Judas had committed suicide, and it was adjacent to a cemetery. What more appropriate than to add this field to the cemetery and use it for the burial of strangers, especially for Jews who died on a pilgrimage to the holy city? It is possible that Judas was buried here, although some time must have passed before the field was acquired. Memory of the place and its associations lingered, and the field became known as Haceldama, or field of blood. It well deserved the name, for it was purchased with the money paid for the betrayal of Christ, and it was the scene of the death of the betrayer.

Chapter 13

CHRIST BROUGHT BEFORE PILATE

When the captors of Jesus had tired of striking and spitting on Him, He was led to a prison cell and locked up as a common criminal to await the next step in the moves to bring about His death. The first rays of dawn were beginning to light the skies over the Mount of Olives beyond the Temple when the hum of activity began again in the palace of Annas and Caiaphas. In its night session the Sanhedrin had formally condemned Jesus Christ to death as a blasphemer. The next step must be to take the case before the tribunal of the Roman procurator, Pontius Pilate. As the meeting of the Sanhedrin broke up, its members agreed to a short rest period until dawn, after which they would reassemble. Their aim was clear — the death of Jesus Christ. That had been decided to their complete satisfaction. The only matter to be decided now was the very practical question of what tactics to use to secure a death sentence from Pontius Pilate. That would be taken up in the morning.

The decision of the morning meeting was to act immediately. The Roman procurator would have no concern for an accusation of blasphemy, so the Sanhedrists decided to rest their case on an accusation that Jesus claimed to be the Messiah, a political role that could be made to appear aimed at the authority of Roman rulers.

Action followed immediately. A deputation of chief priests, Scribes, and ancients was selected to conduct Jesus to the praetorium of Pilate and to press the case before his tribunal. A guard was quickly formed from the police and the retainers of the high priest. Jesus was led from His cell and carefully bound again. The group gathered in the courtyard. An officer barked orders, and the motley crowd formed into a line with Jesus in the middle. They marched out into the vestibule and then through the main gate into the street outside. They turned eastward for a while and then northward through the narrow streets. Dawn was breaking over the city by now, and the first rays of the sun were reflected from the pinnacles of the Temple. Some shops were just being opened along the way, and shopkeepers and some passersby looked with curiosity at the line of marchers with a bound prisoner in their midst. Some probably joined the group, impelled by curiosity or by an interest in what was taking place. The cortege descended the cobbled streets that led into the valley that cut Jerusalem in two, crossed the valley quickly, and then mounted the streets that led to the castle on the hill just to the north of the Temple. A half hour after their departure from the palace of the high priest, the group stood before the western entrance of the Antonia, which served as the praetorium and residence of the Roman procurator, Pontius Pilate,[33] when he came to Jerusalem to preserve peace on the great Jewish holy days.[34]

[33] There is a difference of opinion on this point, which we discuss below.

[34] In narrating the events that took place during the night of Christ's trial, we have followed the order that appears to us the most probable. Even a cursory reading of the Gospel texts reveals the

When Jesus and His accusers stood at the entrance to the Antonia, the sight before them was impressive. To their right, running north-south, was the west part of the wall that surrounded
the Temple area. This high wall had been built by Herod the
Great in the Roman style, and some of its huge stones are still
visible at the Wailing Wall of the Jews. At a point a little to the
right of the group, this wall joined the west wall of the Antonia.

This was a logical place for a fortress, and there had been one
in this locality centuries before, even at the time of the kings.
The high ground here dominated the Temple area just as the
Temple area dominated the lower city. Through the centuries
before Christ, and even during the final fateful days of the Roman
siege that ended in the destruction of Jerusalem in A.D. 70, the
fortress that occupied this ground was the key to the city. History

---

difficulty of determining the exact order of events. Matthew and
Mark, for instance, speak of a night meeting of the Sanhedrin at
which Christ is condemned, and then a morning meeting. St.
Luke speaks only of a morning meeting, and it is at this meeting
that he places the trial and condemnation of Jesus. It seems to
us that Luke has no special source for this event and that his arrangement is determined by his own purposes.

In harmonizing the Gospels, commentators usually follow
one of three orders:

1. A night trial as related by Matthew and Mark, and also
   a dawn trial as related by Luke.
2. A night trial only, as related by Matthew and Mark.
   According to this theory, what is related by Luke took
   place at this night trial. Some think there was an informal gathering in the morning to determine procedure.
   This is the order we have followed.
3. A morning trial only, as related by Luke. What is related by Matthew and Mark really took place in the
   morning.

records the names of several fortresses that had been built and destroyed here.

When Herod the Great had secured his appointment as king in the year 40 B.C., he still had the task of conquering his rivals. He accomplished this with the help of Roman legions by the conquest of the city of Jerusalem in July of 37 B.C., after a siege of five months. Herod took up residence in the Hasmonean palace on the east slope of the west hill of the city. He did not find this palace to his taste, especially since his mother-in-law lived there, so he built a massive palace-fortress for himself at the northwest corner of the Temple area and named it Antonia after his friend and patron Marc Antony. This first great Herodian structure in Palestine was probably erected between 37 and 35 B.C.

The Jewish historian Josephus was quite familiar with the Antonia and gives a detailed description of it. "The Antonia," he wrote,

> lay at the angle where two porticoes, the western and the northern, of the first court of the Temple met; it was built upon a rock fifty cubits high [a cubit is eighteen inches] and on all sides precipitous. It was the work of King Herod and a crowning exhibition of the innate grandeur of his genius. For, to begin with, the rock was covered from its base upward with smooth flagstones, both for ornament and in order that anyone attempting to ascend or descend it might slip off. Next, in front of the actual edifice, there was a wall three cubits high [probably meaning "thick"] and behind this the tower of the Antonia rose majestically to an altitude of forty cubits. The interior resembled a palace in its spaciousness and appointments, being divided into apartments of every description and for every

purpose, including cloisters, baths, and broad courtyards for the accommodation of troops; so that, from its possession of all conveniences, it seemed a town; from its magnificence, a palace. The general appearance of the whole was that of a tower with other towers at each of the four corners; three of these turrets were fifty cubits high, while that at the southeast angle rose to seventy cubits, and so commanded a view of the whole area of the Temple. At the point where it impinged upon the porticoes of the Temple, there were stairs leading down to both of them, by which the guards descended; for a Roman cohort was permanently quartered there and at the festivals took up positions in arms around the porticoes to watch the people and repress any insurrectionary movement. For if the Temple lay as a fortress over the city, the Antonia dominated the Temple, and the occupants of that post were the guards of all three; the upper town had its own fortress—Herod's palace. The hill Bezetha was, as I have said, cut off from the Antonia; the highest of all the hills, it was encroached on by part of the new town and formed on the north the only obstruction to the view of the Temple.[35]

This was not a mere "fortress" or "tower," as it was called in popular parlance because of its past and is still called today in some quarters. This was a vast structure that dominated the eastern half of the city and had all the characteristics of both a

---

[35] *Wars*, 5, 5, 8. For detailed analysis of this text, for archeological finds, and for tentative reconstruction, see Père Vincent, *Revue Biblique* (1952): 513ff.; (1954): 87ff.; *Jerusalem de l'Ancien Testament*, I, pp. 193ff.

fort and a palace. Because of its size and resources, it was almost a city within a city. The vast cisterns for its water supply are still extant.

The Antonia stretched east-west for about 185 yards and north-south for about 95. The interior was divided into two distinct zones. The southern part, constructed on an elevated, rocky esplanade, was the luxurious palatine residence. The larger part, to the north and completely separated, was the barracks for the troops. On the west side, at the point where Christ and His captors awaited word to enter, was a monumental entrance that led into a vast courtyard of over 2,700 square yards, paved with immense stones. A road, constructed of great serrated stones, led from the entrance straight through to a gate between the eastern towers. These gates and the road between them were the connecting links between the Antonia and the city.[36]

---

[36] There is a division of opinion among experts as to whether the praetorium of Pilate was at the Antonia or at the palace that Herod later built for himself at the northwest angle of the city wall and that became known as the palace of Herod. On the resolution of this difficulty depends the localization of the trial of Christ.

The mistake is often made of attempting to identify the praetorium with an official building of the city, especially with the Antonia or the palace of Herod. As a matter of fact, a praetorium was any place used by the procurator to set up a platform and curule chair for the exercise of his official functions. The word "praetorium" was used for the residence of a general, whether in a city or a camp.

We are of the opinion that the local tradition is correct and that the trial of Christ took place at the Antonia. The purpose of maintaining order on the feast of the Passover could best be accomplished at the Antonia, since it overlooked and was connected with the Temple area, where trouble was most likely.

Pontius Pilate is known to us from each of the four Gospels and also from the writings of other contemporary historians. He was the fifth procurator to hold office after Rome had deposed Archelaus, son of Herod the Great, in the year A.D. 6. Pilate held office from 26 to 36. Although his jurisdiction extended over Samaria also, his official title was procurator of the Province of Judea. Pilate was appointed to office by the emperor Tiberius, who ordinarily left provincial governors in office a long time. He believed that governors were like flies on a wounded animal; once they were satiated they became less greedy, whereas new officials started the gouging afresh.

We know nothing of the early life of Pontius Pilate: his training, the offices he had held before he became procurator, his successes or failures elsewhere. His position as procurator of an imperial province implied that he was of equestrian rank and therefore a person of modest importance in the hierarchy of the administration of the empire.

Pilate was little better or worse than most of the other procurators just before and after his time. Roman law, Roman justice, and Roman principles of stern but fair and considerate rule over subject peoples were an ideal often lost sight of in actual practice. Pilate evidently thought that the best manner of ruling the Jews was to disregard their feelings and use force. He may have been encouraged in this by the fact that the emperor Tiberius, under the influence of his favorite, Sejanus, disliked the Jews. The Jewish writer Philo quotes Agrippa I, a contemporary, to the effect

---

Another powerful argument is that archeological discoveries in this area harmonize accurately and in many details with the Gospel narratives. The great flagstones of the road and courtyard can still be seen here.

that Pilate was an "unbending and recklessly hard character," and he accuses him of "corruptibility, violence, robberies, ill-treatment of the people, grievances, continuous executions without even the form of a trial, endless and intolerable cruelties."

Pilate did not understand, or even try to understand, the people he ruled. What is worse, he despised them, their customs, and their religion. No doubt he had considerable provocation. The Jews were not an easy people to govern. They firmly believed that, instead of being ruled by others, it was their destiny as the Chosen People of God to rule all others. This conviction revealed itself often and unpleasantly in their relations with their Roman masters. Pilate was undoubtedly hard and arrogant. Yet there was a certain weakness and irresolution in his character that the Jews discovered soon after he had taken office and which they used for their own purposes at the trial of Christ. Pilate's predecessors had accommodated themselves to the religious convictions of the Jews and had refrained from introducing idolatrous images — even the military standards bearing the image of the emperor — into the holy city. Pilate evidently thought this a weakness unworthy of his office and dignity. He sent troops into Jerusalem during the night bearing the forbidden images. There was a great disturbance when the morning light revealed the presence of the pagan symbols. Excitement ran so high that crowds of people flocked over the roads to Caesarea and for five days and five nights besought Pilate to remove the offensive standards. Pilate's patience gave way on the sixth day. He admitted the Jews to his presence in a public place and ordered his soldiers with concealed weapons to surround them. Pilate threatened them with death if they did not cease annoying him and depart in peace. Instead of obeying him, they bared their necks and declared that they would prefer death to seeing their laws transgressed. Pilate yielded—as he was to yield later to their threats—and ordered the idolatrous standards returned to Caesarea.

Pilate was not a man to give up easily. On another occasion, he introduced into the palace of Herod votive shields, without images but bearing an inscription of the emperor's name. Again the people were in an uproar. They sent a delegation of nobles, including four sons of Herod, to Pilate, requesting that he remove the shields. When he refused, the Jews appealed to the emperor Tiberius, who rebuked Pilate and ordered the shields to be taken to the Temple of Augustus in Caesarea.

On one occasion Pilate won out over the opposition of the Jews. He had taken money from the sacred Temple treasury to build an aqueduct to bring water into Jerusalem. This use of the sacred money was a sacrilege to the Jews. When Pilate appeared in Jerusalem, he was surrounded by a howling mob complaining of the sacrilege. Pilate had advance information of what would happen and had ordered his soldiers, armed with clubs, to mingle with the people. At a prearranged signal, the soldiers set upon the crowd, beating them unmercifully and killing great numbers of them. Pilate won his point, but only at the cost of intensified hatred and opposition. St. Luke mentions an incident, on which we have no further information, of some Galileans whose blood Pilate had mingled with their sacrifices (13:1).

In A.D. 35, a Samaritan pseudo-prophet promised the people that if they would assemble on Mount Gerizim, he would show them the sacred vessels that Moses was supposed to have buried before his death. The credulous multitude believed him and assembled in a village at the foot of the mount. Pilate got word of the affair and sent a detachment of soldiers, who attacked the crowd, wounding and killing many. The Samaritans sent a complaint to Vitellius, the legate in Syria. Vitellius ordered Pilate to go to Rome to render an account of his conduct. While Pilate was on his way to Rome, the emperor Tiberius died. We do not know what happened to Pilate. There is an ancient tradition, recorded by the historian Eusebius (fourth century), that he was exiled to Vienne in Gaul and there took his life. Legends abound concerning Pilate's later life and his death, but they are completely untrustworthy.

Standing before the great western portals of the Antonia, Christ's accusers suffer a scruple. According to their reckoning, the next day was the Passover, and therefore they should eat the Paschal meal at sundown this very day. Entrance into the house of a pagan caused a legal impurity that would prevent this. What were they to do? A hasty conference brought a solution, a solution characteristic of these unworthy religious leaders. They decided that they would not contract a legal impurity if they did not enter the great open court where trials were held. With a little indulgence on Pilate's part, this could be avoided. They could remain in the two parallel vaulted gateways that served as corridors between the outside street and the great paved courtyard of the palace-fortress. There was an open space here of about 275 square yards, more than enough room for a group that hardly numbered more than two hundred people at most. Pilate could set up his tribunal in the great court just inside the entrance, and they could then present the case to him without entering and incurring legal defilement.[37]

---

[37] The Gospel of St. John states that "they therefore led Jesus from Caiaphas to the praetorium" (18:28).

We can be sure that up to this point in the capture and trial of Christ, all used Aramaic, the language of the country. What language was used in the trial before Pilate? In the Eastern part

Having settled their case of conscience, the leaders of the group immediately got down to the business at hand. They addressed themselves to the officer in charge of the guard, requesting that he inform the procurator that they had a prisoner to be tried before his tribunal. They asked also that the trial might be held at the portal so that they would not be forced to enter the courtyard and incur a legal impurity. They pushed Jesus Christ forward and delivered Him, bound, into the custody of the Roman soldiers.

The officer went up the stairs at the right leading to the quarters of the procurator. In a few minutes, Pontius Pilate, the procurator of Judea, surrounded by a few of his legal advisers and assistants, descended the stairs and walked across the great flagstones of the courtyard toward the Jews assembled at the west portal. Evidently, Pilate had made up his mind in this instance to follow the Roman custom of respecting the religious sensibilities of a subject people.

And now began the greatest trial in history. It was a strange confrontation. In a gallery under the great arched entrance to the palace-fortress were the chief priests, Scribes, and ancients who had been sent to represent the Sanhedrin as accusers of Jesus Christ. Their role had changed. Just a few hours before, they had acted as judges. Now they were reduced to the role of accusers. In the courtyard facing them stood Pontius Pilate with a few advisers. Nearby, surrounded by soldiers of the guard, was Jesus. In Roman law, Pilate alone acted as judge and jury. He could ask

---

of the empire, Greek was used ordinarily in the administration of justice, and it is highly probable that Pilate spoke Greek. It is unlikely that he spoke Aramaic—at least, not well enough for a formal trial. We think it is more likely that Greek was used and that interpreters immediately translated what was said into Aramaic for those who did not understand Greek.

advice of his assistants if he wished, but to him alone belonged the right to conduct the trial and to make the final judgment. Life and death were in his hands and in his hands alone. His was to be a momentous decision.

Pontius Pilate began the trial by asking: "What accusation do you bring against this man?" (John 18:29). One wonders immediately if Pilate had no prior information concerning Jesus and His difficulties with the leaders of the Jews. We think it highly unlikely—the more so if Roman soldiers were involved in the arrest of Jesus. The conflict between Jesus and the Jewish leaders had on occasion caused considerable turmoil, and such a matter must have been reported to the procurator, since he was responsible for maintaining public order and administering justice in local cases. In fact, it is not unlikely that Pilate had been told, at least sketchily, of the events of the preceding night. It would be his business to be informed of cases pending and probable.

Pilate's words had a particular significance. They were the opening words of a formal trial. He demanded that the plaintiffs step forward and make their accusations. Pilate could have accepted the judgment of the local court; he could have verified its sentence and ordered its execution; or he could simply have taken the word of these accusers who were among the great of the land. Pilate did none of these things. He exercised his right to try the case himself. This meant that the trial would be conducted according to Roman procedure; according to Roman, not Jewish, law.[38]

---

[38] Various trials mentioned in the Acts of the Apostles were based on Roman law: 18:15; 23:29; 25:18–20.

Since the Romans alone had the right over life and death, why did the Jews go through the motions of a trial of their own?

The Jews were taken aback by Pilate's words — or at least gave the impression that they were. They replied: "If he were not a criminal, we should not have handed him over to thee" (John 18:30). This reply is often interpreted as a bit of insolence. It is not likely, however, that these wily leaders of the Jews, who wanted to secure Christ's death through Pilate, would have begun by offending him. The sense is rather: If we who are Jews hand over to you, the Roman procurator, one of our own, we do it only because He is guilty and deserves condemnation. In other words, Pilate can really trust them in this matter.

But Pilate was not going to get involved so easily. "Take him yourselves," he said, "and judge him according to your law" (John 18:31). Up to the present, Pilate had not been informed, at least not officially, that it was a case of capital punishment, so he could very well tell Christ's accusers to deal with Him according to their own laws. If he had been informed, then his answer was a deliberate slap at them as leaders of a subject people who had lost the right over life or death. Christ's accusers then made a confession that showed that it was the death penalty that they

---

One of the chief reasons is that in the eyes of devout Jews, *only* the trial before the Sanhedrin had any validity in conscience. Also, the sentence of the Sanhedrin was a means of exercising a certain pressure on the procurator (John 19:7). It was a potent weapon, too, for destroying Jesus' reputation with the populace. It probably soothed the wounded pride of the members of the Sanhedrin to go through the externals of a formal trial, even though their decision could not be put into effect.

Objection has been made that Jesus could not be tried by both the Jewish and Roman tribunals because Roman law forbade that a man be tried twice for the same offense. But Jesus was tried before the Sanhedrin on a charge of blasphemy and before the procurator on a charge of treason.

wanted and that they wanted it from Pilate since they had no power to inflict it. "It is not lawful for us," they confessed, "to put anyone to death" (John 18:31).

After this first exchange of words, the Jewish leaders recognized the fact that Pilate was determined to be a judge rather than an executioner. Doubtless they were not wholly unprepared for this outcome. They knew that the charge of blasphemy, for which they had condemned Jesus, would have no effect on the pagan Pilate, so they formulated new accusations. "We have found this man perverting our nation," they said, "and forbidding the payment of taxes to Caesar, and saying that he is Christ, a king" (Luke 23:2). The accusations were cleverly fabricated for the purpose of impressing the Roman procurator and proving beyond a doubt the competence of his tribunal. It belonged to the procurator to preserve order and peace. They accused Jesus of stirring up the people, leaving the impression that He stirred them up politically. It was a special duty of the procurator to assure proper collection of taxes. They accused Jesus of preventing this, although He had upheld Caesar's right to taxes but a few days before. It was the duty of the procurator to protect Roman sovereignty against usurpers. They accused Christ of claiming to be Messiah-King, although He had fled those who would have made Him king. (In the eyes of his accusers, Messiah and king were synonymous, however, as they expected a Messiah who would rule them and who would free them from the foreign yoke and payment of tribute.) The third accusation was the most serious, as it was really a charge of treason, one of the greatest crimes in Roman criminal law.

Pilate was faced with a dilemma. He knew that these Jews hated him and all that he stood for. He knew that their newly discovered patriotism, their sudden concern for Roman authority, was a sham. But the accusations against Jesus were extremely serious, and the accusers offered themselves as witnesses with the words: "We have found this man ..."

Pilate deliberated for a few moments on the best course to pursue. He made up his mind to interrogate the prisoner privately. He ordered the guard to bring Jesus after him as he and his retinue turned and headed for the stairs leading to his private quarters about thirty yards from the portal where the trial had been started. Pilate entered his own apartments, followed by Jesus and His guards.

The procurator immediately got to the heart of the matter. He realized that the third accusation included the other two implicitly, so he asked Jesus directly and simply: "Art thou the King of the Jews?" This was in reality a request for a plea of guilty or not guilty, for a confession or a denial.

Christ's answer was neither yes nor no. To answer the question He must know the sense in which it was asked. So Christ's answer was a question on His part: "Dost thou say this of thyself, or have others told thee of me?" (John 18:34). If Pilate asked the question in the sense in which He would understand it, then Christ must answer no. He was not a king in the political sense. If he was asking the question in the sense in which the Jews understood—or should have understood—the role of the Messiah-King, then the answer must be yes.

A practical man, Pilate had little use for philosophical distinctions. His reply manifests impatience. "Am I a Jew?" he said. Am I a Jew, that I should be interested in these religious affairs? Am I a Jew, that I should be worried about the Messiah and his kingdom? Pilate then goes on to place the blame exactly where it belonged: "Thy own people and the chief priests have delivered thee to me." Annoyed at what he considered a digression, Pilate tried now to get at the facts in the case: "What hast thou done?"

he said directly to Jesus. In other words: What have You done that Your own people have turned You over to me? Pilate knew well it was not for the reasons given in the accusation.

Having insisted on the proper distinctions, Jesus returned now to the original question and answered Pilate: "My kingdom is not of this world. If my kingdom were of this world, my followers would have fought that I might not be delivered to the Jews. But, as it is, my kingdom is not from here" (John 18:36).

By declaring that He had a kingdom, Christ admitted that He was a king. He declared, however, that His kingdom was not of this world but from on high. As proof of this, Christ offered the fact that His followers had not fought to prevent His delivery into the hands of the Jews. If His kingdom were an earthly one like Caesar's, His retainers would have done battle to protect Him. The mere fact that He had been delivered into the hands of the Jews, whose king He was accused of being, was proof that His kingdom was not of this world.

Pilate's practical mind had little use for the distinctions Christ made. He said to Jesus: "Thou art then a king?" Pilate evidently felt that Jesus could make all the distinctions He liked, but still He was endangering Himself by claiming to be a king in any sense of the word. In the original Greek there is a touch of irony, mingled perhaps with pity or contempt. The word "thou" is emphasized: *"Thou . . . a king?"*

Christ's reply is an unequivocal affirmation of His royalty: "Thou sayest it; I am a king." And then Jesus goes on to explain to an uncomprehending Pilate the nature of His kingdom and royalty: "This is why I was born, and why I have come into the world, to bear witness to the truth. Everyone who is of the truth hears my voice" (John 18:37). What Jesus said, in effect, was that He was born and appeared before the world in His public ministry in order to bear witness to the truth. Christ revealed and taught the highest form of truth—religious truth. His life and deeds bore witness to the truth of His teaching. Those who seek, find and accept the truth that Christ revealed and taught; they hear his voice—i.e., become His disciples, citizens of His kingdom.

Christ's words presented a subtle invitation to Pilate, but the cautious procurator would have no part of it. Often he had heard of Greek and Roman philosophers who had found and taught "the truth"! He had no regard for their speculations. Pilate was a busy administrator, a practical man. If he had no time for the Greek and Roman truth-seekers, how much less should he now give ear to this idle dreamer who was despised and betrayed even by His own people. Pilate expressed contempt in his brief, cynical question to Christ: "What is truth?" (John 18:38).

The procurator did not wait for an answer. He did not expect one. Indeed, he considered the question unanswerable. Ordering the guards to bring Jesus along, he left his chambers, went down the stairs leading to the great courtyard, and strode to the portal where the Jews awaited him. He immediately announced his decision: "I find no guilt in this man." We can well imagine that this announcement left the accusers stunned and silent. Was their victim to escape them now, despite their well-laid plans and devious machinations?

They recovered quickly. Pilate's decision had not been accompanied by the formalities of a final and definite judgment. It was a simple statement of his opinion following a private questioning of Jesus. The Jews refused absolutely to concur in that opinion. They returned to their accusations, repeating them, emphasizing them, enlarging them. They insisted most tenaciously and forcefully that Jesus had aroused the people. Undoubtedly, they felt that they could present acceptable proof of this charge. Christ had indeed stirred the people, although not politically.

As the medley of accusing voices rose to a strident clamor, Pilate looked at Jesus, expecting some defense. Pilate had often presided at trials. He was accustomed to hear the accused multiply excuses and denials as the accusations mounted. What he witnessed now astounded and perplexed him. Jesus stood as quietly and calmly as a disinterested spectator at the trial of another. Hardly believing what he saw, Pilate said to Jesus: "'Dost thou not hear how many things they prefer against thee?' But he did not answer him a single word, so that the procurator wondered exceedingly" (Matt. 27:13–14).

It may seem a little strange that Jesus not only refused to reply to the accusations of the Jews but also refused to answer Pilate's question. The fact is, of course, that Christ had already replied to Pilate's queries. He had given him sufficient information concerning His kingship and kingdom to convince him that He was innocent, and Pilate had already so declared. Pilate's clear duty was to release Jesus. Instead, he now went over the same ground again, listening to the same accusations and requesting the same information from Jesus. Perplexed as he was, Pilate could not resist a feeling of admiration for Christ's coolness and courage.

Christ's silence had only an adverse effect on his accusers. Like a refrain, they returned again and again to the accusation that Jesus had stirred up the people. And to prove that the disturbances were of vast importance, they added that Christ had stirred up the people "throughout all Judea, and beginning from Galilee even to this place" (Luke 23:5). The purpose of the high priests was to emphasize to Pilate that the "crimes" of which they accused the prisoner were great and had taken place in Judea under his jurisdiction.

Pilate was in a quandary. On the one hand, he was convinced that Christ was innocent and that the leaders of the Jews had delivered Him to trial out of evil motives. Furthermore, he hated them, and his pride was hurt by the thought that they were trying to force him to do their will. On the other hand, the charges were extremely grave and the accusers were of the highest rank. A denunciation to the emperor might be fatal to his career.

As Pilate turned the matter over in his mind, his ear caught the word "Galilee" on the lips of the chief priests. That gave him an idea, and his face lit up with pleasure at the thought that Christ's accusers had themselves provided him with a stratagem for ridding himself of this unpleasant affair. If Jesus was from Galilee, he was a subject of Herod Antipas, who was in Jerusalem for the Passover. Pilate had the right to try Jesus, but he could forego the right and send Him to Herod Antipas. This would be a gesture of deference to Antipas and would provide a way out for himself. We can well imagine a disdainful smile on the lips of Pilate as he waved the Jews aside and ordered Jesus led from His tribunal to the court of Herod Antipas.[39]

---

[39] It appears clear to us from the Gospel of St. Luke that Pilate had two motives in sending Jesus to Herod Antipas. He wanted to rid himself of a trial he found distasteful, and he wanted to pay a compliment to Herod, with whom he had had difficulties. In ordinary circumstances, a ruler did not have jurisdiction outside his territory, but there were exceptions and Pilate could invite Herod to try a case that involved one of his subjects. In these circumstances, Herod could have held court in Jerusalem or he could have brought the prisoner back into his own territory of Galilee or Perea. Pilate was so convinced of Christ's innocence that he expected an acquittal from Herod. He knew that if Christ were guilty of the crimes of which He was accused, Herod would long ago have proceeded against Him.

The LAST HOURS *of* JESUS

Pilate may well have flattered himself for his cleverness, but his decision was cowardly and unjust. The moment he was convinced that Christ was innocent, he should have freed Him. He did not. That was the beginning of his guilt.

Chapter 14

HEROD ANTIPAS

In an earlier chapter we identified the Herod with whom we are concerned in the Passion of Christ as the son of Herod the Great, infamous for many cruel and evil deeds but especially for the slaughter of the Innocents at Bethlehem. Herod Antipas[40] was a cunning and clever man. By obsequiousness to the Romans and an external deference for the religious sensibilities of the Jews, he maintained himself in power from 4 B.C. to A.D. 39. Like his father, Antipas was a builder. To defend Galilee, he rebuilt Sepphoris, a fortified town only three miles from Nazareth, where Jesus spent his hidden life. He built fortifications along his eastern frontiers to protect his territory from Arab attacks. As a further measure of protection, he married the daughter of the Arabian king, Aretas. He built himself a capital on the west shore of the Sea of Galilee and called it Tiberias after the emperor. Devout Jews refused to live in the city, however, as it was built over sepulchers,

---

[40] The Gospels refer to him as Herod; Josephus calls him Antipas. The two names are usually combined to distinguish him from his father.

and contact with a grave occasioned a legal impurity for seven days.

Some of the greatest crises and crimes of Herod's career resulted from an illicit love affair. He resided for a while with his half brother, Herod Philip.[41] Antipas fell passionately in love with Herodias, wife of Herod Philip, and she returned his love. He promised to divorce his wife and marry her. In the meantime, however, his wife had heard of what was going on and fled to her father. King Aretas never forgave the injury done his daughter, and some years later he inflicted an overwhelming defeat on the armies of Herod Antipas. Antipas married Herodias, who was not only his sister-in-law but also his niece.

At this time, St. John the Baptist was preaching and baptizing in the area around the Jordan River, which was the dividing line between Judea and Perea. When John was on the east bank of the Jordan, he was in the territory of Herod Antipas. The adulterous and incestuous marriage of Herod and Herodias was a matter of public scandal, and in the spirit of the prophets, John denounced it in scathing terms to the multitudes who came out to hear him. The scandal was the greater because Herod posed as a champion and defender of the Jewish religion. John did not content himself with denunciations at a safe distance, before a sympathetic audience. He sought out Herod in one of his palaces and rebuked him to his face. It must have been a strange scene. On the one hand, the tetrarch in his rich robes and courtly surroundings. On the other, the bearded preacher from the desert, whose gaunt figure was clothed in a rough garment of camel's hair held about him by a leather belt.

---

[41] He is called Herod in Josephus and Philip in the Gospel. It is likely that Philip was his surname.

John was thrown into prison for his pains, perhaps at the instigation of Herod's wife. Herodias was infuriated. John's rebukes and public denunciations wounded her pride and endangered her position. Her reaction was direct and fierce, her solution simple. She determined to kill John. The only difficulty was to find a way to do it.

Her difficulty proved to be Herod himself. St. Mark tells us that Herod "feared John, knowing that he was a just and holy man, and protected him; and when he heard him talk, he did many things, and he liked to hear him" (6:20). These words throw light on the character of Herod. He was not wholly depraved. He recognized and respected virtue. He felt a sincere attraction, especially under the influence of John, to do right, to follow the course his conscience pointed out to him. But Herod was a weakling. He had accustomed himself to seeking the pleasant and avoiding the difficult. He would swim with the current rather than against it. He lacked the courage and energy to master himself. Instead of releasing John to continue his work of preaching and baptizing, he kept him in prison. We do not know just when or why, but we do know from Josephus that Herod transferred John to a prison at Machaerus, a vast palace-fortress built by Herod the Great at the southern border of his kingdom, on the plains of Moab overlooking the precipitous slopes to the Dead Sea.[42]

It was at Machaerus that the final scene in John's life took place. Herod celebrated his birthday with a great banquet, to which he invited many of the more important people of his dominions. As part of the entertainment, probably as its climax, Salome, daughter of Herodias by a former marriage, danced for Herod and his guests. Stimulated by the wine and intrigued by

---

[42] *Antiquities*, 18, 5, 2.

the sight of a girl of such high rank dancing before them, Herod and his guests greeted the act with a burst of applause. Herod wanted to show his appreciation. He knew it would please not only the girl but also her mother. Calling Salome to him, he told her to ask for anything she liked, and added with an oath that he would give it to her "even though it be the half of my kingdom" (Mark 6:23). By this time, the wine had befogged Herod's senses and deprived him of prudent restraint. He committed himself publicly and blatantly to giving the girl whatever she asked for.

Salome was a girl of about fifteen at this time and under the influence of her cunning and determined mother. She sought her mother's advice as to what she should request. Herodias was ready. In fact, she had planned it this way and had hoped for this outcome. Without a moment's hesitation, she told her daughter to ask for the head of John the Baptist. Salome reentered the banquet hall, approached Herod hastily, and said: "I want thee right away to give me on a dish the head of John the Baptist" (Mark 6:25). Herod was caught in the trap he had helped to set for himself. He did not want to displease Salome, and least of all her mother. He did not want to go back on a promise made in the presence of so many guests. He weakly gave his consent and ordered that John be executed. His head was brought to Salome on a dish, and Salome presented it to her mother. Herod grieved, but his grief was neither deep nor lasting.

There is no reason to believe that Christ and Herod had ever met before the trial of Christ. It is altogether possible that as a boy Jesus had seen Herod. From the hills above Nazareth, one could get a clear view of Sepphoris, three miles to the northwest, with its new walls and great citadel. Herod had rebuilt it and had made it his capital until the year A.D. 18. It was the largest and wealthiest city of the province, and it is not at all unlikely that the Holy Family went there occasionally to shop for household goods and material for Joseph's shop. On some of these occasions, Jesus may have seen Herod.

A considerable amount of discontent marked the rule of Herod Antipas, and he kept a constant watch throughout his territories. It was not long after the beginning of Christ's public ministry that Herod began receiving reports of His preaching, and especially of the miracles He performed. These reports aroused in Herod a superstitious fear, and he jumped to the conclusion that John the Baptist, whom he had murdered, had risen from the dead. Herod went so far as to express a desire to see Jesus (Luke 9:9). Jesus would have nothing to do with him, and even warned His followers to "beware of the leaven of the Pharisees, and of the leaven of Herod" (Mark 8:15).

Late in the last year of His public ministry, Christ was in Perea, across the Jordan. Some Pharisees came to Him and warned Him: "Depart and be on thy way, for Herod wants to kill thee" (Luke 13:31). They were in the territory of Herod Antipas and not far from Machaerus, where John the Baptist had been put to death. Jesus could very well have been in a dangerous situation.

But Jesus recognized a plot. He knew that the warning was not sincere. The Pharisees hated Him and would prefer to have Him leave for Judea, where they had a better chance of killing Him. They were conniving with Herod against their common enemy. But Herod did not want more bloodshed, and he felt that if Christ fled before a mere threat, He would lose the respect of His followers and His movement would collapse.

Jesus' answer showed that He saw through their scheming: "Go and say to that fox, 'Behold, I cast out devils and perform cures today and tomorrow, and the third day I am to end my course. Nevertheless, I must go my way today and tomorrow and the next day, for it cannot be that a prophet perish outside Jerusalem'" (Luke 13:32–33). Jesus would go; but He would go at a time determined by Himself and not by Herod or the Pharisees.

Luke 23:5–12 does not tell us where Herod resided in Jerusalem, but in all probability it was at the Hasmonean palace. This palace was about four hundred yards from the Antonia and was built on the northeast shoulder of the west hill of the city. It stood high above the deep valley that cut the city in two, and from its walls and windows one could look down into the Temple area just across the valley to the east.

No doubt Pilate sent an official message to Herod informing him of what was taking place. Again, a procession was formed, marched out through the great west portal of the Antonia, and turned south down the valley. Jesus, bound, was surrounded by Roman soldiers. Following after was a motley crowd of chief priests, Scribes, Pharisees, their retainers, and a group of the curious and of hangers-on. After a few hundred yards, the procession turned west and labored up the steep hill to the palace. Its portals quickly opened, as they were expected. The soldiers, with Jesus and His principal accusers, were ushered into the great hall, into the presence of Herod Antipas.

For the first time, Jesus and Herod found themselves face-to-face. Herod was about fifty and had been ruler of Galilee and Perea since he was seventeen. He greatly coveted the title of king; it was never granted him except in popular speech, but he surrounded himself with all the pomp and luxury of royalty. We can imagine that for an occasion such as this he sat on a chair on a slightly elevated dais, in a rich but informal garb. Officers of the guard, courtiers, and probably even some women of the court—possibly Herodias—lolled about, awaiting the beginning of an affair that might provide them with a few moments of diversion.

Jesus was brought forward and stood facing Herod. St. Luke tells us that Herod was very glad to see Him. He had heard a great deal about Him, and he had been impressed. But it was not the teachings of Jesus that had impressed him. It was only the miracles. Herod was probably a man of no faith at all and thought that Jesus was a magician, a conjurer, a sleight-of-hand artist who had earned His influence and reputation by trickery. But He must be clever, Herod thought, to gain the reputation He had throughout the land. It would be fun to have a private showing, here and now, of His magical arts.

Give Him room, Herod ordered. Unbind Him and give Him a chance to show us what He can do. St. Luke tells us that Herod put many questions to Jesus. At this point they probably had nothing to do with the accusation brought against Jesus. Herod was interested only in Christ's occult powers. What had He really done? Were the rumors about Him true? What was the source of His power? Where had He learned His "trade"? Wouldn't He give some samples of it now? He had worked wonders for the ordinary people; here was an opportunity to make an impression on those who really counted.

Jesus maintained complete silence. He ignored Herod. He acted as if he did not exist. We can well imagine that a shocked silence filled the room. This carpenter from Nazareth, this ordinary workman who had no riches, power, or position, this accused whose life was in Herod's hands, dared to show contempt for the tetrarch by ignoring his requests and refusing even to answer when spoken to. Herod must have felt humiliated in his own eyes and in the eyes of those present. He had received Jesus graciously. He had shown pleasure at seeing Him. He had not acted as judge or inquisitor. In fact, he had spoken to him in a rather friendly manner. And now Jesus treated him this way!

Jesus' silences are often as instructive as His words. One of the obvious reasons He remained silent now was that Herod treated Him as a mere conjurer. Jesus could have answered and raised the conversation to a higher plane, but He did not. He knew Herod. In Herod's vice-laden soul there was still a faint aspiration for higher things, but it had been all but extinguished by a debauched, worldly, and impure life. He was incapable of a sincere effort in search of the truth. Even at this solemn moment, with the life of Christ hanging in the balance, he seeks only a passing moment of entertainment for himself and his court. He did not deserve a word from the mouth of Christ.

Herod's reaction was one of annoyance and anger. The chief priests and Scribes were pleased with this turn of events and pushed forward, pressing their charges against Christ. They probably made the same accusations that they had made before Pilate, perhaps adding the charge of blasphemy, since Herod was at least nominally a Jew in religion.

Herod paid no attention to the charges. His network of spies would have reported Jesus' activities long ago if He were guilty. To Herod He was a visionary, a fanatic whose religious views conflicted with those of the Jewish leaders. Herod had no thought of a trial, either here in Jerusalem or later in his own territory. Anyway, why should he get entangled with Jesus as he had with John the Baptist, whose death had caused deep resentment among those who considered him a prophet? Then, too, he had no thought of taking Pilate's friendly gesture too seriously. He was well aware that Pilate had his own selfish reasons for sending Jesus to him.

Although he refused to condemn Jesus, Herod sought revenge, and his revenge reflected the character of the man. He had wanted amusement for himself and his court, and he would

have it. Among the accusations brought against Jesus, one captured Herod's attention. Jesus claimed to be a king. Surely this
was the height of the ridiculous. Herod had sought kingship, and
even he had not attained it. And this poor deluded person before
him claimed it as His right.

This was really a laughing matter. From anger Herod turned
quickly to merriment. This was a joke to be enjoyed and acted
out. Get a brilliant garment such as kings wear, Herod ordered,
and clothe Jesus in it. The officers of the guard quickly obeyed,
found a suitable garment, perhaps even one that Herod had cast
off, and clothed Jesus in it. Then Herod motioned to all to join
in paying mock obeisance to the king.

How long this scene of mockery lasted we do not know, but
it was probably brief. Herod and his friends were soon sated with
any pleasure and quickly turned to something else. When Herod
finally called a halt, he ordered that Jesus be returned to Pilate. To
add to his revenge, he ordered that Jesus be led to Pilate through
the streets of Jerusalem still wearing the bright robe of His mock
kingship.[43]

St. Luke adds a strange epilogue to the incident we have just
described. "And Herod and Pilate became friends that very day;
whereas previously they had been at enmity with each other"
(23:12). The Evangelist gives no reason for the hostility. It could
have been an incident that Luke relates earlier when he refers
to the "Galileans whose blood Pilate had mingled with their
sacrifices" (13:1). As Galileans, they were subjects of Herod. The
Jewish historian Philo relates also that when Pilate attempted to

---

[43] The Greek word describing the garment in which Herod clothed
Jesus is best translated "brilliant." It could refer to a brilliant
white or any brightly colored garment.

bring the idolatrous shields into the holy city, the sons of Herod the Great sided with the Jews against Pilate.

Whatever the reason for the quarrel, Pilate's act of politeness and deference in sending Jesus to Herod ended it. There was really little reason for either to be particularly elated. Pilate's plan had not worked as he had hoped, and he had Jesus back in his courtyard for trial. And Herod knew that Pilate was wishing on him a troublesome case. It was likely that each was anxious to be reconciled. Herod knew well that Pilate was a representative of the Roman power and must have some influence in Rome to obtain and hold his position as procurator. Pilate knew that Herod was a favorite of the emperor Tiberius. We know that later Herod sent secret reports to the emperor about Vitellius, legate of Syria. Perhaps Pilate suspected that he was now doing the same concerning him. It is a sad commentary on their characters that these two men limited their interest in the presence of Jesus Christ before them to a reconciliation in favor of their personal ambitions.[44]

---

[44] Herod Antipas came to an unhappy end. When his brother Philip, also a tetrarch, died, the emperor Caligula appointed Agrippa, Herod's nephew, in his place with the title of king. This was a title Herod had long wanted. Goaded on by his wife Herodias, Herod set out for Rome to ask the emperor for the same title for himself. Getting wind of what was going on, Agrippa sent messengers to the emperor accusing Herod of plotting a revolt. The emperor deposed Herod, confiscated his territories and possessions, and sent him into exile to a city in Gaul called Lugdunum, probably the place today called Saint-Bertrand-de-Comminges, not far from the Spanish border. Herodias was granted her freedom, but she chose exile with the man over whom she had exercised such an evil influence. History leaves them in their exile, unknown and forgotten.

Chapter 15

CHRIST RETURNED TO PILATE

Pilate's satisfaction at his reconciliation with Herod was offset by the fact that his ruse had not worked, and he now found himself again in the courtyard of the Antonia surrounded by his guards and counselors, facing the chief priests, Scribes, and ancients. Jesus stood to one side, still bound and guarded by Roman soldiers. Pilate found it difficult to get the affair off dead center. The Sanhedrists accused Jesus, Pilate disbelieved their charges, and Jesus remained silent. It was not very easy to decide the case either way. It went against the grain for Pilate to declare Jesus guilty, since he believed Him innocent and hated His accusers. Neither was it easy to declare Him innocent in view of the gravity of the charges, the rank of His accusers, and the publicity the affair already had.

Pilate's resources were not at an end. He now played the part the weak judge and wily diplomat. He called together Jesus' accusers so that he could speak to them more intimately. He assumed an air of reasonableness and concession. "You have brought before me this man," he said, "as one who perverts the people; and behold, I upon examining him in your presence have found no guilt in this man as touching those things of which you accuse him. Neither has Herod; for I sent you back to him, and behold, nothing deserving of death has been committed by him" (Luke 23:14–15).

Pilate's words were a survey of the trial up to the present. He had examined Christ in their presence and found Him innocent of the charges they preferred. He had sent him to Herod, and the tetrarch had found no cause for capital punishment. Pilate's statement was certainly an implicit finding of not guilty.

That is why his next words are so astonishing. Too timid to decide the case definitely in Christ's favor, he now threw a sop to his accusers by adding: "I will therefore chastise him and release him" (Luke 23:16). He has declared Christ innocent, and yet he concludes that he will have Him scourged—for that is the meaning of the word used. We cannot see into the workings of Pilate's mind, and it is difficult to conceive how he could possibly have justified his proposal even to himself. Perhaps he told himself that where there is smoke there is fire, that there must be some reason for such a great to-do, that in any case Jesus was a fanatic who had involved Himself in this situation through His own fault and needed to be taught a lesson. A guilty conscience never wants for excuses.

At this point, there was an interruption in the trial. Pilate and the others could hear the sounds of a crowd coming up from the city and pushing its way into the open spaces that led into the great courtyard. Some of the newcomers mingled with the group of Christ's accusers already gathered there, while others, less scrupulous about a legal impurity, pushed into the great flagstone yard where Pilate faced Christ's accusers.

Word had gone out in the city that Pilate was at the Antonia for a few days and was even now conducting trials. Some of the people recalled the privilege accorded them of demanding the release of a prisoner on the occasion of the Passover. This concession on the part of the Romans was particularly appropriate for this feast, which celebrated the release of the Israelites from the bondage of Egypt. The custom of freeing a prisoner in honor of some great occasion was known to the Romans and to other nations of antiquity. In Roman law, an *abolitio* was granted prior to condemnation and had the effect of discontinuing the proceedings; an *indulgentia* was a pardon after condemnation. The *indulgentia* was much rarer and, at least later, could be granted only by the emperor.[45] It would appear that this practice was a special concession of the Romans to the Jews, as St. John records that Pilate said to them, "You have a custom that I should release someone to you at the Passover" (John 18:39). A similar custom existed in Egypt shortly after this time. A papyrus, dating from A.D. 86 to 88, gives an account of a trial before Septimus Vegetus, prefect of Egypt. A certain Phibion had attempted to obtain justice by laying hands on his adversary and his womenfolk. The prefect declared that he deserved scourging, but added, "I pardon you as a favor to the crowd."

The presence of the new group of people jostling their way forward and mingling with the accusers of Jesus had a different effect on the Jewish rulers and on Pilate. Christ's enemies were surely not pleased at this interruption. The newcomers were ordinary people, and some of them might be friendly to Jesus.

---

[45] In the case of Christ and Barabbas, there was question of the *abolitio*. Christ had not been condemned, and it appears that Barabbas had not yet been brought to trial. He is referred to only as a prisoner.

There might even be some of His Galilean followers in the group, pilgrims in Jerusalem for the festival. Pilate, however, welcomed the interruption. He sensed immediately that it might provide him the means of escape he was seeking. In any case, from this time on, the trial of Jesus Christ entered a new phase. There was now a different element—a group of the people of Jerusalem facing Pilate, and from this moment on, they take an active and influential part in deciding the fate of Jesus Christ.

Pilate took advantage of the sudden turn of events to propose Jesus to the crowd as the prisoner to be released. "Do you wish," he said, "that I release to you the king of the Jews?" (Mark 15:9). Pilate hoped that the people would answer yes. He expected such a reply, as he must have known that Jesus was favorably regarded by the ordinary people. Yet Pilate's contempt for the Jews showed itself even now when he was seeking to influence them, as he referred to Jesus as "King of the Jews." His audience would certainly not be won over by presenting a bound and humiliated prisoner as their king.

At this point the name Barabbas was heard on the lips of the crowd. It is possible that it was Pilate's idea to propose a choice between Jesus and Barabbas, but it seems more likely that some in the crowd had come with the express purpose of asking the release of Barabbas. It is even likely that some of his partisans were among them. As the cries for Barabbas mounted and multiplied, Pilate asked, a little incredulously, "Whom do you wish that I release to you? Barabbas, or Jesus who is called Christ?" (Matt. 27:17).[46]

---

[46] In some early manuscripts, this text reads, "Whom do you wish that I release to you, Jesus Barabbas or Jesus who is called Christ?" The weight of manuscript authority is against this reading.

Who was this man who appeared briefly on the stage of history and disappeared so suddenly and completely? The name Barabbas was very common at the time and means simply "son of the father." The Gospels give us little information about him. St. Matthew refers to him as "a notorious prisoner" (27:16). The Greek adjective used by the Evangelist is more frequently used in the sense of "famous." St. Mark says that Barabbas "was imprisoned with some rioters, one who in the riot had committed murder" (15:7). St. Luke mentions him as "one who had been thrown into prison for a certain riot that had occurred in the city, and for murder" (23:19). St. John says simply, "Barabbas was a robber" (18:40). St. Peter refers to him in an address to the Jews in the Temple area after the resurrection of Christ. "You disowned the Holy and Just One," he says, "and asked that a murderer should be granted to you" (Acts 3:14).

The Gospels do not give us sufficient information to identify Barabbas with certainty, but it seems highly probable that he was a member of the sect of Zealots. The Zealots were drawn, for the most part, from among the Pharisees. They were extremists, however, and considered their fellow Pharisees too weak and passive. The Zealots believed in action. Let the Pharisees go to the Temple to pray; they would settle the issue, sword in hand.

The Zealots believed that the Jewish people should be subject to no human master, but to God alone. They persuaded the people to refuse tribute to the Romans. They were fierce nationalists, burning with a spirit of independence. They identified completely the interests of God and of the nation. They were guilty of political murders, seditions, riots, robbery, and other crimes. Wherever they achieved power, they became cruel and relentless tyrants. They had much to do with inciting the Jewish people to the rebellion against the Romans that ended in the awful catastrophe of the destruction of the city and Temple in A.D. 70.

At this point in the trial, there was another interruption, one that gave the leaders of the Jews an opportunity to persuade the people to cry out in favor of Barabbas. Pilate had been standing during the trial. Now, in order to give the people a few minutes in which to make up their minds, he sat on his curule chair, which had been placed on an elevated platform called the tribunal. While he was seated there, a messenger strode up to him and passed him a note from his wife. It read, "Have nothing to do with that just man, for I have suffered many things in a dream today because of him" (Matt. 27:19).

Under the Roman Republic it had been forbidden for magistrates to take their wives to the provinces, but this law ceased to be operative under the empire. It was not at all surprising that Pilate's wife should have accompanied him from Caesarea to Jerusalem and taken up her abode in the palatial southern part of the Antonia. From its windows and walls, she had a clear view of the entire Temple area where were concentrated the activities and ceremonies of this festive period. There is a fairly early tradition that her name was Procula (or Procla) and that she had become a convert to the Jewish religion.

Was her dream of natural or supernatural origin? It is possible that it was natural. Living at Caesarea, it is not at all improbable that she had heard of Jesus and even become interested in His teaching. She may very well have learned of the arrest of Christ the preceding night. Worry over the part her husband was taking in these events could have caused her dream. It is much more likely, however, that her dream was of supernatural origin. It was evidently such in the mind of St. Matthew, or he would not have bothered to record it. This dream was a warning given to

Pilate to change the course on which he was embarked before it was too late. The Evangelist does not record his reaction. It is likely that he was affected by it and even strengthened somewhat to resist the evil pressure exerted by the enemies of Christ. It is noteworthy that St. Matthew, who alone records the dream of Pilate's wife, is the only Evangelist to record Pilate's washing of his hands at the end of the trial. It may have been St. Matthew's thought that the dream increased Pilate's sense of responsibility and caused him to attempt to wash away his guilt.

While Pilate was seated on his curule chair awaiting the decision of the people and reading the note from his wife, the enemies of Christ had been busy. They had no difficulty in persuading their own group to choose Barabbas. The chief priests, Scribes, and ancients mingled with the new arrivals, those who had come to secure the release of a prisoner, and persuaded them to ask for Barabbas rather than Jesus. When Pilate felt that the people had had sufficient time to make their choice, he arose, called for silence, and asked them, "Which of the two do you wish that I release to you?" (Matt. 27:21).

The answer was "Barabbas," and it rose loud and emphatic from hundreds of throats. St. Luke makes it clear that there was no doubt or hesitation or difference of opinion: "The whole mob cried out together, saying, 'Away with this man, and release to us Barabbas!'" (23:18). It was an uproar rather than an answer, and in that uproar only one name was heard again, almost like a chant, "Barabbas, Barabbas!" In their excitement the mob did not just cry for the release of Barabbas; they cried out against Christ, "Away with this man!" They could not have done more to show their complete agreement with Christ's accusers.

Pilate was startled by this turn of events. He had thought such a choice impossible. He had felt confident that a crowd of ordinary people would not share the malice and hatred of the Sanhedrists. Now he had gotten himself deeper into difficulties. He had to contend not only with the Sanhedrists and their followers but also with this group of late arrivals on whom he had depended to extricate him from his dilemma. Instead of being a help, they had become a hindrance.

Pilate's next words show the extent to which he had lost his calm and self-composure: "What then am I to do with Jesus who is called Christ?" (Matt. 27:22). In his confused state of mind, Pilate virtually abdicated his prerogative of judge. He asked a howling mob what he was to do with the accused. He placed his fate in their hands. They had been granted the right to ask the release of a prisoner; they had never been granted the right to decide what should be done with another.

If Pilate did not realize his mistake the moment the words had left his lips, he did not have long to wait. The answer was quick and cruel: "Crucify him!" (Mark 15:13). At first they had cried simply: "Away with him!" Now, egged on by the Sanhedrists, they cried out those terrible words: "Crucify him!"

Whipped to a fury by the chief priests, Scribes, and ancients, the mob would not be satisfied even with death. They wanted the cruel and awful death on the cross for Jesus. Pilate was hesitant, confused. He asked again the futile question: "Why, what evil has this man done?" And then he repeated the inanity that, since he found Him innocent, he would chastise Him and release Him (Luke 23:22). But the crowd and its leaders knew Pilate. They had dealt with him before. They knew that he was weakening before their insistence. They refused even to argue with him or to prefer further charges against Jesus. They simply cried out again and again: "Crucify him, crucify him! Let him be crucified, let him be crucified!" Their blood-cry rumbled through the great archways of the vaulted entrance, where most of the crowd was assembled, and echoed back from the high stone walls of the Antonia. Nothing but the blood of their victim could satisfy their rage now.

Pilate agreed to go along with them, but not all the way. He would insist on his proposal that Christ be chastised and released. Turning to the guards who held Jesus captive, he gave them the order to scourge Him. At the same time, he ordered the release of Barabbas.

It is strange indeed that there should have been such a difference between the receptions Jesus received from the people on Palm Sunday and on Good Friday, only five days later—the "hosannas" and the "blesseds" of Palm Sunday wholly reversed by "Away with him, crucify him" on Good Friday. What could possibly have produced such a complete turnabout? The reasons must be sought chiefly in the person of Barabbas and in the makeup of the crowd at the trial.

Barabbas has often been pictured as a petty sneak-thief. He probably was not that at all, as we have seen. While some of the more prudent might think him a menace and regret his activities, it is not at all improbable that he was something of a hero to many of the people. In a choice between the firebrand, who caught their imagination by bloody acts of violence against the Romans, and Jesus, who counseled peace and love, the people were easily persuaded to vote for the man of violence rather than the man of peace.

The Gospels give us little information about the crowd that arrived during the trial to demand the release of a prisoner according to custom. There is small likelihood that it was anything approaching a general concourse of the people. It was probably made up of those who had a special interest in the custom because they had a particular prisoner in mind. We cannot conclude with certainty, but it may well be that the crowd was composed largely of friends or partisans of Barabbas and had come to the Antonia for the express purpose of requesting his release. If this is true, and it was Pilate's idea to make the matter one of a choice of Jesus or Barabbas in the hope of diverting the appeal for clemency toward Jesus, it goes without saying that his chances would be slight. Furthermore, it was foolish of Pilate to think that he could influence this mob of patriotic, Rome-hating Jews to follow his wishes rather than those of their own leaders.

The crowds that hailed Jesus on Palm Sunday were probably in very large part Galilean pilgrims who were camped outside the city. Jesus was from Nazareth and had spent nearly all His life in Galilee. He was one of their own, their prophet. The crowd that went up to the Antonia to demand release of a prisoner was probably made up of people of Jerusalem. They were not as friendly to Jesus; He had not, in fact, spent a great deal of time among them. They despised Galileans and looked with suspicion and disdain on anything that came out of Galilee. Furthermore, their Messianic ideas were probably closer to those of the Zealots than to Christ's teachings concerning the Kingdom of God. Anyway, how could this man possibly be the Messiah? There He was, defenseless in the hands of the Roman soldiers. Furthermore, He had been condemned as a blasphemer by the highest Jewish court in the land, made up of the most respected men of the nation, men who were the guardians and even the embodiment of the most sacred traditions of their race and religion. If any of the people had been inclined to doubt or to favor Jesus, they soon became victims of mob psychology and joined with the others in demanding His death.

Three Evangelists record that Jesus was scourged. St. Luke alone omits a direct reference to this event, although he relates that Pilate said twice that he would have Jesus scourged and released (23:16, 22). Even the three Evangelists who mention the scourging refer to it in a matter-of-fact manner. It was undoubtedly only with a feeling of shock that they could record, even years later, that Jesus Christ the Son of God was subjected to this shameful torture. Then too, the early readers of the Gospels had no need to be informed of the details of a Roman scourging, which was a common form of punishment, seen frequently in every town and city of the empire.

Jesus was scourged in the very courtyard in which the trial was taking place and before the gloating eyes of His enemies. Roman scourging was a public affair. It was administered in the forum or before the tribunal of the judge who had passed sentence. From what happened later, it is evident that Pilate did not remain to witness the scourging of Jesus. He probably returned to the palace to attend to other affairs awaiting his attention during his brief stay in Jerusalem.

The Romans inflicted scourging for various reasons. It was used as a torture for eliciting a confession or for securing other information (Acts 22:24). It was also a death penalty in itself. Verres, governor of Sicily (73–71 B.C.), declared to a certain Servilius: *"Moriere virgis"* (Thou shalt be beaten to death), and six husky lictors saw to it that he was. Scourging was also used as a preliminary punishment for those condemned to death. Indeed, it was the ordinary prelude to crucifixion. In some cases, it was imposed by a judge as a punishment in itself. If we had only the

Gospels of St. Matthew and St. Mark, we would surmise that Christ's scourging was inflicted after He had been condemned to crucifixion. The Gospel of St. John makes it evident that, at this point in the trial, Pilate condemned Jesus to be scourged only, and that he did it in the hope that the Jews would be satisfied with a penalty less than death.

Since Jesus was condemned by a Roman judge, He was scourged in the Roman manner, and this manner of scourging was barbarous. The victim was first stripped of his garments and then tied securely to a low post or pillar, so that he had to bend over, exposing his back and shoulders more readily to the whips. In the provinces, and in the case of slaves and criminals, either the flagellum or the flagrum was used. The flagellum was a whip of leather thongs. The flagrum was of two kinds: one consisted of leather thongs to which were attached small pieces of bone or metal; the other was made of small iron chains with metal pieces at the ends. We do not know whether the flagellum or the flagrum was used to scourge Jesus. As a matter of fact, it made little difference, as both inflicted intense pain. The flagellum cut fine lashes across the skin and had the effect almost of flaying the victim alive. The flagrum bruised and dug under the skin to such an extent that bits of flesh were sometimes torn from the body.

Jewish law limited the number of strokes in scourging to forty, and in practice only thirty-nine were inflicted, lest the law be broken by a mistaken count. Roman law made no such limitation. The only limit was that the victim be kept alive if he had still to undergo capital punishment. It was not uncommon, however, for the one scourged to die under the lash. The Gospels give us no information regarding the number of strokes inflicted on Jesus Christ. On the one hand, He was considerably weakened, as He was unable to carry His cross as far as Calvary; and on the other hand, He was not scourged almost to death, as Pilate was surprised to learn that He had died on the cross after only three hours. The scourging of Jesus was committed to the soldiers. The Roman soldiers stationed in Palestine were auxiliaries, recruited from among the neighboring peoples who hated the Jews, so we can be sure that they were not at all inclined to be merciful toward their victim.

It is possible to gain a clearer idea of what happened at the scourging of Jesus from some incidents related in history. In his denunciation of Verres, Cicero tells us that while Servilius was speaking at the tribunal in his own defense:

> he was surrounded by six very muscular lictors, with a great deal of experience in beating and striking men. They beat him most cruelly with rods; finally the first lictor, Sextius,... turned his rod around and began savagely to lash in the poor wretch's eyes. The latter fell to the ground, his face and eyes streaming with blood; but despite all that, they continued to beat against his sides, even after he had collapsed.... Then, reduced to that state, he was carried out of there, and he actually did die shortly afterward.[47]

And this incident described by Cicero was a beating with rods, not a flagellation, which was even worse.

Other incidents throw light on the horrible cruelty of a Roman scourging. Philo, writing about Alexandrian Jews who were scourged by order of the prefect Flaccus, relates that some died under the scourges and the rest recovered only after a long

[47] *Verrem*, 2, 5, 54.

illness.[48] Josephus records that Albinus, the Roman procurator of Judea, had a false prophet, Jesus son of Ananias, "flayed to the bone with scourges."[49] In the *Martyrdom of Polycarp* we read of early Christians who "were torn by scourging until the mechanism of their flesh was seen, even to the very veins and arteries."

The Evangelists refrain from giving us details concerning the scourging of Jesus. It was a Roman scourging, inflicted by Roman soldiers on the orders of a Roman judge, so we have some idea of what it must have been. There was the shame of nudity, the horrible physical pain, and the infamy of condemnation to the punishment of slaves and criminals.

Jesus must have been a pitiable sight when the soldiers finally threw down their lashes and wiped the perspiration from their brows. He was covered with blood. His blood dripped from His wounds onto the ground. His chest, neck, shoulders, back, hips, and legs were slashed as if with knives and streaked with blue welts and swollen bruises. Even His face was cut and disfigured by the lashes that had rained down upon Him. He was in such a state that He could scarcely have been recognized even by those who knew Him best.

After the scourging of Jesus there was a lull in the trial. Pilate had gone to his offices in the palatial southern part of the Antonia and had not returned. The soldiers threw Jesus His garments and stood leisurely while He clothed Himself. They were tired of their unexciting duty. One of them suddenly made a suggestion for

---

[48] *In Flaccum*, 10, 75.
[49] *Wars*, 6, 5, 3.

having some fun while passing the time, and the idea caught on with the other soldiers. They pushed Jesus toward the northeast corner of the courtyard to the end opposite the portal, where His accusers were congregated. In this area the soldiers would be free from close observation by Pilate and the Jews, and they would be withdrawn from the direct route of traffic between the west gates and the entrance to the procurator's quarters. This area of the Antonia was part of the barracks of the soldiers. St. Matthew speaks of it as the "praetorium" (27:27), and St. Mark calls it the "courtyard of the praetorium" (15:16). It was probably an extension of the flagstone courtyard into one of the more interior sections of the Antonia.

In this area, some very interesting discoveries have been made in recent years. Engraved on the great flagstones are outlines used in playing Roman games similar to those found elsewhere, especially in military establishments. Particularly significant is the outline of a game covering three of the flagstones near the stairway. At the summit is a bristling crown, and all the lines converge near the bottom toward a sword. The letter B, probably for "Basileus," the Greek word for "king," appears in several places, indicating that the game played here was the game of chance known as the royal game, the play of the king, Basiliscus. The crown and the sword recall the Sacees of the Persians and the Saturnalia of the Romans, burlesque carnivals in which a condemned man was dressed in the tinseled trappings of a king, given the privileges and honors of royal power, only to be killed with the sword in the end.

It is stretching the imagination far too much to see any connection between the events that took place in the barracks of the Antonia on that first Good Friday and the Sacees of the Persians or Saturnalia of the Romans. The game that the soldiers played in the outlines traced on the flagstones was simply a soldiers' game of chance played with dice or knucklebones. It is possible that the soldiers thought that it would be a lot more fun to play a king game with a real, live, make-believe king than with dice or bones. It is not necessary to presume this, however. All morning the soldiers had heard repeated charges against Christ that He claimed to be a king. These Roman soldiers were Greeks and Samaritans, and they hated the Jews. In the pitiable state in which they saw Jesus at the moment, He looked just about right to be King of the Jews. One of the soldiers proposed that they should treat Him as a king. The suggestion was received with acclaim, a call went out to other soldiers of the cohort[50] to come and join in the farce, and then the cruel sport began.

As soon as a large enough group had gathered, the soldiers stripped Jesus. They removed only His outer garments, as that was all that was necessary for their purpose. Then they threw a scarlet mantle over His shoulders.[51] The mantle was probably

---

[50] The Evangelists speak of a cohort, a tenth part of a legion. The cohort numbered ordinarily six hundred men, but often fell below this full complement. The Greek word used here, however, is often used of a maniple, or third part of a cohort. There were five cohorts garrisoned at Caesarea and one at the Antonia. Pilate probably brought one to Jerusalem as an escort, and it may be to this cohort that reference is made. It is likely that the duty of scourging Christ was committed to a small detail of soldiers and that these were the ringleaders in the crowning with thorns and the mockery. Other soldiers who were at leisure stood around enjoying the spectacle, and some of them probably got into the act.

[51] Matt. 27:28. St. Mark calls it a purple cloak (15:17). There is no contradiction, as the ancients made very little distinction between these colors.

the cast-off chlamys of one of the soldiers, as even soldiers wore such bright-colored garments. The chlamys was held by a clasp over the right shoulder and hung down over the left side of the body. The color was an imitation of the royal purple — a mockery of the kingly pretensions of Jesus.

The most important part of the farce was a crown, and the soldiers looked about for something that would serve this purpose. One of them came up with an idea. Nearby was a bundle of thorn branches used as kindling wood. Handling them carefully, they molded a few branches into a crown. They then pulled out a stool or bench to serve as a throne, seated Jesus on it, and pressed the crown of thorns onto His head.[52] At this point their purpose was to mock Jesus rather than to inflict physical torture. Nevertheless, it was impossible to press a crown of thorns on His head without puncturing the scalp and forehead and causing severe pain. Nothing was lacking now to the full regalia of royalty but a scepter. A soldier soon found something suitable — a reed. They placed it in His unresisting right hand and closed the hand over it to hold it firmly. The soldiers who were leading the farce then stepped back, looked at Jesus critically, and concluded that they had done a good job in making Him a mock king. Turning to the large circle of soldiers who stood by watching, they invited all to join in the fun.

Now began the mockery of Jesus. One by one, the soldiers presented themselves before Him, bowing to Him and bending

[52] We cannot be sure whether it was a diadem that encircled the head or a crown that covered it. Learned dissertations have been written on the species of thorns used in the crowning of Jesus. They can only arrive at the conclusion that since the Evangelists do not tell us, we do not know. A large variety of thorn bushes grow in the vicinity of Jerusalem, and many kinds are possibilities.

their knees before Him, calling out as they did, "Hail, King of the Jews!" in mocking imitation of the Roman salutation, "Hail, Caesar!" Although Roman soldiers, they were orientals and aware of the oriental custom of greeting a monarch with a ceremonial kiss. They approached Jesus as if to kiss Him, but, instead of kissing Him, they spat on Him. Taking the reed from His hand, they struck Him with its heavy end, driving the thorns into His head, and then struck Him again with their hands and fists.

We do not know how long this scene of mockery and torture lasted — probably until the soldiers tired of their cruel sport or Pilate sent for Christ. The terms used by the Evangelists indicate that the acts of cruelty and insult were often repeated. There is no record that Christ uttered a single word. He had foreseen and foretold what was to happen to Him. In Gethsemane, He had struggled to bring His will into complete harmony with the will of His Father. He had succeeded. Now He suffered silently, without protest or recrimination.[53] After or during the scourging

---

[53] Objections to the Gospel accounts of the crowning with thorns have been made on the ground that the Romans would never permit a prisoner to be treated in this way. Historical records reveal that the facts completely justify the Evangelists. Mistreatment of prisoners, especially of those condemned to death, was the rule rather than the exception.

The crowning and mocking of Jesus had nothing to do with the Persian feast of the Sacees nor the Roman Saturnalia, but the soldiers must have been familiar with them and may possibly have derived some of their inspiration from them.

A text of Dio Chrysostom (*De Regno*, 4, 66) relates that in celebrating the feast of the Sacees, the Persians took a prisoner condemned to death, sat him on a royal throne, clothed him in the garments of royalty, permitted him to command what he wanted — to drink, to repose, to use the royal concubines — and

of Jesus, Pilate ascended the stairs into his own quarters to take care of matters that required his official attention. This business had taken longer than expected, as the soldiers had time, not only for the scourging, but also for the crowning with thorns and the mockery of Jesus as King of the Jews. His other affairs finished, Pilate ordered that Jesus should be brought out again into the open part of the courtyard before his tribunal. As he emerged from his apartments onto the landing of the stairs that led down into the flagstone courtyard, Pilate could get a good view of all below him. He could see the chief priests, Scribes, and ancients, together with their followers and retainers, grouped together in the vaulted entrances at the west gate. Around them, and spilling inward into the court, was the crowd of common people who had come up to demand the release of a prisoner. All were silent now in expectation of what was about to take place. From the other side of the courtyard and to Pilate's right,

---

no one dared to stop him from doing what he liked. Afterward, he was stripped, scourged, and hanged. The Roman feast of the Saturnalia was celebrated in a similar manner.

An incident related by the Alexandrian Jew Philo (*In Flaccum*, 5, 6) illustrates the mentality of the times. Agrippa, who had just been appointed king in the place of the tetrarch, Herod Antipas, was passing through Alexandria in Egypt. To mock Agrippa and Jewish pretensions to royalty, the crowd laid hands on a poor idiot named Carabas and took him to the gymnasium. There they placed him on an elevated place as a throne, clothed him with a mat for a robe, and placed a papyrus crown on his head and a reed in his hand. Some of the young men, with sticks over their shoulders, made up a bodyguard for him, while others requested that he render justice and pass on various affairs of state. To make sure that all would know at whom the mockery was aimed, they saluted him with the Syriac title "Marin," meaning "Lord."

a small detachment of soldiers emerged into the open area with Jesus in their midst. As they came nearer, Pilate got a clear view of Jesus. He had ordered the scourging, but it is unlikely that he knew anything about the crowning and mockeries. He had expected to see Jesus bedraggled and bloody, but what he saw now was beyond his expectations. Jesus still wore the crown of thorns and the purple garment of a mock king. Pilate may have felt some natural reaction of sympathy, but he was not displeased at what he saw. He had the decency and the stubbornness still to want to release Jesus, and the pitiable plight in which he beheld Him could well be of help. Facing the crowd, Pilate declared, "Behold, I bring him out to you, that you may know that I find no guilt in him" (John 19:4). Then he ordered the soldiers to bring Jesus up the stairs and told Him to turn about so that He faced His enemies. And then Pilate cried out in a loud voice, "Behold the man!" (John 19:5).

Alone of the Evangelists, St. John, the beloved disciple, records these words of Pilate. They have come down to us through the centuries, like the words of a prophet. It would almost seem that Pilate, like Caiaphas, was used by God as an instrument of prophecy and that his words go far beyond any meaning he intended they should have. It was almost as if he were saying to those present and to generations yet to come: "Behold the man; behold more than a man: behold Him whose coming and whose present situation were foretold by the prophets, especially Isaiah; behold Him from whom alone comes the salvation of the world."

What was the meaning Pilate himself gave his words "Behold the man"? Many think that he was appealing to the good nature and pity of Christ's enemies, that, in effect, he was saying: Look at what this man has suffered. Look at the bloody and miserable and weakened state to which He has been reduced. Can you demand more punishment for such a wretched victim?

Perhaps there is some truth in this interpretation. It may be that Pilate underrated the hatred and hardness of heart of the enemies of Jesus. We think, however, that he was taking another tack and that what he really meant was: Look at this miserable man, this caricature of a king. Can He be taken seriously? Can He be a rival to Caesar or a danger to the peace of the country? Looking at Him now, you can't possibly take your accusations seriously.

In either case, Pilate had underestimated Christ's enemies and their capacity for hatred. He had his answer, and he had it quickly. St. John tells us that it came from the chief priests and their attendants, and it came in a single word repeated again and again: "Crucify, crucify!" (19:6). The rest of the crowd took up the word and repeated it until it became a raucous chant assailing the ears of the procurator.

Pilate was angered by their increasing obstinacy. "Take him yourselves and crucify him," he cried out, "for I find no guilt in him" (John 19:6). Pilate's words were not to be taken literally. His answer was ironical and expressed his contempt for those who could demand death for an innocent man. What Pilate really meant was: If you can do such an evil act, do it, but I want no part of it. Unfortunately for Pilate, unless he had part of it, it could not be done.

The Jews understood perfectly what Pilate meant. They knew he was not giving them permission to crucify Jesus. They felt that they were not making much progress and that their victim might still escape their grasp. It is likely that at this point there was an urgent conference among their leaders. Pilate refused to take their accusations seriously and on three separate occasions had declared his belief in Christ's innocence. What could be done? What means could they use to bend the stubborn Pilate to do their will?

The enemies of Jesus decided on a change of tactics. They had condemned Jesus before their own tribunal for blasphemy because He claimed to be the Son of God. They had changed their accusations before the Roman tribunal and had charged Jesus with treason. They seemed to be losing their case, especially since the scourging and the crowning with thorns had made such a mockery of any royal pretensions He could possibly still entertain. Now they determined to go back to the original charge, without, however, dropping the political accusations. After all, the Romans made a great to-do about upholding local laws and customs, especially in matters that pertained to religion. Let Pilate be a good Roman now and judge according to local law. Their spokesman, undoubtedly one of the chief priests, cried out to Pilate, "We have a law, and according to that law he must die, because he has made himself Son of God" (John 19:7).

The new accusation had an effect beyond anything anticipated. There was a brief interval of shocked silence. Pilate looked closely at Jesus and, as St. John says, "He feared the more" (19:8). It is strange that St. John should say that "he feared *the more*" when he has not told us that Pilate feared at all. This little aside of St. John throws a light on what had preceded as well as on what was going on at the moment. St. John indicates that Pilate's actions up to the present in refusing to condemn Jesus had been motivated at least in part by fear. He feared to condemn an innocent man, but more than that, and especially now, he feared to condemn one who might be more than human.

Pilate had good reason to fear. He was a man of above-average intelligence, and he must have realized from the beginning of the trial that this man who stood before him was no ordinary prisoner cringing before his judge and multiplying answers to accusations. Jesus had remained as calm and silent as if another had been on trial. His patience and serenity, His disregard of the repeated charges of His enemies, His quiet majesty even when scourged and crowned with thorns and mocked as a royal pretender must have made a deep impression on Pilate. And when He did speak, His words did nothing to allay Pilate's fears, for He had said: "My kingdom is not of this world" (John 18:36). The note from Pilate's wife telling him to "have nothing to do with that just man" had increased his disquiet. He may have been indifferent to contending philosophical systems, as was evidenced by his words "What is truth?" but he was a man of his times, and in the paganism of that day, belief in sons of gods and goddesses, and in their appearance in human form, was common. Now Pilate was struck with a chill fear that this man whom he had already scourged and maltreated and whose death was sought from him by the Jews might indeed be more than an ordinary mortal.

During the exchange between Pilate and the Jews, Jesus and Pilate were still standing on the stairway leading up to the private quarters of the procurator. Now Pilate turned on his heel and reentered the palace, ordering Jesus to be brought after him. Pilate feared but was ashamed of his fear. He was compelled to find out the truth, but he did not want to exhibit his fears to the Jews. The best course, he thought, was to question Jesus privately. Once they were inside, Pilate turned to Jesus and said: "Where art thou from?" He evidently wished to conceal his fears even from Jesus. His question did not refer merely to Christ's place of birth. Without compromising himself with a direct question, he tried to lead Jesus into a discussion of His origin.

Now, as on other occasions during His trials, Jesus was silent. He simply ignored Pilate's question. Pilate did not deserve an answer. His question was not frank and was probably inspired by nothing higher than a vague superstitious fear. Furthermore, Pilate had shown clearly that he did not sincerely seek the truth when he shrugged off Christ's explanations with a contemptuous "What is truth?"

Pilate was annoyed at Christ's silence. He thought: Doesn't this man realize the situation He is in? Doesn't He know that He faces crucifixion? Doesn't He appreciate the fact that I am trying to help Him? Doesn't He understand that I alone have the power to decide His case? Pilate put his thoughts into words directed to Jesus: "Dost thou not speak to me? Dost thou not know that I have power to crucify thee and that I have power to release thee?" (John 19:10).

Pilate's boast of power drew a reply from Jesus. "Thou wouldst have no power at all over me," He said, "were it not given thee from above" (John 19:11). Pilate spoke as if his power could be used in any way he liked. Christ reminded him that all power of man over man is from above. As a magistrate, he must do justice not merely in the name of Tiberius, from whom he derived his authority, but in the name of God, from whom Tiberius derived his power. It is possible that Jesus' words had a more specific sense because he referred explicitly to Pilate's power over Him. In this case, Jesus' words really meant: If you have power to dispose of my life, it is because of the permissive will of God, and if you condemn me, it is because my hour has come.

Acting as the judge rather than the accused, Christ goes on to apportion blame for what is taking place: "Therefore, he who betrayed me to thee has the greater sin" (John 19:11). Pilate was guilty because he was acting against his conscience. He had repeatedly declared his belief in Christ's innocence but had not dismissed the case and freed Him, as He was bound to do. But there was another, Caiaphas, whose guilt was double. He had the same obligation as Pilate of judging justly. He had the further obligation, as high priest, of recognizing the Messiah and proclaiming Him to Israel. Caiaphas failed on both counts, and he therefore had the "greater sin."[54]

---

[54] Some think that Christ referred here to Judas. We think this unlikely, because he was speaking to Pilate, and Pilate probably knew nothing of Judas.

Chapter 16

CHRIST CONDEMNED

From this point on, the trial of Jesus moved swiftly to a conclusion. After speaking with Jesus, Pilate renewed his determination to release Him. It was simply a case now of doing it in a way that would least offend the leaders of the Jews. Pilate left Jesus behind in the procurator's quarters of the Antonia and again went out and descended to face Jesus' accusers near the west gates of the courtyard. St. John writes briefly at this point and does not record the first part of the dialogue that must have taken place between Pilate and Christ's accusers. What follows, however, makes it clear that Christ's enemies had not been inactive while Pilate was questioning Him. They had scented trouble over their accusation that Christ claimed to be the Son of God. They suspected that Pilate had taken the matter seriously and might be favorably impressed by Christ's words and deportment. They decided on another change of tactics. They would play their trump card even at the risk of giving serious offense to Pilate. If it failed, Jesus would go free; if it succeeded, Jesus would be crucified.

After some parrying between Pilate and Christ's accusers, it was probably one of the chief priests who called for silence and then in solemn, menacing tones addressed Pilate: "If thou release this man, thou art no friend of Caesar; for everyone who makes himself king sets himself against Caesar" (John 19:12). The Jews abandoned the charge that Christ claimed to be the Son of God and returned to their original accusation that He made Himself king. Now they added a new note by bringing the emperor into the case. To be "Caesar's friend" was a mark of great distinction and an assurance of protection and advancement. Pilate could hardly be "Caesar's friend" unless he showed proper solicitude for the interests of the emperor in a case of treason. For a man in Pilate's position, not to be "Caesar's friend" meant ruin, perhaps even exile or death. The Jews did not say expressly that if Pilate released Jesus, they would denounce him to Tiberius, but the threat was implied. Pilate had been conscious of the danger all along. He turned over the situation in his mind. On the one hand, all the inconvenience and danger of a denunciation to Tiberius, who was particularly severe in searching out and punishing treason; on the other hand, the life of a single Jew, denounced by the leaders of His own people, a man who, whatever His qualities, might be suffering from hallucinations of royalty and even divinity.

Pilate made up his mind, and this time he did not change it. He abandoned Jesus. He decided to condemn him to death on the cross. There was no more doubt or hesitation. In a choice between himself and his career and the life of Jesus Christ, he chose himself and his career. In the end, he lost both. Until the end of time, Christians will express their faith in Jesus Christ in words that recall that he "suffered under Pontius Pilate."

St. John is often referred to as more of a theologian than a historian. At this point, however, it is to him rather than to the other Evangelists that we must turn for the setting of this tragic and dramatic scene. As elsewhere in his Gospel, one has here a feeling that St. John was present and that we have an eyewitness account. It is probable that he had followed the cortege from the palace of Caiaphas to the Antonia and that he had mingled with the crowd to observe what was taking place. In solemn and measured words that identify the time and place and the actors in this scene, St. John says that "Pilate ... brought Jesus outside, and sat down on the judgment-seat, at a place called Lithostrotos, but in Hebrew, Gabbatha. Now it was the Preparation Day for the Passover, about the sixth hour" (19:13, 14).

The place where the condemnation of Jesus took place had a twofold name. Some called it Lithostrotos, a Greek word meaning "paved with stones," "pavement." For the pavement to have given its name to the place, it must have been something very special. As we have said, this fact helps us to identify the locality as the courtyard of the Antonia. Excavations on this site have revealed the tremendous courtyard, paved with great flagstones, many of them more than three feet square and eighteen inches thick. This great Roman pavement must have been a subject of wonder and comment to the local people, who would quite naturally refer therefore to the courtyard as "the pavement." Nowhere else in Jerusalem has anything like it been found.

The other word that St. John uses is "Gabbatha."[55] There is no relation between the words Lithostrotos and Gabbatha as regards their meaning. "Gabbatha" means "a high place." The

---

[55] The word is Aramaic rather than Hebrew. St. John follows a common practice of the time in referring to Aramaic as Hebrew. The Jews learned Aramaic, a sister language of Hebrew, during the Babylonian captivity and continued to use it. By the time of Christ, Hebrew was a dead language used in religious services, much as Latin is used by the Catholic Church today.

palace-fortress Antonia, as we have seen from the description of the historian Josephus, was built on the highest hill in Jerusalem. It is only natural that this area should have been called "the high place." It was probably the more commonly used name, as the people would naturally prefer an Aramaic to a Greek word.

St. John is equally precise regarding the time. It was, he says, "the Preparation Day for the Passover." According to the reckoning of some, it was the day before the Passover, and not the Passover day itself. The accusers of Jesus followed this reckoning of time, as they had refused to enter the courtyard lest they incur a legal impurity. St. John further tells us that it was "about the sixth hour." We cannot be sure what method of reckoning the hours is used by St. John, as many were current in various parts of the Roman Empire at the time. The simplest explanation is that he followed the method that began computing the hours from six in the morning, which would mean that the condemnation of Jesus took place around noontime. St. Mark says that our Lord was crucified at the third hour (15:25). Mark evidently followed the method that divided the day and night into four parts of three hours each. According to this method, the first division of time was called the first hour (six to nine by our reckoning), the second was called the third hour (nine to twelve by our reckoning). Each period received its name from the hour at which it began. According to Mark's reckoning, anything that happened from nine to twelve (our time) would be ascribed to the third hour. The ancients were not very accurate about the exact time, so that when St. John says that our Lord was condemned at about the sixth hour, it could very well have been between eleven and twelve o'clock.

Once he had made up his mind to condemn Jesus, Pilate took immediate steps to proceed with the formalities. A platform had already been erected on the flagstones of the great courtyard of the Antonia, and on it rested his curule chair. Ordinary cases could be tried anywhere, but those of greater import were decided formally by a judge seated on this chair in the view of all present. Pilate had undoubtedly conducted part of the trial of Jesus seated thus, but during much of it he had walked back and forth before the Jews and had even taken the prisoner into his own quarters for personal interrogation.

Now Pilate sat to make formal announcement of his judgment. He was surrounded by a few assistants and by a guard of soldiers. He ordered that Jesus be brought from the procurator's private quarters, where he had left Him after the last interrogation. Jesus emerged, still wearing the purple garment and the crown of thorns. The soldiers conducted Him to a place beside Pilate, facing the crowd of accusers.

Pilate looked at Jesus and could not help feeling how incongruous was the situation. This man was being condemned for aspiring to be a king. Looking out at the mob before him, Pilate felt bitter resentment toward them and their leaders, who were forcing him to act against his judgment and conscience. This is just the sort of king they deserve, he thought, and then gave himself the petty pleasure of taunting them. "Behold your king," he cried out to them (John 19:14).

The barb of Pilate's ridicule struck home. The Jews were furious. They looked at this pitiable figure of a man presented to them as their king, and they yelled back at Pilate: "Away with him! Away with him! Crucify him!" Almost as one voice the cry of rejection went up from the mob, repudiating Jesus Christ as their king, demanding instead that He be crucified. Pilate was delighted that his shafts had hit home, so he continued the farce. In mock wonderment, he asked them: "Shall I crucify your king?" placing heavy emphasis on the last two words. Now the mob was silent, and the answer came back from the chief priests, the representatives of the nation, the official spokesmen of the Jewish theocracy. "We have no king but Caesar," they declared (John 19:15).

Those were fateful words. The official representatives of the Jews not only rejected Christ as their Messiah and King; they also abandoned, publicly and to an official representative of Rome, their hopes of the Christ. They rejected the Kingdom of God and its Ruler to become members of the kingdom of this world and subjects of its ruler. Their choice was fatal to them and to Israel.

Pilate could see that his mockery and his stinging barbs were working the crowd into a fury. If he kept it up, he might have a riot on his hands. Since he had already made up his mind to condemn Jesus to death, he was gaining nothing except the momentary satisfaction of taunting these people.

St. Matthew, who alone records the incident of the note from Pilate's wife, is the only Evangelist to record another episode that illustrates the disturbed state of Pilate's conscience. St. Matthew tells us that Pilate "took water and washed his hands in the sight of the crowd, saying: 'I am innocent of the blood of this just man; see to it yourselves'" (27:24–25). Independently of any custom that existed at the time, Pilate's words and actions made his meaning perfectly clear. He was completely convinced that Jesus was innocent and that the sentence of death he was about to pass on Him was unjust. Pilate was not a religious man, but he had some sense of justice. He was disturbed, and his superstitions were aroused, by Christ's words and manner and by the note he had received from his wife. He wanted to dissociate himself in a public and dramatic manner from responsibility in the affair. He was simple enough and superstitious enough to think that he could do it by washing his hands, declaring himself innocent, and telling the crowd to take the responsibility.[56] Pilate's words to the crowd, "See to it yourselves," remind us of the words of the chief priests and ancients to Judas confessing his betrayal of innocent blood: "What is that to us? See to it thyself" (Matt. 27:4). In the crime in which all are involved, each seeks to shift the blame to another.

The people, however, have no such scruples. They have been angered by Pilate's taunts and aroused to a white heat of hatred by their wily leaders. They understand Pilate's hesitations and scruples and his desire to be quit of all responsibility. They will take it willingly, all of them. "All the people answered," St. Matthew tells us, "and said, 'His blood be on us and on our children.'" They would not only take on themselves the responsibility of Christ's blood; they would take it even for their children.

To swear by that which is dear to oneself is not extraordinary. To call down responsibility for another's blood not only on oneself but on one's children is perhaps unique in history. Who would say that their imprecation had no effect? Some of these people and their children must have been present at the siege of Jerusalem by the Romans forty years later. Was it the irony of fate, or divine retribution, that the Romans could scarcely find sufficient wood to make crosses to crucify the Jews who had rebelled against Caesar? Did any looking down from their crosses

---

[56] Practices similar to Pilate's action were known among the Greeks and Romans and also among the Jews. Such a practice is prescribed in the legislation contained in Deuteronomy (21:1ff.). When the corpse of a murdered man was found and the murderer could not be discovered, the ancients of the nearest town washed their hands over a slain heifer, saying, "Our hands did not shed this blood, nor did our eyes see it."

recall this day forty years earlier when their fathers had cried out for the crucifixion of the Messiah?

Pilate acted quickly now to bring the unsavory business to an end. He wanted to be rid of it and forget it if he could. Sitting on his curule chair as official representative of the Roman emperor, he pronounced the final fateful words of sentence: *"Ibis in crucem,"* "To the cross thou shalt go." It was a sentence from which there was no appeal. Jesus was condemned officially to death on the cross.

Volumes have been written on the trials of Christ before the Sanhedrin and before the Roman procurator. Great efforts have been expended in examining every detail of the trials and in assessing responsibility of all who participated. The Gospel accounts make it clear that Jesus Christ was condemned to death for blasphemy by the Sanhedrin, highest court of the Jews, because He claimed to be the Son of God in the true and strict sense of these words. He was condemned by the Roman procurator in a wholly different trial on a wholly different charge: treason. The reason for the Roman trial was that the Jews no longer had the right over life and death and the enemies of Christ would not be satisfied with anything less than death.

In assessing the moral responsibility, the leaders of the Jews were far guiltier than Pontius Pilate. The Scribes and Pharisees hated Jesus, despised His teaching, and were jealous of His influence with the people. They succeeded in forming an alliance with the chief priests, and even with the high priest himself, to do away with Jesus for what they persuaded themselves were reasons of state (John 11:45–53). The betrayal by Judas put Jesus in their hands and led to His trial and condemnation.

Pilate too was guilty. Again and again, he proclaimed Christ's innocence, but out of cowardice in the face of a threat of denunciation to the emperor, he condemned Jesus Christ to death. We think that Christ Himself settled any argument as to who was guiltier when He said to Pilate, "He who betrayed me to thee has the greater sin" (John 19:11).

Chapter 17

THE WAY OF THE CROSS

Pilate had not finished with the trial of Jesus Christ when he pronounced on Him the sentence of death by crucifixion. There were details and formalities to be worked out, and Pilate, still seated on his curule chair, busied himself with his assistants. The time of the execution was no problem. It was Roman custom that the execution should follow the sentence immediately. Pilate decreed that Christ be executed this very day. He then directed a clerk to write the official record of the case for his own archives and to make a transcript to be sent to the emperor with his regular reports.

Jesus was condemned to death and executed by Romans and therefore was put to death in the Roman manner. It was the Roman custom to prepare a placard on which was inscribed the name of the condemned and the reason for the death sentence. This was either hung around his neck or carried raised up before him on the way to the place of execution so that all would know his identity and the reason for his condemnation. Pilate ordered that such a placard be prepared for Jesus. It was probably a board painted white with writing in black or red characters. Pilate himself dictated the wording, "Jesus of Nazareth, the King of the Jews," and he had it inscribed in the three principal languages used in Palestine at the time, Hebrew (Aramaic), Greek, and Latin, so that all could read it.

Under similar sentence of death by crucifixion were two robbers. The Gospels give us no information as to who they were or when they had been condemned. Because the Romans executed immediately after sentence, it is likely that they had been tried and condemned that very morning. Pilate had time for their trials after Christ had been sent to Herod Antipas, and later during the scourging and crowning with thorns. He decided to proceed with the crucifixion of all three at once.

Executions were a military function, and Pilate committed the execution of the condemned three to a centurion. As the title implied, this officer commanded a hundred men. It appears that the centurion—the *exactor mortis*, he was called, exercising this function—appointed four soldiers for each of the condemned, as we find later that our Lord's garments were divided among the four soldiers who performed the execution. Since executions took place in public and attracted crowds, and since the condemned were led through the streets to the place of execution, it is likely that the centurion ordered his full contingent of a hundred soldiers to be ready to accompany the cortege and maintain order.

A great deal of information about crucifixions is available from contemporary sources, so that it is not difficult to reconstruct with considerable exactness the scene that took place at the praetorium of Pilate after the condemnation of Christ. St. John informs us that Jesus carried His own cross (19:17). Contemporary writers often referred to part of the cross as the whole, and probably that is what St. John does here. We agree with the more commonly accepted opinion that Jesus carried only the crossbeam. This part probably weighed between seventy-five and a hundred pounds, and the whole cross two hundred pounds or more. It is doubtful if a man weakened by scourging could have stood up under the weight of the entire cross. The soldiers in charge of Jesus' execution raised the beam and placed it across His shoulders. In order to hold it steady, it was necessary for Jesus to stretch out His arms and grasp it. It is possible that His arms were fastened by ropes to the crossbeam, as often happened.

The usual Roman procedure was to scourge the prisoner before the march to the place of execution, and even sometimes during it, but this was now omitted in the case of Jesus, who had already been scourged. It was common practice elsewhere to strip the victim of his clothes and drag him naked to the place of execution, but this was not done in Jerusalem out of consideration for Jewish modesty. In fact, the Gospels tell us explicitly that Jesus' garments were returned to Him. The Gospels do not inform us whether the crown of thorns was taken from His head, but it is very likely that it was, when the purple garment of mockery was removed. The crowning with thorns and the mockery had been part of the private sport of the soldiers and had nothing to do with the official sentence now being executed. The upright part of the cross was carried by the soldiers or by onlookers whom they pressed into service for this menial task. It is wholly unlikely that the upright of the cross was kept in one place as a permanent fixture, as happened at Rome. This would have been abhorrent to the Jews. Furthermore, the place where Christ was crucified was certainly not a public place of execution. Sometimes a rope was bound around the waist of the condemned so that a soldier could drag on the unwilling victim. We do not know whether Christ was bound in this manner.

Preparations for the execution of the three men were made quickly. Part of Pilate's duties while he was in Jerusalem was to try capital cases, and condemnations to death did not come unexpectedly. Within a short time after the sentences had been passed, everything was in readiness. Under the command of the centurion, the procession formed in the vast flagstone courtyard and faced toward the western portals. The soldiers were fully armed and prepared to prevent attempts at rescue, or demonstrations that would interfere with their work. A detachment of soldiers to clear the way went first, followed by the centurion, probably on horseback. The prisoners followed, carrying the crossbeams of their crosses, each surrounded by the four soldiers who had immediate charge of their execution. Another detachment of soldiers brought up the rear.

The cortege filed out through the portals, pushing its way through the crowd of chief priests, Scribes, and ancients who were gloating now over the successful outcome of their plot. It had been difficult to bend Pilate to their purposes, but they had finally done it. We can well imagine that they snarled their hatred at Jesus as He passed slowly, weighed down under the heavy beam of the cross.

Out in the narrow cobblestone streets of the city, the procession turned left. Had it turned right, it could have gone out of the city through the Fish Gate, only about one hundred yards away, which led to roads leading north from Jerusalem. Crucifixions took place outside the city, and any place that was near a frequented road and where the crucified could be prominently displayed was satisfactory. But it was the purpose of the Romans, too, to make a display of the condemned by leading them through the streets of the city. So the centurion selected a longer way, one that led down into the Tyropean Valley and then up again toward the right in a westerly direction toward the Ephraim Gate, which opened onto a road leading to the northwest. This was a thickly populated area of the city, its streets closely connected with the Temple and with two great gates leading into and out of the city. Bazaars lined both sides of the streets, and above them were the living quarters of their owners. Jerusalemites and pilgrim strangers from near and far jostled one another in crowds that made it almost impossible to pass. It was through these narrow and crowded streets, not altogether dissimilar to the present Way of the Cross in Jerusalem, that Christ slowly passed, bearing the weight of His own cross.[57]

The distance from the Antonia to Calvary was five or six hundred yards, somewhat longer if we take into account the intervening valley and the tortuous city streets. The procession had covered most of the distance and was near the Ephraim Gate when it became evident that Jesus was so weak He could no longer bear the weight of the cross. This was not surprising, since the last part of the way was uphill, and also in view of the scourging, the crowning with thorns, the buffetings, the sadness "even unto death" of the agony in the garden. The scourging alone was sufficient to weaken or even kill a strong man. The Gospels do not tell us how Jesus manifested this weakness, but later Christian tradition is probably correct in assuming that He stumbled and fell under the burden of the cross, and perhaps several times.

The centurion was quick to note the situation. It was his business to see that everything was done with dispatch. It was evident that Jesus could no longer carry the cross, but the centurion

---

[57] We are of the opinion that the Way of the Cross in Jerusalem follows approximately at least the way followed by Jesus from the Antonia to Calvary.

hesitated to order one of his soldiers to do it. Carrying the cross to the place of execution was part of the punishment of a criminal and was considered degrading. Looking about him, the centurion saw a peasant coming through the gate from the fields outside the city walls. The Gospels identify him as Simon of Cyrene. He had evidently been working in fields or gardens to the northwest of the city and was coming in now either to make purchases or because he lived within the walls. The centurion impressed him into service and ordered him to take Christ's cross and carry it to the place of execution. The soldiers removed the crossbeam from Jesus and placed it on the shoulders of Simon, who fell in line after Jesus as the procession continued on its way.[58]

Who was this Simon who carried the cross in Jesus' place? The Gospels give us little information about him. They refer to him as a Cyrenean, so he or his family must have come from Cyrene, a city in northern Africa, capital of the surrounding region called Cyrenaica, situated between Egypt on the east and Carthage on the west. For centuries, Cyrene had been a city of considerable importance, maintaining extensive commercial relations with other cities of the eastern Mediterranean. The Cyrenaic school of philosophy, deriving its name from this city, taught hedonism, that pleasure is the chief good. It was not until 74 B.C. that Cyrenaica became a Roman province. There was a large colony of Jews in Cyrene, and there were so many people from that city living in Jerusalem that they had their own synagogue there (Acts 2:10; 6:9; 11:20).

St. Mark refers to Simon as the father of Alexander and Rufus (15:21). Since St. Mark wrote for the Christian community at

---

[58] It is a mistake to picture Simon simply helping Jesus to carry the cross. Simon took over the entire burden and followed after Him.

Rome, it would appear that these two were known there and, very probably, belonged to the church of that city. In that case, it is extremely likely that Simon too became a Christian. It is possible that it is to Simon's son Rufus that St. Paul refers in his epistle to the Romans, when he writes, "Greet Rufus, the elect of the Lord, and her who is his mother and mine" (16:13). If these conjectures are true, then Simon and his family were generously repaid for the service he rendered the Divine Master, especially in view of the fact that the Gospel texts make it evident that the task was forced on Simon as a compulsory service. At least he fulfilled literally and physically Christ's admonition: "If anyone wishes to come after me, let him deny himself and take up his cross, and follow me" (Matt. 16:24).

At this point St. Luke makes the remark that "there was following him a great crowd of the people" (23:27). This is not surprising, as nearly all looked upon an execution as a spectacle, a sort of free circus provided for popular entertainment. Instead of sympathizing with the condemned, onlookers mocked him and tried to add to his tortures. The authorities made efforts to give executions the greatest possible publicity in order to terrify would-be criminals.

We have no definite information as to just how big a crowd followed Jesus to Calvary, but the wording of St. Luke indicates that it was considerable. The way led through a busy section of the city; it was near midday, and everybody was astir; there were great multitudes of pilgrims in the city from Judea and all the Near East. The Passover was greater than Pentecost, and on the latter feast, fifty days later, St. Luke tells us (Acts 2:9–11) that there were in Jerusalem "Parthians and Medes and Elamites, and inhabitants of Mesopotamia, Judea, and Cappadocia, Pontus and Asia, Phrygia and Pamphilia, Egypt and the parts of Libya about Cyrene, and visitors from Rome, Jews also and proselytes, Cretans and Arabians." Rumors of what had been going on at the praetorium of Pilate must have circulated through the city, so that those interested and the morbidly curious crowded the streets just outside the western portals of the Antonia. St. Luke tells us that on the following Sunday evening, Cleophas, one of the disciples who met the Risen Christ on the road to Emmaus, was astonished that even a stranger in Jerusalem could be ignorant of the events that had taken place the preceding Friday (24:18).

We can be pretty certain of some who were in that crowd on the way of the cross. The representatives of the Sanhedrin—the chief priests, Scribes, and ancients—were at the praetorium and later at Calvary, so they undoubtedly followed the procession closely. We can say the same for their retainers and sympathizers, as well as for many of the people who had come up to Pilate's praetorium to demand the release of a prisoner in honor of the Passover. All these people had joined forces in demanding Christ's death and were now on their way with Him to the spot where they would enjoy the spectacle of His crucifixion.

What of the disciples of Jesus? Were there none there? As we shall see presently, St. Luke speaks of some women of Jerusalem who sympathized with Jesus. But where were His Apostles and disciples? Where were the people who had listened to Him and applauded Him even when He castigated their leaders who were now doing Him to death? Where were the crowds who but a few days before had cast their garments on the ground before Him and hailed Him as the Messiah and Son of David?

We can be sure that there were some in that crowd who were still completely devoted to Jesus in spite of His miserable state. There were the Galilean women, because we find them later at

Calvary (Matt. 27:55–56; Mark 15:40–41; Luke 23:49), and chief among them Christ's own mother, probably with St. John at her side here as on Calvary. Belief in a meeting of Jesus and Mary on the way of the cross is not supported by sound documentary evidence but rests on solid historical probabilities.[59]

Except for the likelihood that St. John was in that crowd with the Mother of Jesus, there is no evidence whatever that any of the other Apostles, even the brave and boastful Peter, were present. There is a possibility that Joseph of Arimathea and Nicodemus were there, as they showed considerable courage on Calvary after the death of Christ.

The ordinary people, those who had listened to Jesus admiringly and had hailed Him as a conquering hero on the preceding Sunday, had gone over to His enemies. The events of the preceding night and morning had wrought a complete change in public sentiment. Today Jesus stood before them as one condemned to death by the highest court of the land, and again by the Roman procurator. Now they believed that they had been deceived by this false prophet from Nazareth, and they showed their resentment by noisily joining forces with Christ's executioners. It helps us to understand the situation if we recall once more that Jesus was not very well known to many of the people of Jerusalem, as He had spent only short periods there occasionally (see Matt. 21:10–11). Furthermore, as we have said, they looked on Him as a Galilean and therefore, in this respect at least, inferior to themselves.

St. Luke also relates the incident of the women of Jerusalem who met Jesus and sympathized with Him on the way of the

---

[59] Mention of the meeting of Jesus and Mary on the way to Calvary is made first in the *Acta Pilati*, dating from the fourth century. This work, however, is generally legendary in character.

cross. It is not surprising to find this event narrated by St. Luke, as he emphasized the part played by women in the Gospel. These women were the first to offer sympathy to Jesus in His Sacred Passion. (It is worthy of note that no woman spoke or acted offensively to Christ in His Passion or at any other time.)

St. Luke places this incident immediately after the reference to Simon of Cyrene, so it probably took place near the gate leading out of Jerusalem to Calvary. The crossbeam had been removed from Jesus' shoulders and placed on those of Simon. Leaning forward under the heavy burden, Jesus had been unable to look about Him. Now He straightened up, and His glance ranged over those who lined the sides of the street. In the midst of the crowd He saw a group "of women, who were bewailing and lamenting him" (23:27). Who were these women? Unfortunately St. Luke gives us little information. They were certainly not the Galilean women mentioned as present on Calvary, as Jesus addressed this group as "daughters of Jerusalem," meaning "women of Jerusalem." Some think they may have been an organization of pious women who tried to alleviate the sufferings of the condemned by a manifestation of sympathy and by giving him a special drink, such as the wine mingled with myrrh offered to Christ on Calvary. It is much more likely that these women knew Christ and accepted His teachings. Respecting and loving Him as they did, they could not restrain an outward manifestation of their grief and shock at the awful sight that met their eyes as Jesus passed by.

Jesus respected their sympathy, for He stopped, turned toward them, and spoke to them. This was the first time that Jesus had spoken for quite a while, and His words were a reward for their fidelity and courage. Even in the dire extremity in which He was, Jesus forgot Himself and thought of others. "Do not weep for me," He said, "but weep for yourselves and for your children." Then He went on to give the reason they should weep for themselves and their children rather than for Him: "For behold, days are coming in which men will say, 'Blessed are the barren, and the wombs that never bore, and the breasts that never nursed'" (Luke 23:28–29).

Jesus referred to the destruction of the city of Jerusalem, which would occur forty years later, in terms similar to those He had already used elsewhere: "Woe to those who are with child, or have infants at the breast in those days" (Luke 21:23). To the Jews, motherhood was among God's greatest blessings and sterility an opprobrium and a curse. So great would be the evils that were to befall the city that the natural order of things would be reversed and barrenness would be considered a blessing.

Jesus continued, "Then they will begin to say to the mountains, 'Fall upon us,' and to the hills, 'Cover us.'" These words are a proverbial expression of despair, as we find them used in the prophet Osee ([Hos.] 10:8) and in St. John's Apocalypse ([Rev.] 6:16). They foretell the despair that the calamities to come will engender in those who suffer them. So great will be the miseries of that time that people will look upon death as a liberation and seek it as a blessing.

Christ concludes His words to the women of Jerusalem by adding, "For if in the case of green wood they do these things, what is to happen in the case of the dry?" (Luke 23:31). In the Old Testament, the green and fruitful tree was the image of the just man. Here the green wood refers to Christ Himself, the dry wood to the people of Jerusalem. If the justice of God reaches even the green wood, Christ, what will it do to the dry wood, the people of Jerusalem? The answer came forty years later, in the year 70, when Titus and his army laid waste the city and its temple and slaughtered or sold into slavery its inhabitants. This siege and its aftermath, as recorded by the Jewish historian Josephus, constitute one of the most terrible pages of history.[60]

It was probably immediately after Jesus had spoken to the women of Jerusalem that the procession threaded its way slowly through the Ephraim Gate. This gate was slightly to the north of the angle where the north-south wall met the east-west wall. Close by was a tower that had been built to reinforce this part of the wall. Beyond the gate the procession continued along the great highway leading out of the city toward Jaffa to the northwest. About a hundred yards in the open country beyond the gate, the centurion gave the signal to stop. Since leaving the city he had looked about him for a suitable place for the execution. A spot to his right had all the necessary qualifications. It was outside the city but near it; it was along-side a highway where those crucified could be seen by all who

---

[60] The Stations of the Cross as constituted at present date only from the Middle Ages and cannot therefore be cited as historical proof for the incidents commemorated. Some of these incidents are certain because related in the Gospels: the condemnation to death, the carrying of the cross, Simon of Cyrene, the women of Jerusalem, the stripping of Jesus, the nailing to the cross, the death on the cross, the taking down from the cross, and the burial. The meeting of Jesus and His mother is not recorded in the Gospels but is historically logical, as Mary was later at Calvary. The falls beneath the cross are not found in the Gospels, but they too are historically likely. As we have pointed out, it was undoubtedly because Christ fell beneath the weight of the cross once or several times that it became necessary to transfer the burden to Simon. The incident of Veronica and the veil is not mentioned in the Gospels and has no sound historical foundation.

passed; it was a little elevated above the surrounding territory so that the crucified would be exhibited clearly to the eyes of all. The procession stopped. The soldiers led the condemned a little off the road and began preparations for the grim task of crucifixion.

Chapter 18

CALVARY

The Gospels inform us that Jesus was crucified at a place called Calvary—in Hebrew, Golgotha. Both words have the same meaning: the skull. The Gospels refer to the locality as a "place," never as a mount or mountain. The name Calvary or Golgotha referred to an area wider than the spot where the cross of Christ was raised, as St. John tells us that "in the place where he was crucified there was a garden and in the garden a new tomb" (19:41). In all likelihood, Calvary was the name of the area just beyond the angle where the walls met and just outside the gate through which Christ had passed.

Why was the place called "the Skull"? Certainly not because the skulls of executed criminals lay about, as some have asserted. The Jews would never have permitted the bones of the executed to lie unburied, as they caused a legal defilement. Furthermore, Calvary was not a fixed place of execution but one selected at random. Neither can we accept the opinion of some of the Fathers of the Church, who believed that it got its name from the fact that the skull of Adam was buried in the grotto under the rock of Calvary. Such an opinion is pure figment of the imagination.

The place got its name because this area or some particular feature of it resembled a skull. Even today in the Holy Land, place names are often derived from parts of the human body, such as head, shoulder, belly, and so forth. In fact, the area where Calvary is situated is still called at times *ras*, or "head." The hill in this region was the northern part of the north-south hill on which the western part of the city was built. At the point with which we are concerned, the hill sloped gradually in a southeasterly direction. About a hundred yards before the walls, a little rocky promontory, a hillock of no great dimensions, jutted out toward the east. This projection was roughly shaped like a skull and gave its name to the area immediately surrounding it.

Calvary was only a slight elevation, probably no more than about fifteen feet above the ground along its sides. The top of this little hillock was wide enough for the crucifixion of three men and elevated enough to exhibit them to the public without causing inconvenience to the executioners. Calvary was a suburban area of gardens and tombs, its quiet disturbed by the heavy traffic on the Jerusalem-Jaffa road, which passed directly beneath the hillock from which its name was derived. Joseph of Arimathea had a little country estate here in which he had built his tomb. Even at this time, however, the area was becoming more and more urbanized, as only about twelve years later Herod Agrippa found it necessary to include it within a new wall that he built.

The Gospels do not provide us with the exact localization of Calvary. They do tell us that it was outside the walls of the city, and they imply that it was near a highway, as the passersby insulted Jesus on the cross (Matt. 27:39; Mark 15:29). Christian tradition is quite explicit as to the localization of Calvary, and we accept that tradition as valid. Père Vincent of the *Ecole Biblique* in Jerusalem, the greatest of all Palestinian archeologists, well says, "The authenticity of Calvary and the Holy Sepulchre is endowed with the best guarantees of certitude which one can hope for in such a subject."[61]

Knowing that Calvary was outside the walls, it is difficult for the traveler today to picture to himself the traditional site as authentic, since it is in the middle of the modern city. The solution of this difficulty involves a long and complicated study of texts of the Old Testament and of the Jewish historian Josephus, as well as of various archeological data, a study that would be out of place here.[62]

The solution of the problem hinges on the position of the second wall, built at the time of King Ezechias (ca. 700 B.C.) and restored and rebuilt in later epochs. If it included the traditional site of Calvary within the city, then this site is certainly not authentic. We think that texts and archeological remains prove that the second wall started near the present Jaffa Gate and after running north turned east and passed just south of Calvary. At a point at present in the German Savior Church, it turned north. Among the ruins in the Alexander Hospice is the threshold of an ancient gate that may very well have been part of the Ephraim Gate in the second wall. At a point impossible to determine, the wall turned east until it ended at the Antonia.

[61] *Jerusalem II*, p. 89.
[62] See Vincent-Steve, *Jerusalem de l'Ancien Testament, Premiere Partie*, pp. 90ff.; Père Vincent, *Jerusalem Nouvelle*, bk. II, pp. 89ff.; *Dictionnaire de la Bible*, Supplement, "Jerusalem," cols. 926ff.

If the second wall followed this line, then the traditional site of Calvary was definitely outside the city walls.

If a traveler standing in the courtyard outside the entrance to the Church of the Holy Sepulchre in Jerusalem could close his eyes and then open them to see Calvary as it was at the time of Christ, He would be looking on a scene that is not difficult to reconstruct. He would be standing on or near the Jerusalem-Jaffa highway. In back of him would be a ditch protecting the wall, and, above the ditch, the east-west part of the second wall. A hundred yards to his right, the wall and ditch turned north, and a few yards beyond the angle were a gate and a tower. Looking directly in front of him, which would be to the north, our traveler would see, a little to his right, a round, skull-shaped promontory, rather flat on top, which jutted out from the main part of the hill beyond and gave the name Calvary, or Skull, to the area. Beyond this hillock, a little to the left, he would see the opening of a tomb that had been cut in the solid rock of the hill. This area was the site of Christ's crucifixion, burial, and resurrection.

It is incredible that the early Christians should forget or ignore the principal places rendered holy by the presence of Jesus. This is especially true of the spot sanctified by His death and resurrection. Some who had heard and seen Christ, some perhaps who had even witnessed His crucifixion and death, were still alive at the time of the siege of Jerusalem in the year 70. Warned of the impending catastrophe, the Christian community escaped to Pella beyond the Jordan. When peace was restored, they returned to the partially destroyed city and continued their life there under an uninterrupted succession of bishops. Calamity struck again when the Jews revolted against the emperor Hadrian in the year 132. When this insurrection had been put down, Hadrian completely destroyed Jerusalem and on its ruins built a Roman city called Aelia Capitolina. His engineers selected Calvary as the site of the forum and capitol of the new city and, to create a level platform, filled in the area with rubbish and debris. He erected a statue of Jupiter over the Holy Sepulchre and one of Venus over the spot where Christ was crucified. His attention was undoubtedly directed to these spots because of their religious associations. Hadrian made little or no distinction between Christians and Jews and thought their religion was a reason for their repeated rebellions against Roman authority. In an effort to obliterate religious memories, he erected idolatrous statues among the Temple ruins and at the Terebinth of Abraham, where pious Jews honored their ancestor. To prevent Christians from honoring the place where Christ was born at Bethlehem, he built a shrine to Adonis over the sacred grotto.

Hadrian's efforts had exactly the opposite effect. His installations preserved for future generations the very memories he wished to eliminate. When peace came to the Church, and Constantine, in 326, decided to build a basilica at the site of Christ's crucifixion and burial, the Christians of Jerusalem knew the spot to which to direct his engineers. It would have been much more satisfactory for future generations if Constantine had simply cleared the area and then left it in its original state. His engineers cut away the rock surrounding the tomb to the level of the vestibule and then built a beautiful basilica called the Anastasis (Resurrection) over it. To the east of the Anastasis was an outer court surrounded by magnificent porches. The spot where Jesus was crucified was at the southeast angle of this court. Constantine cut the rock of Calvary into the shape of a cube about eighteen by fifteen feet on the top. Later both

Calvary and the Holy Sepulchre were included under one roof, as they are today.

It would seem that to the Persians is due the credit—or dis-credit—for the invention of crucifixion. It was used by Alex-ander the Great and by his successors, the Diadochi, but never in Greece itself. The Syrians also used it. The Carthaginians learned it from the Persians, and the Romans from the Car-thaginians. At the time of Christ, crucifixion was a common form of punishment throughout the Roman Empire. Condemned criminals dying on a cross were a familiar sight in every prov-ince where Roman justice was administered. Crucifixion was unknown to Jewish penal law, although at times the body of the one executed was hung on a tree, in which case he was consid-ered to be cursed: "For he is accursed of God that hangeth on a tree" (Deut. 21:23). This may help to explain why Jesus' enemies were so insistent that Pilate should crucify him. They felt that they could nip in the bud any movement in His favor by arguing that, having hung on the tree of the cross, Christ was accursed of God (see Gal. 3:13).

Among the Romans, crucifixion was originally a punishment inflicted on slaves and was even called the *supplicium servile*, the slave punishment. At Rome, the place where slaves were cruci-fied became a veritable forest of crosses. Gradually, crucifixion became the punishment not only of slaves but of others guilty of major crimes such as desertion, treason, rebellion, highway robbery, sedition, or piracy. Theoretically, at least, it was unlaw-ful to crucify a Roman citizen. Cicero was at his most eloquent on this subject. "For a Roman citizen to be bound," he said, "is a misdemeanor; for him to be struck is a crime; for him to be killed is almost parricide; what must I say then, when he is hung on the cross? There is no epithet whatever which may fittingly describe a thing so infamous."[63]

There is evidence, however, that this punishment was inflicted on Roman citizens, especially on citizens of lower rank, such as freedmen and citizens in the provinces and at times even on citizens of higher rank. The historian Suetonius relates that Caesar Galba, when in Spain, condemned a Roman citizen to be crucified. When he appealed to the fact that he was a Roman citizen, Galba ordered him crucified on a cross much higher than the others and painted white. Verres, governor of Sicily, crucified a Roman on the coast facing Italy in order to show how useless was his appeal to his Roman citizenship. In spite of Cicero and his eloquence, the practice continued. As we have seen in the trial of Christ, there was often a vast difference between theory and practice in the administration of much-vaunted Roman justice.

The Romans used crucifixion a great deal in the provinces, especially in the restless and rebellious province of Judea. Josephus, the Jewish historian, relates many cases of crucifixion. A sedition that broke out at the death of Herod the Great was suppressed by Quintilius Varus, legate of Syria, who crucified two thousand Jews. Tiberius Alexander, procurator of Judea (A.D. 46–48), crucified the two sons of Judas of Galilee. Ummidius Quadratus, governor of Syria, on an official visit to Caesarea, crucified the prisoners who had been captured by the procurator Cumanus (A.D. 48–52). Josephus states that the number crucified by the procurator Felix (A.D. 52–59) was incalculable.

[63] *Verrem*, 2, 5, 66.

The procurator Gessius Florus (A.D. 64–66) scourged before his tribunal in Jerusalem and nailed to the cross Jews on whom had been bestowed the Roman dignity of the equestrian rank.

During the siege of Jerusalem in the year 70, the Romans crucified as many as five hundred captives a day. Josephus tells us that "the soldiers, out of rage and hatred, amused themselves by nailing their prisoners in different postures; and so great was their number that space could not be found for the crosses nor crosses for the bodies." Originally both the Greek and Latin words for "cross" meant simply a stake or pole. In fact, at times the victim was suspended on a single stake or even on a living tree. This upright stake gave its name to the entire instrument of torture, which consisted of an upright stake to which was attached a crossbeam. In ordinary practice, the stake or vertical part of the cross was fixed in the ground and remained stationary; the crossbeam was carried on the shoulders of the victim to the place of execution.

Two kinds of crosses were in ordinary use. One was the *crux commissa*, in which the crossbeam was placed on top of the upright to form a letter T. The other was the *crux immissa*, in which the vertical beam extended upward beyond the crossbeam. We cannot be certain which type of cross was used for the crucifixion of Jesus, but we think the weight of evidence favors the latter. In the *crux immissa*, a socket was cut into the upright near the top, and the crossbeam was fitted into it. There is strong evidence among ancient writers that a peg or hook of wood was inserted halfway down the upright stake of the cross so that the one crucified sat on it. Ancient writers referred to it as a horn because it resembled the horn of a rhinoceros. This peg made the work of crucifixion easier, as it helped to support the weight of the body. It also increased the sufferings of the crucified by prolonging his life, as it decreased the drag on the hands and arms, which brought on asphyxiation. The footrest, pictured so often in reproductions of the crucifixion of Christ, was entirely unknown to the ancients.

The height of the cross varied considerably. There was the low cross (*crux humilis*) and the high cross (*crux sublimis*), and both were used frequently. On the low cross, the feet of the crucified were just above the ground, and often, as part of his punishment, he was exposed thus to the attacks of dogs and wild beasts. On the high cross, the feet of the victim were about a yard above the ground. The high cross was used for those who were to be displayed prominently to the public, either as an added punishment or as a deterrent to others.

In ancient writings, there are frequent references to the fact that the victim was crucified naked—in fact, he was naked when scourged and while carrying his cross to the place of execution. In ordinary practice, at least, it would seem that the nudity was complete, although concessions may have been made to suit local customs. Sometimes the crucified was attached to the cross by nails, sometimes by ropes. When nails were used, the sufferings of the victim were more intense but briefer. In either case the victim could live for a considerable length of time, even for days.

Such was the punishment of death by crucifixion as practiced by the Romans. It was a shameful death, inflicted originally on slaves and the worst criminals. It involved being paraded through the public streets and then being exposed, naked on the cross, to the insults and abuse of executioners and onlookers. It was a painful death, involving scourging and carrying the cross and then long hours nailed to the cross, suffering from the wounds of the nails, weakness, thirst, suffocation, heat and cold, constriction of the muscles, and the gradual, drop-by-drop loss of blood. Many ancients considered crucifixion the most shameful and the most painful form of death. We shall see how right they were as we study the crucifixion and death of Jesus Christ.

Once Calvary had been selected for the crucifixion of Jesus and the two thieves, the Roman soldiers went into immediate action. They surrounded the little hillock and took possession of it so that they could do their work without interference. The crowd that had followed them poured off the road and filled the surrounding area. The soldiers led Jesus and the other two up the slopes of the hillock and selected the spot at which each of the crosses would be erected.

At this moment, before the work of crucifixion began, occurred one of the few incidents of compassion and of human decency during the Passion of Christ. St. Mark informs us that "they gave him wine to drink mixed with myrrh; but he did not take it" (15:23).[64] This mixture of wine and myrrh was well known and liked by the ancients. They thought that it had a narcotic effect, capable of dulling the senses and thus lessening pain. The custom of giving such a drink to those condemned to die was Jewish, not Roman. It probably had its origin in the book of Proverbs: "Give strong drink to them that are sad and wine to them that are grieved in mind. Let them drink and forget their want and remember their sorrow no more" (31:6–7). The

---

[64] The Gospel of Matthew says that the wine was "mixed with gall" (27:34). The word used by Matthew is a generic term referring to any bitter drink and would include myrrh.

Talmud preserved the memory of the practice of giving those to be executed wine in which a grain of incense had been dissolved. According to this source, noble women of Jerusalem prepared the drink and brought it to the place of execution. There can be little doubt that it was the women whom Christ addressed as "daughters of Jerusalem" who now offered him this further mark of compassion and devotion. Not being allowed to mount the little hillock where the preparations for crucifixion were going on, they passed the drink to the soldiers, who offered it to Jesus. To show His appreciation of this kindly gesture, Jesus took the drink, put it to His lips, and tasted it, but refused to drink it. In His agony in the Garden of Gethsemane, He had voluntarily accepted His Passion and all the sufferings it implied. His sacrifice would redeem the world, and He would offer it in the full possession of His powers of intellect and will.

The first act of the executioners was to find a spot for the upright beam of each of the three crosses. It was necessary to fix it several feet in the ground so that it would not sway or fall under the weight of the crucified. The flat surface of the little hillock was rocky, but the soldiers had no great difficulty in finding three places where they could plant the crosses solidly in the ground. Once they were set up, they packed earth and stones around them to give them added solidity.

While this was going on, Jesus was stripped of His garments. Was He stripped entirely naked? That question cannot be answered with certainty. There are many ancient texts that indicate that it was Roman custom to crucify entirely naked. It is the common opinion of the Fathers of the Church that Christ was completely naked. It must be noted, however, that the Fathers of the Church base their opinion on mystical and symbolical interpretations rather than on any historical tradition.

There is strong likelihood that Jesus was allowed to retain a loincloth of some sort when He was stripped of His garments. In interpreting ancient texts, we must bear in mind that in both Greek and Latin the word "naked" can mean relative as well as complete nakedness. The word could be used, for instance, of one clothed only in his undergarments. Furthermore, the Jews had a well-developed sense of modesty and an abhorrence of public nakedness. Later Jewish tradition, recorded in the Talmud, states that the condemned was stripped a few cubits from the place of execution; if it was a man, he was covered in front; if a woman, she was covered both front and back. It is also to be noted that, contrary to Roman practice, Jesus was clothed again after the scourging. Since the concession was made then, it was probably made later at Calvary.

Once the upright of the cross had been set up firmly in the ground and the victim stripped of His garments, the four soldiers appointed to the task proceeded with the work of attaching Christ to the cross. The crossbeam had been thrown on the ground near the upright. Jesus was made to lie down on His back so that His shoulders rested on the middle of the beam and His arms stretched out along it. A soldier reckoned the exact spot where one of Jesus' hands would fit and then dug a hole in the wood with an awl so that the nail would pierce it more easily. While another held the wrist and hand of Jesus firmly against the wood, he then drove a nail with quick, sharp blows of the hammer through Jesus' hand and into the wood. Then one of the soldiers pulled Jesus' free arm out to its full length on the other side of the beam, and the same process of nailing was repeated.[65]

---

[65] Jesus was nailed to the cross, and not tied. Nailing was the more common practice. After the resurrection, Jesus showed the

Then began one of the most delicate and difficult parts of the crucifixion. The crossbeam with its victim nailed to it had to be raised and attached to the upright of the cross. Unless it was done carefully, the crucified would be torn loose and the nailing would have to be done over. Two soldiers grasped the ends of the beam and a third probably took hold of Jesus by the waist, and all lifted together until He was on His feet. Jesus was then made to stand with His back to the upright of the cross. The two soldiers who had held the crossbeam took forked poles or strong pieces of wood, placed them underneath the crossbeam, and pushed upward. As they did, a third soldier again grasped Jesus and lifted Him until He straddled the peg in the middle of the upright and the crossbeam settled into the socket prepared for it. Once this was done, a soldier pressed Jesus' feet against the wood of the upright and drove a nail through each.

Jesus was now nailed firmly to the wood of the cross.[66] It is not difficult to imagine the frightful pain that the nailing and shaking about must have caused Jesus. Except for some little relief from the wooden seat in the upright, the entire weight of His body rested on fresh wounds in His hands and feet. And this was only a beginning of the frightful torture that was to go on increasing in agony for three hours.

wounds in His hands and feet to His disciples (Luke 24:39–40; John 20:20). The thieves crucified with Jesus are often pictured as tied to their crosses. There is no evidence whatever for this. All three were attached to the crosses in the same manner—by nails.

[66] It is more probable that the feet of Jesus were attached to the cross by two nails. This appears to have been the ordinary practice. It would have been clumsy and difficult to use but one nail for both feet.

The LAST HOURS *of* JESUS

While we think it more likely that Christ was crucified in the manner we have described, this is not altogether certain. It is possible that the crossbeam and the upright were already fitted together to form a cross, and that Christ was nailed to it on the ground in the manner ordinarily pictured by artists. Once He was nailed to the cross, it was elevated into position.

It is also possible that the executioners first set the entire cross firmly in the ground and then lifted Jesus up on it in such a way that He straddled the peg that served as a seat in the upright. They then bound Him securely with cords and afterward nailed Him to the cross. Then they removed the cords. This method of crucifixion would not be difficult with a low cross, but the cross on which Jesus died was high.[67]

That Christ was crucified on a high cross (*crux sublimis*) appears evident from an incident that happened later. When Jesus said, "I thirst," a soldier dipped a sponge into the sharp, ordinary wine the soldiers were drinking and put it to Jesus' mouth. To do this, he had to use a spear.[68] If the cross had not been high, he could easily have done this with his hand. We do not know why the high cross was used for Jesus. It is possible that Pilate

---

[67] St. Mark states that Christ was crucified at the "third hour" (15:25). Comparing this assertion with the statement of St. John (19:14), it would appear that Jesus was crucified at approximately the noon hour.

[68] The present text of St. John's Gospel says the soldier used a "stalk of hyssop" to hold the sponge. A stalk of this plant would be too small and weak for the purpose. The Greek words for "hyssop" and "spear" are very similar, and we accept the theory of many commentators that an early scribe mistook the two in transcribing the Gospel of St. John. The Greek word used by Matthew and Mark could be translated "spear" as well as "reed."

wanted as large a number of people as possible to see the derisive inscription nailed above Jesus' head. This was another little revenge he could extract from his abject surrender to the will of the Jewish leaders.

While Jesus was being crucified, the same procedure was being followed for the crucifixion of two robbers. All four Evangelists note the fact that two robbers were crucified with Jesus and add the detail that Jesus' cross was erected in the middle, as if He were the greatest malefactor of the three. The sacred writers were evidently struck by this wanton humiliation of Jesus, but also by the fact, mentioned expressly by Mark (15:28), that this incident was the fulfillment of a prophecy made by Isaiah many centuries before: "He ... was reputed with the wicked" (53:12). From the Greek word used by the Evangelists in referring to them, it is evident that the two were not petty thieves but armed robbers or brigands.

As soon as Jesus had been attached firmly to the cross by His hands and feet, a soldier raised a ladder, mounted it, and nailed immediately above Jesus' head the placard for which Pilate had dictated the wording and which he had had inscribed in Hebrew (Aramaic), Latin, and Greek.[69] The crowd surged forward a little

---

[69] The wording of the inscription varies a little in the Gospel accounts but is substantially the same in all four. The nearest to the original is probably St. John, an eyewitness. It may be that the differences are due to a little variation in the different languages. St. Matthew says the inscription read: "This is Jesus, the King of the Jews" (27:37). There is a striking similarity between this reading and the wording of the inscription of Attalus, who was martyred at Lyons in the second century. The historian Eusebius relates that he was led into the amphitheater, preceded by a tablet on which was written: "This is Attalus the Christian."

to get a better look at it, and the passersby stopped on the road to look up and read it: "Jesus of Nazareth, the King of the Jews." The Gentiles who read it must have chuckled and joked among themselves at the obvious sarcasm. It was really a fine bit of irony to label this man hanging on a cross the King of the Jews. Perhaps some of them even ridiculed the Jews near them.

The Sanhedrists present were infuriated. It was bad enough that the inscription had been borne publicly in the procession to Calvary, but then it had been more or less obscured in the milling crowd. Now it stood out clearly at the top of the cross erected along a main highway near a gate of the city, and in three languages so that no one who could read would miss it. The chief priests decided that this was more than they could or should bear and organized a delegation of their number to return to the praetorium and petition Pilate to change the inscription to read: "He said, I am the King of the Jews." Pilate made short shrift of them. He had had about all of their ways he could stomach, and anyway he was delighted that his shaft had hit home as sharply as he had hoped and intended. With an imperious wave of his hand, he dismissed them with the laconic remark: "What I have written, I have written" (John 19:21-22). The chief priests had to return to Calvary and report their failure to their fellows.

Once Jesus had been elevated on the cross, He must have looked at the scene below and around Him. Right below Him, on the crest of the hillock where the three crosses were planted, were the soldiers who had just finished the work of crucifixion. They were putting away their tools and throwing the garments of the crucified into a little pile for later division. In a few moments, they would take up their guard stations as appointed by the centurion to make sure no one tried to rescue the condemned men.

In the little space between the hillock and the highway, and all about in the surrounding gardens, were crowds of people. Some were actively hostile to Jesus, especially those who had listened to Him willingly but felt now that He was a deceiver. Many were indifferent but went along with popular sentiment and curried favor with the rulers by showing hostility to Jesus. Others were there simply out of morbid curiosity and had no doubt that all three crucified were getting what they deserved. Clustered here and there in small groups were the Jewish leaders—chief priests, Scribes, and ancients—the men who had brought about the condemnation of Jesus. They were pleased now. They congratulated one another, looked up gloatingly at Jesus, and mocked Him as they rubbed their hands in self-satisfied glee at their success.

Looking down from His cross, Jesus could see others, too —friends, disciples, and relatives. Many of them stood at a distance, probably out of fear of the soldiers, but some later approached and stood beneath the cross. A few are mentioned expressly in the Gospels. First among them was Mary, the Mother of Jesus. Then there was her sister, who was probably Salome, the mother of the Apostles John and James (if this is true, St. John was the nephew of the Mother of Jesus). Present also were Mary Magdalen and Mary of Cleophas, who was probably the one referred to as the mother of James the Less and of Joseph. According to a very early Christian source (Hegesippus, second century), Cleophas was a brother of St. Joseph, foster father of Jesus. Mentioned also as present were the Beloved Disciple, whom we have no difficulty in identifying as the Apostle St. John, with Joseph of Arimathea, and Nicodemus. There were undoubtedly others, as St. Luke refers to the presence of "all his acquaintances and the women who had followed him from Galilee" (23:49), and St. Mark, after naming some we have already mentioned, writes of "many other women who had come up with him to Jerusalem" (15:41).We can be sure too that those whom Christ had addressed as "daughters of Jerusalem" were there, perhaps joined now with the Galilean women.

That is all the information we have about the friends Jesus saw before Him as He looked down from the cross. The Gospel narratives are by no means complete, however. It would seem strange to us if Christ's friends of Bethany — Mary, Martha, Lazarus, and Simon the Leper — were not there. Whether any of the Apostles except John had recovered sufficiently from their fright to watch even from a distance we do not know. Perhaps there were also a few of the deaf and the blind and the crippled whom Christ had helped, giving mute testimony now to their gratitude.

Jesus was crucified facing the road that led from the nearby Ephraim Gate onto the main highway to Jaffa and Gaza. As he looked down from His cross, He saw a constant stream of traffic pushing its way past Him, in and out of the city. There was every kind of people: Jew and Gentile, proselyte and pagan, Greek and Roman — men, women, and children. There were soldiers, merchants, businessmen, pilgrims, government officials. Some were on foot, others rode donkeys, horses, or camels. An occasional litter or chariot bearing a wealthy or important person passed by. Some stopped to stare and even joined with the Jews in mocking and reviling Jesus. Others, hardened to sights of this kind and oblivious of the tremendous mystery being enacted on that roadside, glanced up and then passed on, indifferent. Jesus spoke to none of them.

Since Jesus was crucified on a high cross and on a hillock, his head must have been at the height of the city walls, scarcely a hundred yards away. As He was crucified facing the road, He looked to the south. Directly before Him were the highway, the moat and the city wall, and, rising beyond it, the west hill of the city with its elegant residences dominated by the great towers of the palace of Herod to the right. Out beyond where the hill sloped southward, and therefore out of sight, was the house where He had eaten the Last Supper with His Apostles. Somewhat nearer — its roof, perhaps, visible from Calvary — was the palace of the high priest Caiaphas, where He had been condemned by the Sanhedrin. When Jesus looked to His left, he could see the Ephraim Gate near the angle where the walls met, and raising His eyes He could see the towers of the Antonia and, a little to the south, the pinnacles of the Temple. Out beyond the city, etched in green against the blue sky, was the Mount of Olives.

Chapter 19

THE SEVEN LAST WORDS

At the Last Supper and on the way to the Garden of Gethsemane, Jesus discoursed long and lovingly with His Apostles. During His Sacred Passion, however, He spoke rarely and briefly. Indeed, it may well be that the silences of Jesus during His Passion were as eloquent and impressive as His words. During the three hours that He was nailed to the cross, Jesus interrupted long periods of silence by speaking seven times. These utterances are known as His Seven Last Words. We are fortunate that there were those beneath the cross who could recall and record for posterity these last words of Jesus, as they were a fitting climax to His public ministry. All these words are not contained in each of the Gospels, nor in any one of them. In fact, Matthew and Mark relate but one word of Jesus on the cross, and Luke and John each relate three. Because of this we cannot have complete certainty about the order in which each of the words was uttered.

The first word of Jesus from the cross was almost certainly: "Father, forgive them, for they do not know what they are doing." St. Luke alone records it (23:34). It is strange that this word is missing from a few of the oldest and most important manuscripts of the Gospel of St. Luke. The only conclusion we can draw is that some of the early copyists—Christians though they were—omitted these words because they were scandalized by Christ's indulgence toward His enemies. There can be no doubt that this passage is authentic. It is verified not only by a sound manuscript tradition but also by the example of many early martyrs who imitated Christ's forgiveness of His enemies.

It is difficult to determine the exact time at which Christ's first word from the cross was spoken. Some think it was while the soldiers were nailing Him to the cross. One reason for this is that St. Luke relates the incident immediately after stating that they crucified Christ. Another is that our Lord uses the present tense—"what they are doing"—in His prayer. Neither reason is conclusive. The Evangelists are notably indifferent to exact chronological order. And it is unlikely that Christ referred to the soldiers nailing Him to the cross. It was too obvious that they did not know what they were doing. They were carrying out orders; they were fulfilling a duty imposed on them by proper authority. As pagans or Samaritans, it is unlikely that they had come in contact with Christ before. To them He was a criminal, legally condemned by the highest authority of the land, and their duty was to see that the sentence of the court was carried out. Christ would not have felt constrained to ask forgiveness for them in a special way.

We think that this first of the Seven Last Words was spoken just after Jesus had been raised on the cross and as He looked out over that sea of hostile faces turned up at Him. Christ's words must have had an electrifying effect. These people had seen many criminals crucified. They had seen them resist their executioners and attempt to escape. They had heard them howl and scream with pain. They had listened to them curse their tormenters and snarl at them in impotent rage as they spat at them.

What a different scene met their eyes on Calvary! Throughout His sufferings, Jesus maintained a majestic calm. On the way to Calvary, He had forgotten His own sufferings to warn the daughters of Jerusalem of the evils that would befall their city. On the cross, He raised his eyes to heaven and in a firm and self-assured tone addressed God as "Father." He did not pray for Himself; He did not ask to be taken from the cross or to be delivered from His sufferings. He prayed for those who had brought Him to this pass. He prayed to God, His Father, that they should be forgiven, and He even added an excuse for them: "They do not know what they are doing." Jesus had taught forgiveness. "Love your enemies," He had said. "Do good to those who hate you, and pray for those who persecute and calumniate you" (Matt. 5:44). On Calvary, He added to His verbal teaching the power of His example.

For whom did Jesus pray? He prayed for those who were responsible for His condemnation and crucifixion. Surely in the front rank of these were the leaders of the Jews — the chief priests, Scribes, and ancients. It was their duty to recognize Christ's claim to be the Messiah and Son of God, to examine His credentials, and to accept and proclaim Him as such. Yet they opposed Jesus throughout His public ministry. On many occasions they had plotted to put Him to death. They had finally laid hands on Him, condemned Him before their own tribunal, and brought about His execution by threatening the Roman procurator with a denunciation to the emperor.

They had acted out of hatred and envy and malice. They were guilty and needed forgiveness. Yet even for them Christ could plead ignorance. It was a culpable ignorance; they could and should have known better. But at least they did not have a full and immediate awareness of the enormity of what they were doing. Speaking of the crucifixion of Christ to the Jews in the Temple area but a short time later, St. Peter said: "I know that you acted in ignorance, as did also your rulers" (Acts 3:17; cf. Acts 13:27; 1 Cor. 2:8).

To a lesser extent and in varying degrees, the Jewish people who had joined their leaders in persecuting Christ shared their guilt. Many had heard Christ's teachings and had witnessed His miracles. Some may even have been cured by Him. They permitted themselves to be led astray to such an extent that they had helped put pressure on Pilate to secure Christ's condemnation and had accepted for themselves and their children responsibility for the blood of Jesus. Christ had said earlier: "If I had not come and spoken to them, they would have no sin. But now they have no excuse for their sin.... If I had not done among them works such as no one else has done, they would have no sin" (John 15:22, 24). Leaders and led alike shared in the sin, but for the led particularly, ignorance, though culpable, was an extenuating circumstance, and on the cross Christ recalled it in His prayer to the Father for forgiveness of His enemies.

Christ's prayer must have included Pontius Pilate, too, as he had played an unjust part in Christ's condemnation and execution. On three separate occasions he declared Christ innocent, but when faced with the threat of denunciation to the emperor, he capitulated and condemned Him to death. Pilate acted unjustly and against his conscience. Nevertheless, Christ's plea of ignorance would apply to him too, as he did not recognize Jesus as the Messiah and the Son of God. He quite evidently admired Jesus and respected Him; he even had a vague superstitious fear, from his wife's dream and from references to Christ's claim to be the Son of God. We can be sure, however, that he did not appreciate the awful implications of the unjust sentence he passed on our Lord.

Jesus was God as well as man. On the cross, He was offering a sacrifice for the sins of mankind. In a very definite sense all sinners had, therefore, a part in nailing Jesus to the cross. It is not too much, then, to say that Jesus' prayer extended to all sinners. And of sinners, too, it can be said that "they do not know what they are doing," because they do not have a full realization of the malice of sin. If they did, they would not sin.

Jesus' prayer took effect almost immediately. It must have made a tremendous impression on all people of goodwill who heard it. A short time later, one of the robbers crucified along-side Him confessed belief in Him. At the moment of Christ's death, others were converted, partly, no doubt, because of the marvels that occurred at that time. The centurion in charge of the crucifixion declared Jesus to be a just man. The people who had come out of curiosity began to beat their breasts as a sign of repentance (Luke 23:48). Later, large numbers of the people became Christians (Acts 2:41; 4:4), among them many priests (Acts 6:7) and Pharisees (Acts 15:5).

When the four soldiers detailed for the task had raised Christ on the cross and fixed the title above His head, they had accomplished the most laborious part of their work. They were free now to divide among themselves whatever items He possessed when they stripped Him in preparation for the crucifixion. This was a recognized custom of the time. For this we have the authority of the four Gospels and also the fact that the emperor Hadrian found it necessary, a hundred years later, to regulate the custom by decreeing that only items of minor value fell to the execution-ers. The executioners of Christ found only the clothes He was wearing to divide, but these had some value, and they proceeded to distribute them. It must have been a poignant scene for Christ to look down from the cross at the soldiers dividing His garments as if He were already dead.

Christ's garments probably consisted of sandals, a headscarf, an undershirt, a tunic that covered the body from the neck to the ankles, a cincture, and an outer garment or mantle. The first three Gospels inform us that the soldiers divided the garments and that they cast lots to determine what each should take. St. John, who was an eyewitness and who wrote after the other three Evangelists, clarifies the picture for us. It was easy to make a fair division of all of Christ's garments except the tunic, and this the soldiers did. But when it came to the tunic, they were nonplussed. The tunic had more than usual value because it was a seamless garment, woven in one piece from the top. It was probably worth more than all the rest of the garments together. Unfortunately, the Gospels give us no information as to how Jesus acquired this tunic. Informed guesses indicate His own Blessed Mother, or the devoted Galilean women who followed Him, or His friends of Bethany, Mary and Martha. A few think that it was the robe in which Herod had clothed Him as a mock king. This is improbable and also contradicts St. Mark, who states that after the crowning with thorns the soldiers clothed Christ in His own garments (15:20). The difficulty of the soldiers was that it would ruin a seamless garment to cut it into parts. One of them made a suggestion to which all agreed. They would cast lots—probably some form of dice—and the winner would take the tunic. This they proceeded to do. St. John recalls that in doing this, they unwittingly fulfilled a prophecy made centuries before concerning the Suffering Messiah: "They divided my garments among them, and for my vesture they cast lots" (19:24; Ps. 21:19 [22:18]).

The soldiers had finished the work of crucifixion, and now they took their places to guard the crucified. It would probably be a long-drawn-out affair, so they sat down near the crosses and proceeded to make themselves as comfortable as possible. To pass the time, they chatted, gambled, and passed around a jug of the thin, vinegary wine called *posca*, a favorite drink of soldiers.

Today, sympathy for the condemned is ordinary. Among the ancients it was unusual. A condemned man was treated as if he were already a corpse, no longer possessed of the rights and feelings of a human being. Executioners and spectators felt free to add what they could to the sufferings of the condemned in his last hours of life.

During the last hours of Jesus Christ, mockeries and insults were among the cruelest sufferings to which He was subjected. His enemies should have been sated with the sight of His frightful physical torments on the cross. They were not. They dared not approach the victim to strike Him, so they struck Him with the venom of their tongues. Their example was followed by others. In fact, the Gospels distinguish four classes of mockers: "they that passed by," the Jewish leaders, the crucified thieves, and the soldiers.[70]

---

[70] St. Luke mentions here that the soldiers mocked Jesus (23:36–37). He mentions also that they gave him vinegar to drink. This event occurred later, and it may have been then that the soldiers joined in mocking Jesus.

As we have seen, Jesus was crucified on a hillock overlooking a main thoroughfare just outside the city of Jerusalem. The cross was set up so near the road that the passersby could speak to the crucified. Unfortunately, this is exactly what many of them did. The Gospels identify them no further than to tell us that they were people who passed by. They were probably those leaving the city rather than those entering, as their mockery reveals that they were familiar with the accusations against Christ. By this time, the affair had undoubtedly become the talk of the town. These people stopped momentarily, probably in small groups, and looked up at the three men hanging on their crosses. They ignored the two robbers. They were brigands who had finally been caught and brought to justice.

But Jesus of Nazareth, that was different. He had pretended to be a prophet, even the Messiah. He had spoken of Himself as the Son of God. Only the preceding Sunday He had been welcomed into the city with acclaim and shouts of "Hosanna to the Son of David." See now what He had come to. What further need had they of proof that He was an impostor?

Looking up at Him, they wagged their heads—to the Jews a sign of ridicule and derision—and called out to get His attention. The word they used, translated "vah" or "aha," was an expression of admiration, but these people used it ironically. They jeered at His helplessness, crying, "Thou who destroyest the temple and in three days buildest it up again, save thyself." They were familiar with the Temple. They had often seen its massive stone structure dominating the eastern ridge of the city, its pinnacles reaching up toward heaven. What a joke it was that this man, who had boasted that He could destroy it and rebuild it in three days, could not help Himself, now that He was nailed to the cross. They had heard, too, that the Sanhedrin had condemned Him for making Himself out to be the Son of God. So they taunted Him, saying, "If thou art the Son of God, come down from the cross" (Matt. 27:40).

Some mocked Christ on the cross and passed by. Others mocked and remained. Among them were the chief priests, Scribes, and ancients, the principal enemies of Jesus. They had other things to do on what was, in their reckoning, the eve of the Passover. Their Passover meal should be eaten that very night. Even now they should be making preparations. But they could not tear themselves away from Calvary. They remained rooted to the spot. They gloated over their victory and enjoyed every evidence of suffering on the part of the crucified. But they were taking no chances, however slim, that something might still go wrong. They had thought they had Jesus in their clutches on many former occasions, and He had slipped from their grasp. It wouldn't happen again, for this time they would wait and watch to the very end.

There was a difference in the mockery of the passersby and of the leaders of the Jews. The former addressed Jesus directly. The latter spoke to one another, but loud enough for Jesus to hear. "He saved others," they said; "himself he cannot save" (Mark 15:31). They apparently admitted that He had saved others. The proof was too great to be rejected. But now He had evidently lost whatever power He had possessed. His present helplessness made him an object of derision.

Having ridiculed Christ's miraculous powers, the Sanhedrists jeered at His Messianic claims. "If he is the King of Israel," they continued, "let him come down now from the cross, and we will believe him" (Matt. 27:42). They used "King of Israel," the traditional form, rather than "King of the Jews," the form used by Pilate. They were so sure that Jesus could not and would not come down from the cross that they promised to believe in Him if

He did. They were insincere. On the following Sunday morning, He would work the even greater miracle of His resurrection, and still they would not believe in Him.

Encouraged by their own words and by Christ's apparent help-lessness, these Jewish leaders went on to blaspheme His divine Sonship. Still addressing one another, they said, "He trusted in God; let him deliver him now, if he wants him; for he said, 'I am the Son of God'" (Matt. 27:43). They were convinced that God had abandoned Jesus and that they were God's instruments in punishing Him. They were pleased with themselves. They could wait here patiently in this good work and later eat the Passover meal with a clear conscience. Furthermore, Jesus would soon be dead, and their spiritual domination over the people would be assured. It was indeed a good day for them and the beginning of a better future. Had they only known!

St. Luke tells us that the soldiers, too, joined in mocking Jesus (23:36–37). He relates this in conjunction with a somewhat later incident. It is likely that the soldiers got their inspiration from the passersby and from the Jewish leaders, who undoubtedly reviled Christ for a long time.

These Roman soldiers knew nothing of Jesus or His teaching. They must have been surprised to see Him mocked and ridiculed by His own people and even by some of the most eminent members of their high court. The title they had nailed over His cross was something of a paradox to them. Imagine even a king of the Jews in this sorry situation. Taking their cue from the others mocking Jesus, they looked up at Him and taunted Him, saying, "If thou art the King of the Jews, save thyself." They probably soon tired of this game, however, as their mockeries brought no response from Jesus and, unlike the Jews, they had no personal animosity toward Him.

As we have seen, two robbers were crucified with Jesus, one on His right and the other on His left. The three crosses were grouped close together, and conversation between the crucified was easy. The Gospels do not identify the two robbers. There are many legends concerning them in early Christian writings, and they are given a variety of names, the most popular of which are Dismas for the good thief and Gestas for the bad. None of these writings carry historical weight, however, so we are left to the details supplied by the Evangelists.

It is immediately noticeable that there is an apparent contradiction between Matthew and Mark on the one hand and Luke on the other. The first two Evangelists state that the robbers crucified with Jesus reviled Him, implying by the plural that both joined in the reproaches. Luke, on the other hand, relates that one of them reviled Christ and the other reproached him for it. Two solutions are offered for this difficulty. Some think that at first both reviled Jesus. Then one of them, touched by Christ's patience and goodness, and especially by His prayer for the forgiveness of His crucifers, was converted, rebuked the other, and confessed Christ. Another explanation, and the better, we think, is that Matthew and Mark used a generic plural indicating a category rather than individuals. They had mentioned the mockery of the onlookers and of the chief priests, Scribes, and ancients. They go on to mention another type of mocker, robbers, and use the plural although there was question of only one. This is not an unusual practice.

The robbers crucified with Christ observed everything that was taking place. Probably they were glad that most of the attention of the onlookers was directed at Jesus rather than at them. They had read the title above Christ's head, and they had heard the reproaches and taunts of the passersby and of the chief priests, Scribes, and ancients. They had turned all these things over in their minds and with a totally different effect in each case.

One made the extraordinary move of joining the enemies of Christ in reviling and blaspheming Him. Usually the condemned, drawn together by their shared misery, made common cause against executioners and onlookers, cursing and reviling them. But one of the robbers turned his head toward Jesus and said sarcastically, "Aren't you the Christ?"[71] And since he had Jewish ideas concerning the Messiah and had heard the others challenging Jesus to come down from the cross, he added mockingly, "Save thyself," and then as a sort of afterthought, "and us." Jesus ignored him completely.

The other robber did not ignore him. It was probably because of Jesus' silence that he felt constrained to speak. He spoke earnestly to the other robber, rebuking him for what he had said to Jesus: "Dost thou not even fear God, seeing that thou art under the same sentence?" (Luke 23:40). The emphasis was probably on the word "fear." He said in effect, "You may not love God, but in view of your imminent death and judgment you might at least fear Him and not incur the guilt of reviling this fellow sufferer." The others could mock Jesus with a feeling of impunity, but not one who was already hanging on a cross beside Him.

And then this crucified robber went on to speak some of the most beautiful words recorded in the Gospels: "And we indeed justly, for we are receiving what our deeds deserved; but this man has done nothing wrong" (Luke 23:41). He had led an evil life.

---

[71] This reading is preferable to "If thou art the Christ."

Justice had overtaken him, and now he was nailed to a cross, dying. At this moment, instead of reviling Christ and hurling insults at his executioners, he quietly opened his heart and mind to admit a flood of grace and light that came to him from the One on the nearby cross. He confessed his sins, he accepted his sufferings as a just punishment for his wickedness, and before that howling crowd of mockers he proclaimed openly his firm belief in Christ's innocence.

Repentance opened the mind and heart of this crucified robber to the gift of faith, and he went on quickly to profess his belief in Jesus Christ: "Jesus, remember me when thou comest in thy kingdom" (Luke 23:42).[72] There is even a beginning of love evidenced in his words, as he addressed our Lord familiarly as "Jesus." And he did not ask for much; he left it to our Lord. He asked simply that Jesus should give him a thought, should not completely forget him when He should come in His kingdom. With his newfound faith in Christ, he ignored his present situation. He had lost interest in that. He thought only of the future. He believed that Jesus was the Messiah and that he would return in the glory of His Messianic kingdom. This kingdom could only be in the future life, as he could see clearly that, like himself, Jesus was dying on a cross.

The profession of faith of the robber crucified with Christ is one of the most extraordinary events recorded in history. It is difficult to imagine anything so unlikely. When this robber looked at Jesus, he saw One who was apparently a criminal, condemned by His own people and the Roman authorities, dying now on a cross, reviled and mocked by all but a few helpless friends in a little group nearby. Yet he professed his belief that Jesus was the

[72] Here we follow the Greek text, which is preferable.

Messiah and begged Him to remember him at the time of His glorious return in His Messianic kingdom.

Had this man known Christ before Calvary? Had he at least heard of Him and of His teachings? We have no information on this. It is not necessary to presume it. The robber was well aware of what had been going on around him on this fateful day. He knew why Jesus had been condemned and crucified. He could read it in the title nailed to the cross above His head. He could hear it in the taunts and mockeries of the onlookers. He observed all this, and more too. He could see that Jesus was not dying like a criminal. He noted His silence, patience, and goodness. He heard Him address God familiarly as His Father and ask pardon for those who had crucified Him. All this helped to prepare him for the very special divine grace that alone could account for his sudden conversion from sinner to saint.

Except for His prayer for forgiveness of His enemies, Jesus had been silent during the crucifixion and while He hung on the cross. He had ignored those who mocked and taunted Him, even the robber crucified alongside Him. But the words of the Good Thief touched Him and brought an immediate response. Turning His head to look at His newfound disciple, He said: "Amen, I say to thee, this day thou shalt be with me in paradise" (Luke 23:43). There was an urgency and solemnity in Jesus' words, emphasized by the expression, "Amen, I say to thee." The robber had asked for something in the indefinite future. He would not have to wait. He would receive all he asked for, and more, this very day. Before night fell he would be with Jesus in paradise. According to all appearances, Jesus had nothing to offer. He was dying nailed to a cross; even His garments had been taken from Him and divided among the soldiers. Yet in a tone of complete confidence and assurance He promised this man dying at his side that before nightfall he would be His companion in paradise.

What did Jesus mean by "paradise"? This word was of Persian origin and from that language passed into the Hebrew and Greek of the Bible. It meant a garden, especially an enclosed garden planted with trees. Metaphorically, the word came to mean happiness, especially the happiness of heaven. At the time of Christ, it was used of the abode of the just after death, and this is undoubtedly the sense of the word as used by our Lord. After He died, Christ's soul descended into hell — or Limbo, as it is called — and there too went the soul of the Good Thief. It was only after our Lord's Ascension that the souls of the just were admitted to heaven. Before the sun had set on that first Good Friday, the soul of the robber crucified alongside Jesus Christ on Calvary was again associated with Jesus in Limbo and heard Him announce to the just assembled there the good news of redemption.

As we have already remarked, Jesus, looking down from the cross, saw some of His friends watching. The Synoptic Gospels refer to them later and indicate that they remained at a little distance. St. John probably refers to a different time rather than to a different group when He places some so near to the cross that Jesus could easily speak to them: "Now there were standing by the cross of Jesus his mother and his mother's sister, Mary of Cleophas, and Mary Magdalen" (19:25). It was not unusual for the Romans to permit close relatives and friends of one crucified to approach the cross.

Mary the Mother of Jesus stood there looking up at Him. She had been present at the wedding feast at Cana at the very beginning of His public ministry when He had answered her request for a miracle by saying, "My hour has not yet come" (John 2:4). Nonetheless, He had performed the miracle. During His public ministry, she had remained in the background, seeing Him occasionally. She had come up to Jerusalem for the Passover with the other Galileans, knowing in her heart the fate that awaited Jesus. She knew that now, indeed, His hour had come. Standing there, watching Him die, she recalled the words holy Simeon had addressed to her in the Temple: "Thy own soul a sword shall pierce" (Luke 2:35). It was indeed pierced, and pierced again, as she looked up at Jesus and saw the bloody wounds in His hands and feet and the welts of the scourges across His body. It was pierced as she heard the revilings and mockeries of His enemies and even of the strangers who passed by on the road below. It was pierced as she saw Him struggle to push Himself upward on His wounded hands and feet so that He would not be suffocated by the constriction of the muscles in His chest, caused by the sagging weight of His body. Mary saw it all, accepted it, and united herself with it. She knew what Jesus was doing. She had accepted all this when she had accepted her role as Mother of the Savior with the words, "Behold the handmaid of the Lord; be it done to me according to thy word" (Luke 1:38).

Looking down at His mother standing just beneath Him, Jesus said: "Woman, behold thy son." Then looking at John, the Beloved Disciple, he said, "Behold thy mother." St. John adds: "And from that hour the disciple took her into his house" (John 19:26–27). Even at this critical moment, suffering intense pain and not far from death, Jesus still thinks of others. As a loving Son, He is concerned with the state of abandonment in which He is leaving Mary. It is obvious that St. Joseph had already died and that Mary had no other children. Jesus' "brethren," mentioned in the Gospels, could have been only cousins. Jesus commits the care of His mother to the disciple He loved most. And it was not a burden He was giving him but a great honor and privilege.

Jesus' use of the word "woman" in addressing Mary sounds rather stiff and formal to us. In reality, it was a form of address that indicated reverence and solemnity. Jesus could very well have said no more than the words, "Woman, behold thy son." The fact that He said to John, "Behold thy mother," called attention to the fact that He was giving John the greatest possible gift, His own mother. Care for her as he would, she could still do more for him than he could do for her.

John took the Mother of Jesus "into his home." Unfortunately, we know almost nothing of the circumstances. St. John and his family were Galileans and earned their living fishing in the Sea of Galilee. The father, Zebedee, ran the business, assisted by his sons and hired men (Mark 1:20). They had contacts in Jerusalem, perhaps even a home there, as John was undoubtedly the disciple known to the high priest who obtained Peter's admission into the courtyard (John 18:15). Mary stayed in Jerusalem for some time, as we find her in the Upper Room after the Ascension with a group of Apostles and other disciples. With John's family she was among relatives, but she was there not by reason of her relationship of blood but because of the spiritual relationship between her and John instituted by Jesus on the cross. There are contradictory traditions about her later life. According to one, she died at Jerusalem; according to another, at Ephesus. One cannot help feeling that she exercised a tremendous influence on St. John, an influence manifested in his Gospel, which shows a profound insight into the mind and heart of Jesus.

The LAST HOURS of JESUS

It is common belief among Catholics that St. John at the foot of the cross represented the human family, and that in him we were all given to Mary as sons, and she to us as a mother. While it has been questioned whether this truth is expressed in this text, there is no doubt about the spiritual maternity of the Blessed Virgin. The doctrine of Mary's spiritual maternity is founded on the fact that Mary is the mother of the Incarnate Word. We are the adopted sons of God through grace and therefore brethren of Jesus Christ and children of Mary. By her *fiat* to the angel Gabriel, Mary accepted the natural motherhood of Jesus Christ and the motherhood also of Jesus Christ as the Savior of a redeemed humanity, the head of the Mystical Body, of which we are members. She is the mother of Christ in the natural sense of motherhood; she is our mother as members of the Mystical Body.

Since the Middle Ages, there has been a growing belief that St. John, in recording this word of Christ from the cross, had in mind more than the strictly literal sense we have already explained. In the Gospel of St. John, we find that certain individuals, although real persons, are types as well. Thus, Nicodemus is the type of the intelligent and inquiring soul; John is the type of the believing disciple. Furthermore, if the strictly literal sense alone is accepted, we can understand how John would be given to Mary as a son to care for her. But why should Mary be given to John as a mother? He not only had a mother, but she was present at Calvary. It is logical to think that, while Salome is John's natural mother, Mary became his spiritual mother. There is confirmation of this interpretation in the teachings of several popes. We can truthfully say, then, that from the moment of the Incarnation, Mary became mother of Jesus Christ and our spiritual mother, and that this spiritual maternity of Mary was proclaimed solemnly in Christ's third word from the cross.

All of the first three Gospels mention an extraordinary phenomenon that accompanied the crucifixion of Christ. As St. Luke says: "It was now about the sixth hour, and there was darkness over the whole land until the ninth hour. And the sun was darkened" (23:44–45). The texts of both Luke and Mark indicate that Jesus had been nailed to the cross before the sixth hour—that is, a little before noon—and that some time had elapsed before the darkness settled over the land. The Evangelists evidently consider the darkness to have been associated with what was taking place on Calvary, and of supernatural origin. It isn't necessary at all to presume an eclipse of the sun. It would have been necessary for God to disturb the entire order of the universe to produce such an eclipse at the time of the full moon. Some of the ancients thought that God miraculously suspended the luminous effects of the sun; others that He brought about a particularly heavy accumulation of clouds that shut out the sun's rays from the earth.

Having lived in Jerusalem for three years, we are much more inclined to accept the explanation of some modern commentators. About this time of year, a hot wind, laden with dust and sand, blows in over the Holy Land from the east. It is called the *khamsin*, or black sirocco. Often the quantity of dust in the air is so great that it obscures the light of the sun and covers the earth with what appears to be a dark fog. A miraculous increase in the intensity of this natural phenomenon could very well have been the cause of the darkness at the time of Christ's crucifixion. It is not necessary to accept literally the statement of the three Evangelists that the darkness covered the "whole land." The darkness was of local significance and probably extended only to the horizon, as far as the witnesses of the crucifixion could see.

The darkness over the land was surely a sign from heaven. Several explanations have been given by the Fathers of the Church. Some think it was an image of the darkness that would envelop the Jewish nation as a punishment for putting to death Him who was the light of the world; others think it was a protestation of nature itself against the unjust execution of nature's Lord. Surely it manifested in some way a threat of just punishment. In the prophets of the Old Testament, the darkening of the sun is a figure used to describe the manifestation of God's justice: "And it shall come to pass in that day, saith the Lord God, that the sun shall go down at midday, and I will make the earth dark in the day of light" (Amos 8:9; cf. Joel 2:10; 3:15; Isa. 13:10). As we shall see later, the darkness was only one in a series of events that constituted a miraculous witness to Christ on the cross.

When Jesus pronounced His fourth word from the cross, He was nearing the end of His life on earth. This word was spoken at about the ninth hour — that is, about three o'clock in the afternoon. The onlookers could see that Jesus was weakening rapidly. Blood dripped slowly from the wounds in His hands and feet. Now and then He would strive to push Himself upward, in spite of the pain of the wounds in His feet, in order to relieve the suffocating pressure on His chest; but less frequently now, owing to His weakness. For quite some time now, Jesus had suffered without uttering a word. All that those nearby could hear from Him were His pitiful efforts to draw air into His constricted lungs. The others on Calvary were silent too. Probably many were frightened by the extraordinary and threatening darkness that covered the place as if night had fallen before its time. Some of the onlookers had tired of the affair and gone their way. The soldiers, restrained by duty, sat near the crosses, watching and waiting for the end. Christ's enemies, implacable still, watched with unabated hatred and determination. Suddenly Jesus pushed Himself upward on His cross, filled His lungs with air, and cried out in a loud voice, *"Eli, Eli, lama sabachtani?"*—"My God, my God, why hast thou forsaken me?" (Matt. 27:46).[73]

There is something mysterious and, on the face of things, a little shocking in these words of Christ from the cross. He had always enjoyed the greatest union with the Father and manifested the greatest trust in Him. Now He speaks as if that union had been broken, as if the Father had abandoned Him, as if His enemies had been right when they had taunted Him that God had forsaken Him. Some have interpreted Christ's words in this sense and concluded that He died despairing of His work and even of God. All we have to do to refute such an opinion is to recall that, a few moments later, Jesus addressed Himself to God in words of complete trust and confidence: "Father, into thy hands I commend my spirit" (Luke 23:46).

To understand these words, it is important to recall that they are the second verse of the twenty-first psalm[74] and that Jesus quoted them from the psalm. While He spoke aloud only the second verse, it is extremely likely that the entire psalm passed through His mind, or even that He repeated it to Himself just as we might use a psalm or a prayer from the liturgy to express our

---

[73] Mark uses the form *Eloi,* a variation of Aramaic, the ordinary language of the country at the time of Christ. Our Lord undoubtedly used the form *Eli,* as some bystanders pretended that He was calling on Elijah (Matt. 27:47). This would have been rather far-fetched if He had used the form *Eloi.*

[74] Psalm 22 in other versions.

sentiments. This is indicated by the fact that two other words from the cross come from this psalm. For this reason, it would be a mistake to interpret Christ's words from the cross or the other words of this psalm in too literal a sense, as if they had been spoken originally by Christ Himself.

There can be no doubt that this psalm is Messianic. It is not certain whether it is a prophecy in the literal and direct sense or whether the situation of the psalmist is prophetic of the situation of Jesus in His Passion. In any case, it reads in part almost like a historical account of the Passion. Here are a few of the more pertinent verses:

> My God, my God, why hast thou forsaken me? Thou art far from my pleas and the words of my cry.

> O my God, I cry by day, and thou hearest not, and by night and thou heedest me not.

> But I am a worm and no man, the reproach of men and the outcast of the people.

> All who see me laugh me to scorn, they draw apart their lips and wag their heads. "He trusts in the Lord; let him free him; let him deliver him if he loves him."

> They open their mouths against me, as a lion ravening and roaring.

> My throat is dried up like a potsherd, and my tongue cleaves to my jaws, and thou hast brought me down to the dust of death.

> For many dogs surround me, a band of evildoers hems me in. They have dug my hands and feet.

I can number all my bones. Yet they watch me, and seeing me, they rejoice.

They divide my garments amongst them and cast lots for my vesture.

In quoting the opening words, Christ applies the entire psalm to Himself. This is particularly significant, as the first part of this psalm describes the grief and sufferings of Jesus, while the second part declares the mediatorial value of His sufferings. In the psalm, triumph follows suffering; in the life of Jesus, the resurrection and the salvation of men followed His Passion.

The fact that Christ used these words of the psalmist and that He spoke the second verse aloud indicates that He made these sentiments His own and that He suffered acutely a feeling of abandonment. Indeed, there was little more left for Him to suffer. He had been rejected and condemned by the leaders of His people, delivered into the hands of strangers, deserted by His followers, mocked by those about Him, and left dying publicly on a cross. And if He now felt abandoned by God, it was only in the sense that His Father had not protected Him from all this but had permitted Him to be delivered up to His Passion for the salvation of men. Christ's words were not a reproach, or a complaint, or an expression of despair. They were a heartrending but confident appeal from the depths of His misery to the Father, in whom He had supreme confidence.

Jesus' fourth word from the cross stirred His enemies to renew their mockeries. Some of them said to one another: "This man is calling [Elijah]" (Matt. 27:47). The Evangelists identify them only as "bystanders." Did they really think that Christ was calling Elijah? It is not likely. Most of them must have known that He was quoting the words of a psalm, and He must have been easily heard, as He spoke with a loud voice. They deliberately misinterpreted *Eli* for Eliljah in order to make a joke of Christ's cry. Many Jews believed that the Messiah would at first lead a hidden and obscure life and that Elijah would come to deliver Him from it and to make Him known. Some of the bystanders thought it was a great joke to think of Elijah coming to find the Messiah on a cross. No doubt they laughed heartily at their own wit.

From the Gospel accounts, it appears that the last four words of Jesus from the cross were spoken in quick succession and a short time before His death. There was a close connection between Christ's plaint of abandonment and His cry "I thirst," as some of the onlookers associated the two words in their ridicule concerning Elijah. St. John alone recounts Our Lord's fifth word: "Jesus, knowing that all things were now accomplished, that the Scripture might be fulfilled, said, 'I thirst'" (19:28). Although he was extremely weak and near death, Jesus' mind was clear. He had been recalling the prophecies concerning Himself, as He had just cried out words from the twenty-first psalm, one of the most explicit prophecies of the Old Testament, and He was undoubtedly reflecting on its words if not actually reciting them to Himself. He knew that there was another prophecy yet to be fulfilled, and to accomplish this He said, "I thirst." Passages in two psalms referred to Christ's thirst: "In my thirst they gave me vinegar to drink" (68:21 [69:21]). This prophecy would be fulfilled in a few moments by the response to Christ's avowal of thirst. The psalm Jesus had just recalled also referred to the present situation, "My throat is dried up like a potsherd, and my tongue cleaves to my jaws" (21:15 [22:15]).

Thirst was one of the most frightful sufferings of crucifixion, and it must have caused Jesus untold physical torment. So far as we know, He had had nothing to drink since the preceding evening. He had lost considerable blood at the scourging, and for three hours on the cross His blood had dripped slowly from His wounds. Perspiration from weakness as well as exposure to the sun increased His thirst. It is not any wonder that Jesus should have spoken those agonizing words, "I thirst."

As we have said, the soldiers had a jug of *posca*, a mixture of sour wine or vinegar and water, to quench their thirst during the long hours of waiting. (Even today, the Arabs of the Holy Land rarely leave their homes for work or travel without a jug of water.) Christ's words "I thirst" aroused pity in one of the soldiers. It must have been a soldier rather than one of the onlookers, as only a soldier would have dared to touch the jug of *posca*. He fixed the sponge used as a stopper for the jug on the end of his spear, filled the sponge with the drink, and approached the cross. Some of those who had been mocking Jesus called out to him, "Wait! Let us see whether [Elijah] is coming to save him" (Matt. 27:49). From the Gospel of St. Mark, it is evident that the soldier was overcome by human respect and joined in the mockery (15:36). In spite of this, however, he performed his act of mercy. He pushed the sponge against Christ's lips, and Christ drank of the vinegar.

The drink that Jesus took probably had the effect of reviving slightly His fast-ebbing strength. Almost immediately He spoke again, saying, "It is consummated" (John 19:30). Since the subject of the verb is not expressed, we are not told explicitly what had been consummated. We know, however, from the circumstances and from the mind of St. John, who alone records this word of Jesus from the cross, that Jesus certainly referred to the fulfillment of the Old Testament prophecies concerning Himself. The two preceding words indicate that Jesus at this time was thinking of these prophecies and their fulfillment. No doubt He referred also to the fact that He had fulfilled all the prophecies that He himself had made concerning His Passion.

The significance of this word of Christ should not be limited to the fulfillment of prophecy. Now, a few moments before His death, Jesus looks back over His life's work and sees that He has accomplished, perfectly and completely, what He had come into this world to do. This included His death, which was now only minutes away. It would be a mistake, however, to refer these words to the completion of all of Christ's work as Savior. There was still the resurrection, the work of the risen life, the Ascension, the sending of the Holy Spirit, and what St. Paul refers to as Christ's appearance in Heaven "before the face of God on our behalf" (Heb. 9:24). Only when the kingdom of God on earth is merged into the kingdom of God in heaven will Jesus be able to say of His role of Savior, "It is consummated."

Jesus had cried out His fourth word from the cross with a loud voice. Now, a moment before death, He cries out again in a loud voice, saying, "Father, into thy hands I commend my spirit" (Luke 23:46). Such an occurrence was unusual, if not miraculous. Death by crucifixion was a slow process of exhaustion ending in complete depletion of physical strength. Jesus' cry indicated that even in dying He was acting with liberty, that He was in complete control of what was happening to Him. He had well said: "I lay down my life that I may take it up again. No one takes it from me, but I lay it down of myself" (John 10:18).

Jesus' very last words are from a psalm (30:6 [31:5]) except that he adds the word "Father." He had felt abandoned during the Agony in the garden and again on the cross, but he still addresses himself with filial love and confidence to his "Father." In the Greek text of Luke, a certain deliberateness is indicated. Literally translated, our Lord says: "Father, in thy hands I place my soul." Jesus' words were an expression of complete confidence in His heavenly Father and of absolute union with His divine will. Ever since, Christ's followers have found strength and consolation at the moment of death by repeating these last words He spoke on Calvary.

It was immediately after His last word from the cross that Jesus died. Here too there is a deliberateness that indicates that even in dying He is acting freely. His head does not drop on His chest after death. Jesus bows His head and then dies. As St. John says: "Bowing his head, he gave up his spirit" (19:30).

AFTER
CHRIST'S
DEATH

Chapter 20

THE PRODIGIES

To those who believe that Jesus Christ, who died on Calvary, is the Son of God, it is not strange that prodigies accompanied His death. The curtain of the Temple was rent, the earth quaked, rocks were split, and, after the resurrection of Jesus, tombs opened and the dead came out and appeared to many in the holy city. The centurion, the officer in charge of Christ's execution, declared: "Truly he was the Son of God" (Matt. 27:54), and the multitudes present returned to the city striking their breasts.

At the very moment of Christ's death, "the curtain of the temple was torn in two from top to bottom" (Matt. 27:51). To the Israelites the Temple was not a building in which the people gathered to worship. It was the dwelling place of divinity. It was approached by a flight of stairs beyond which was a vestibule. A great curtain separated the vestibule from the Holy and another curtain separated this part of the Temple from the Holy of Holies, which was regarded as the dwelling place of divinity, although it had been empty since the loss of the ark of the covenant. The people congregated for worship in especially designated areas in front of the Temple, but were not allowed to enter it. From the outside, however, they could see the curtain that separated the vestibule from the Holy. Josephus tells us that it was "of Babylonian tapestry, with embroidery of blue and fine linen of scarlet also and purple, wrought with marvelous skill."[75] The other veil separating the Holy from the Holy of Holies, which Josephus mentions but does not describe, could be seen only by the priests, who entered the Holy twice daily to burn incense on the altar of perfumes, and by the high priest, who entered the Holy of Holies once yearly, on the feast of the Atonement, to burn incense.

Which of these two curtains was rent at the moment of Christ's death? We do not know. The text of the Gospels throws no light on the subject, and commentators who make a choice do so for symbolical reasons. Most think that it was the interior curtain, because this would indicate better that the old law and worship had been abrogated, true expiation performed by Christ's sacrificial death on the cross, and the approach to the heavenly sanctuary opened to all. Those who think it was the exterior curtain distinguish between our present state and the heavenly state in which those redeemed by Christ shall stand before God. To them, the Holy of Holies is the image of Heaven, to which we shall be admitted by the rending of the second curtain after this life. The rending of the exterior curtain would also be a much more public event, visible to all Israelites present. Only the priests could have seen the rent interior veil. It must be admitted, however, that it would have been impossible to keep such a prodigy secret.

[75] *Wars,* 5, 5, 4.

In either case, it must have been shocking to see the great curtain split in the middle, hanging in two parts from its fastenings above and at the sides. An earthquake could rend rocks and open tombs but could not split a curtain. Those who saw what happened must have sensed a divine intervention.

St. Matthew alone recounts another prodigy that took place at the death of Jesus: "The earth quaked, and the rocks were rent, and the tombs were opened, and many bodies of the saints who had fallen asleep arose; and coming forth out of the tombs after his resurrection, they came into the holy city, and appeared to many" (27:51–53).

By the earthquake as well as by the darkness over the earth, it seemed that even inanimate nature expressed its horror and sorrow at the death of the Lord. We may be sure that this event was a further warning to Christ's enemies and a reassurance to His followers that even on the cross He was God, the Lord of all. Those familiar with the Scriptures knew that the earthquake in the Old Testament was often a sign of God's majesty as a judge and legislator.

It is likely that the earthquake was confined to the Jerusalem area. Since the fourth century, Christian writers have called attention to a split in the rock of Calvary attributed to the earthquake at the time of Jesus' death. In fact, a cleft in the rock is still visible to visitors to the Church of the Holy Sepulchre. The larger and more important tombs in the vicinity of Jerusalem were cut in the solid rock. The earthquake split open some of them and, in other cases, rolled aside the large circular stone that closed them. While the earthquake opened the tombs at the time of Christ's death, the dead did not arise until after Christ's resurrection on Easter morning. St. Matthew groups all these events together because of their logical connection, without regard to strict chronological sequence.

There are various opinions concerning the resurrection of the dead mentioned here by St. Matthew. Some think that these dead, like Lazarus, arose with unglorified bodies and would die again. But St. Matthew says that they *"appeared* to many," an expression he would not use of one in the present life. Others think that they assumed apparent, ethereal bodies, as when angels appear to men. This opinion does not harmonize well with the Gospel text, which seems to refer to real bodies. Furthermore, mere phantoms would hardly be a proper accompaniment of Christ's resurrection. The third and most commonly accepted opinion is that these saints arose with glorified bodies after Christ's resurrection and entered heaven with Him on the day of His Ascension. The fact that they "appeared to many" indicates that they were known and therefore not long dead. They were witnesses of Christ's resurrection and of His triumph over death.

The firstfruits of Christ's death on the cross were the centurion, undoubtedly the officer in charge of the execution, and some of the soldiers. It is not too difficult to understand the centurion's sentiments. He had seen many executions, but never one like this. St. Mark indicates that he watched Jesus closely because he says that he "stood facing him" (15:39). He knew what had taken place before Pilate, and he had observed that man's doubts and fear. He knew of Jesus' claim to be the Son of God from the trial and from the mockery of His enemies. He saw the patience and gentleness of Jesus; he heard Him pray for forgiveness for His enemies and promise paradise to the crucified robber. He saw that His death was a deliberate act, accompanied by prodigies of nature. All these things passed through his mind as he stood before the cross, looking up. As Jesus died, he could not refrain from crying out, "Truly this man was the Son of God"

(Mark 15:39). Some of the soldiers joined in his confession, and they all feared because of the part they had played in putting Jesus to death.[76]

St. Luke alone refers to the conversion of the multitude: "And all the crowd that collected for the sight, when they beheld what things had happened, began to return, beating their breasts" (23:48). The word "all" is not to be taken with absolute literalness, especially as it is a characteristic of Luke's style.

There is no reference here to the attitude of Christ's enemies. They were hardened to the very end. The change of heart took place in the ordinary people, the curious onlookers. At the instigation of Christ's enemies, they had cried out for His blood before the tribunal of Pilate. Even on Calvary they had joined the priests, Scribes, and ancients in mocking Jesus. But, like the centurion, they too had watched Jesus closely and had been impressed. They were touched by Jesus' patience and goodness and frightened by the prodigies that accompanied His death. Now that it was all over, they had second thoughts on the matter and regretted the part they had played. As they left Calvary and headed into Jerusalem through the Ephraim Gate, they struck their breasts in fear and sorrow.

---

[76] St. Luke quotes the centurion as saying, "Truly this was a just man" (23:47). Some think the centurion and the soldiers who joined him used both expressions. The centurion did not have an exact knowledge of Christ's divine Sonship. He probably thought that Jesus was a just man and therefore He was what He claimed to be, the Son of God. It may be, too, that Luke avoided the expression "Son of God" because he thought it equivocal on the lips of a pagan. We have no authentic information on the later life of the centurion.

Chapter 21

THE BURIAL OF JESUS

At the death of Jesus, the crowd thinned out at Calvary. The two robbers crucified with Him were still alive, but Jesus had been the main attraction for the multitude. It was the Roman practice to leave the body of the crucified on the cross until it decomposed or was eaten by animals. No one could take it down or bury it without explicit authorization of the proper authority. On the other hand, it was Jewish law that the body should be buried by sundown, and it is likely that the Romans made little or no difficulty in permitting this. The soldiers remained to watch the two robbers and to see that nothing was done to the body of Jesus without proper authorization of the procurator.

As the crowd dispersed, the friends and relatives of Jesus probably assembled in a little group beneath the cross to take counsel as to what should be done. Unless they could secure the procurator's permission to take Jesus' body from the cross and bury it, it would be thrown into a common grave or ditch reserved for executed criminals.

Joseph of Arimathea offered the solution to their problem. He is mentioned by all four Evangelists, and each adds a little to

our knowledge of him. As his name signified, Joseph was originally from Arimathea, identified as the modern town of Rentis,
northeast of Lydda. He was a wealthy, distinguished member of
the Sanhedrin, no doubt as one of the ancients. St. Luke says
that he was a "good and just man" and that he had not been a
party to the Sanhedrin's action against Jesus (23:50–51). We do
not know whether Joseph had not been invited to the meeting
that condemned Jesus, whether he deliberately absented himself, or whether he voted no to the verdict. In fact, Joseph was
a disciple of Jesus, but secretly, for fear of the Jews. When the
Gospels tell us that he was "looking for the kingdom of God"
(Luke 23:51), they mean that he looked for it through Jesus
Christ. We do not know whether he still retained his faith in
Christ after the events of this fateful day, but he at least kept his
love and respect for Him.

Joseph of Arimathea now offered to solve the problem that
faced Jesus' friends and relatives. His own new tomb, freshly
hewn in the solid rock, was in the garden adjacent to the spot
where Jesus had been crucified. He offered it for the burial of
Jesus. Furthermore, he volunteered to approach Pilate with a
request for the body of Jesus. The others would have been willing
to venture it, but there was little likelihood that they could even
secure an audience with the procurator. Joseph, as a distinguished
member of the Sanhedrin, had an excellent chance of seeing
Pilate personally and of obtaining his request.

Joseph hurried off to the Antonia to present his request to
Pontius Pilate. He was immediately admitted. We cannot help
wondering what reasons he gave for his interest in the case.
Did he admit openly that he was a disciple of the man Pilate
had just crucified? He had not had the courage to profess his
faith to the Jews and probably did not profess it to Pilate. He

may have given reasons of humanity, or national solidarity, or merely said that the crucifixion had taken place on or near his property and he wanted the body buried before sundown. Anyway, it required courage to do what he did, and he should be given credit for it.

Pilate was surprised that Jesus was already dead. He wanted official verification and sent for the centurion who had charge of the execution to question him. When the centurion informed him that Jesus had died, Pilate granted Joseph his request and so informed the centurion. Joseph hurried back to Calvary to tell the news to the others and to begin the work of burial.

Before relating the incident of Joseph of Arimathea, two of the Evangelists state that it was getting on toward evening. By this time, it must have been the last period of the day, between three and six, probably about four o'clock. Some of the leaders of the Jews had remained on Calvary and now they were suffering an acute attack of legalistic scruples. This was the Preparation Day, that is, a Friday, and not an ordinary Preparation Day but the day before a Sabbath that was also the fifteenth Nisan, the great feast of the Passover. Under any circumstances, it would have been embarrassing if bodies remained on the crosses after sundown, but it would be particularly shocking on such a day as this. It would be most humiliating to have their law flouted in such a public place and before the crowds of visitors in the city for the feast. For more than one reason, they rejoiced when they saw Jesus die. But the two robbers showed no signs of dying soon. Something had to be done, as the great feast and Sabbath would begin at sundown, only a couple of hours away.

The leaders of the Jews decided to have recourse to Pilate to solve their difficulty. Whether they saw him personally to explain the situation, we do not know. By this time, he was probably surfeited with the whole affair and wished to have it over and forgotten. He ordered that the legs of the crucified should be broken in order to hasten their death. The Gospels do not tell us whether this work was committed to a special crew or left to the soldiers who had conducted the execution. It was a common enough practice to inflict this punishment on slaves and deserters. When the legs of a crucified man were broken, he died quickly from asphyxiation, as the full weight of his body on his arms constricted his chest muscles and hampered his breathing.

Soldiers approached the robber on one side of Jesus' cross and struck him on the legs with repeated blows of a club or beam of wood. They repeated the same process with the other. Looking closely at Jesus, they saw that there could be no doubt that he was dead and that to break His legs would be a useless waste of energy. Then one of the soldiers did something wholly unexpected, in fact, somewhat mysterious. Perhaps he had a sincere doubt about Jesus' death. Anyway, he braced himself under the cross, took aim, and drove his lance into Jesus' heart. If Jesus had not been dead, the blow would surely have killed Him, as the wound was big enough for doubting Thomas to put his hand into later (John 20:25, 27). Then a most extraordinary thing happened. Blood and water flowed from the wound.

Was the flow of blood and water a miracle, and what was its significance? St. John does not answer either question, but he makes it clear that he considered the event important, because he offers special testimony to its truth, saying, "He who saw it has borne witness, and his witness is true; and he knows that he tells the truth, that you also may believe" (19:35). In saying "*He* knows that he tells the truth," St. John calls on Jesus Christ to witness the truth of his account. Whether the flow of blood and water was a miracle is a medical matter and the findings of medical science would indicate that it was not.[77]

Sad to say, we are not even certain of the exact significance St. John attached to the flow of blood and water. No doubt the early Christians were familiar with it from the oral tradition. Many explanations have been given, but they can all be reduced more or less to a symbolical interpretation of the meaning of the blood and water. In both the Old and New Testaments, blood is a means of propitiation: "With blood almost everything is cleansed according to the Law, and without the shedding of blood there is no forgiveness" (Heb. 9:22). Jesus referred to His blood as "My blood of the new covenant, which is being shed for many unto the forgiveness of sins" (Matt. 26:28). By its very nature water is a universal means of purification. As Jesus said to Nicodemus, "Unless a man be born again of water and the Spirit, he cannot enter into the kingdom of God" (John 3:5). The meaning of the blood and water could be summed up briefly by saying that the blood is the symbol of the Eucharist and the water the symbol of baptism.

John gives the reason he is so insistent about the truth of what he related: "For these things came to pass that the Scripture might be fulfilled" (19:36). He then quotes two texts from the Old Testament. The first is "Not a bone of him shall you break" (Exod. 12:46; Num. 9:12), a part of the Mosaic legislation referring to the Paschal lamb. This was not a direct Messianic prophecy. The Paschal lamb was a type of Jesus, the Messiah, and what was said of it was accomplished in a spiritual sense in

---

[77] The medical aspects of the crucifixion and death of Christ are discussed in many books. One of the best is *A Doctor at Calvary*, by Pierre Barbet, M.D.

Jesus the true Lamb (Apoc. [Rev.] 5:6, 12) slain for the salvation of His people (1 Cor. 5:7). The other text is from the prophet Zacharias, "They shall look upon him whom they have pierced" ([Zech.] 12:10). This part of Zacharias is certainly a Messianic prophecy. It foretells that at the time of the Messiah the Jewish nation will bear the weight of a great crime, the crime of putting the Messiah to death. It was fulfilled in Jesus in a striking fashion, as He was "pierced" on Calvary.

The Evangelists are sparing in details regarding the time of day, but we can reasonably conjecture that it was about four to four-thirty when the friends of Jesus began the work of taking His body from the cross and preparing it for burial. Because of the approaching feast and Sabbath, activity had to cease by sundown, which would be sometime between six and seven o'clock. We can easily imagine that anxious glances were cast occasionally toward the sun, which was descending all too rapidly toward the western horizon.

The friends and relatives of Jesus remained at Calvary until after the burial. The Gospels mention only a few of them at this point because their presence had a particular significance now. Christ's mother remained to the end, watching and helping with maternal solicitude. The Gospels do not tell us whether any of the Apostles, save John, had mustered enough courage to appear. Joseph of Arimathea and Nicodemus took a public and prominent part, though both had been afraid to confess Christ openly during His public ministry.

Joseph was responsible for the burial of Christ, as Pontius Pilate had given him this right. We can be sure that, in all he did, he showed a deferential respect for the wishes of Jesus' mother. Associated with Joseph was a man named Nicodemus, mentioned earlier in the Gospel of St. John. Near the beginning of Christ's public ministry, Nicodemus had come to him by night — evidently from fear or human respect — to discuss the Kingdom of God (3:1–13). Because of Christ's miracles, Nicodemus believed that He was "a teacher from God." Nicodemus was a Pharisee, a doctor of the law, and a member of the Sanhedrin, and, as we shall see from his contribution to the burial of Christ, he was evidently rich. In spite of his timidity in visiting Jesus at night, he had courage. On one occasion, when his fellow Sanhedrists talked of laying hands on Jesus, he asked them, "Does our law judge a man unless it first give him a hearing and know what he does?" (John 7:50–52). For that question he was reviled by his fellow Sanhedrists. Two such wealthy and important men as Joseph and Nicodemus must have had servants present to assist in the burial of Jesus.

Under the direction of Joseph, the work began immediately. The first step was to remove the body from the cross. They began by drawing the nails from the feet. The crossbeam, with Jesus' hands still nailed to it, was removed from the socket in which it rested and lowered gently to the ground. Then the nails were removed. There was probably some difficulty in pushing the arms down alongside the body, as the muscles must have become stiffened from three hours in the one position and because rigidity was already beginning to set in.

The exposed place overlooking a highway where Jesus had been crucified was unsuitable for the pious task of preparing His body for burial. Joseph, with the consent of the others, directed that the body be carried into the garden containing the tomb he had constructed, only about forty-five yards away. This garden was probably enclosed by a low stone wall and contained a few trees and shrubs, which gave it an atmosphere of privacy. It is possible that they deposited the body in the outer chamber of the tomb, but this is unlikely, as the space was so limited that movement would have been difficult, and time was an important element now. It is more likely that the body was laid on a bench or on the grass just outside the door of the tomb.

Joseph and Nicodemus had used to advantage what little time they had to make the necessary preparations. Joseph had purchased a linen shroud and probably also the linen cloths. Nicodemus had brought a hundred pounds of myrrh and aloes—a tremendous amount, indicating that his act was the homage of a wealthy man. Myrrh was an aromatic resin, aloes a scented wood. They were widely used for burials at this period to delay decomposition of the body and to offset bad odors.

The next step was to wash the body of Jesus to remove the blood that had hardened on the skin. Jesus' head and limbs were bound with linen cloths. It is likely that the mixture of myrrh and aloes had been ground to a powder and that this was sprinkled on the body and on the linen cloths. Then the body was wrapped in the linen shroud, which covered it from head to foot. Everything was ready now for the final act—the placing of the body in the tomb.

Joseph had made a timely and generous gesture in offering his tomb for the burial of Jesus. Although originally from Arimathea, he evidently resided now in Jerusalem, since he had prepared his final resting place so near the city. The Gospels tell us that the sepulcher was new and that it had been hewn out of the solid rock. It was not too difficult to cut a tomb out of the rock, as the stone in this area is comparatively soft until exposed to the air. The tomb in which Jesus was laid was cut horizontally into the slope of the hill. It was opened and closed by rolling a great round stone, like a millstone, back and forth in a groove. Just inside the opening was a vestibule or antechamber. Beyond this vestibule, and connected with it by a low opening cut in the rock, was the burial chamber. A niche had been cut in the side of the wall to receive the body. Jesus' body was carried into the vestibule and then passed into the burial chamber. It was placed in the niche in the side wall and sprinkled generously with the mixture of myrrh and aloes. All withdrew from the tomb. It was probably some of the servants of Joseph who pushed the great round stone into place to close the tomb.

The first three Gospels add a poignant detail. The holy women who had followed Jesus from Galilee sat over against the sepulcher, watching every detail and noting particularly just how and where Jesus' body had been laid. They were grateful to Joseph and Nicodemus. They knew that they had done all that could be done in the circumstances. But these devoted women felt just a little left out. They too wanted to contribute their share to the burial of their Friend and Master. They talked it over and decided to purchase their own spices and ointments for the body of Jesus and to return to the sepulcher after the Sabbath rest.

By this time, it must have been about six o'clock. The sun was low in the west. When it had sunk below the horizon, the quiet and rest of the Great Sabbath would begin. One could see lamps being lighted already in neighboring houses, lest this work be done after the beginning of the Sabbath rest. There was a strange quiet now after the noise and excitement of the day. Only a few late stragglers hurried by toward the city. The little group of Jesus' friends and disciples left the garden and took the road that led through the Ephraim Gate. We can well imagine that before they passed through the gate they turned for a last look at Calvary and then sadly entered the city.

That night the enemies of Jesus rejoiced. In their calendar, it was the evening of the Passover meal as well as the beginning of the Sabbath. They ate and drank with a feeling that they had performed a difficult but necessary duty in ridding themselves of Jesus Christ. No longer would He pervert the people; no longer would He badger them in the presence of the multitudes or interfere with their lucrative trade in the Temple area. But as so often happens when evil men rejoice at the success of evil, some of them began to get second thoughts. Jesus had outwitted them so often that they feared Him dead in the tomb. Some recalled uneasily Jesus' prophecy that He would rise three days after His death. Jesus had, indeed, foretold His resurrection—on one occasion to the Scribes and Pharisees themselves (Matt. 12:40). Now someone brought up the subject, and a feeling of apprehension spread to all. They did not believe that Jesus would rise from the dead, but that was not the point. His disciples could steal His body and then spread the word among the people that He had arisen as He had prophesied.

Although it was the Passover and the Sabbath, some of the Sanhedrists met early in the morning to determine what was to be done. It was not a formal meeting of the Sanhedrin. St. Matthew mentions only the chief priests and Pharisees (27:62). It was ironical that chief priests were present; they were Sadducees and did not believe in the resurrection of the body. They knew the people did, however, and went along with the Pharisees in recognizing the danger. The conclusion of the meeting was that they would send a deputation to Pilate to explain the situation and request action.

The deputation of chief priests and Pharisees was granted an audience with Pilate. "Sir," they said obsequiously, "we have remembered how that deceiver said, while he was yet alive, 'After three days I will rise again.' Give orders, therefore, that the sepulcher be guarded until the third day, or else his disciples may come and steal him away, and say to the people, 'He has risen from the dead'; and the last imposture will be worse than the first" (Matt. 27:63–64). They did not have to mention Jesus by name, but called Him "that deceiver." Pilate knew quite well who was on their minds. When they said, "The last imposture will be worse than the first," they meant that popular belief in Christ's resurrection would be even worse than the popular belief that He was the Messiah.

Pilate was probably surprised that their hatred and fear of Jesus survived even His crucifixion and death. He was evidently in an evil mood. He had not expected them to bother him on their festival day. He answered them curtly: "You have a guard; go, guard it as well as you know how" (Matt. 27:65). Pilate despised them and their fears, yet he felt there was no use starting to resist them now. He had gone along with them in much more important matters. When he said, "You have a guard," he referred to Roman soldiers, as is evident from St. Matthew's account of what happened after Jesus' resurrection (28:11–15). It is likely that Pilate referred to the guard of Roman soldiers present at the arrest of Jesus and which had probably been placed at the disposal of the Jewish leaders to maintain peace, especially during the festival days. The Sanhedrists were free to use this guard if they wished.

The Jewish leaders mustered the guard Pilate had granted them permission to use and set off for Calvary. They stationed the guard around the tomb and instructed the soldiers to take utmost precautions against anyone who might attempt to steal Christ's body. Fearing that disciples of Jesus might bribe the soldiers, they took a double precaution. Cutting strips of cloth into ribbons, they stretched them across the round stone that closed the sepulcher and then fixed them to the wall of the tomb with seals. No one could open the tomb now without breaking the seals, thus revealing that the tomb had been tampered with. The Sanhedrists surveyed their work with satisfaction and returned to the city. It never occurred to them that what they had just done would help to offer solid proof of Christ's resurrection, which was now only a few hours away.

Biographical Note

FR. RALPH GORMAN, C.P.
(1897–1972)

Ralph Gorman was born in Binghamton, New York, in 1897. He attended the Catholic University of America and was ordained a priest of the Passionist Order in 1924. He studied further at the École Biblique et Archéologique in Jerusalem and taught Scripture at St. Michael's Monastery in Union City, New Jersey. He served as editor of the *Sign* for twenty-four years and wrote two books: *The Last Hours of Jesus* and *The Trial of Christ — Reappraised*. Fr. Gorman died in 1972.

Sophia Institute

Sophia Institute is a nonprofit institution that seeks to nurture the spiritual, moral, and cultural life of souls and to spread the Gospel of Christ in conformity with the authentic teachings of the Roman Catholic Church.

Sophia Institute Press fulfills this mission by offering translations, reprints, and new publications that afford readers a rich source of the enduring wisdom of mankind.

Sophia Institute also operates two popular online Catholic resources: CrisisMagazine.com and CatholicExchange.com.

Crisis Magazine provides insightful cultural analysis that arms readers with the arguments necessary for navigating the ideological and theological minefields of the day. *Catholic Exchange* provides world news from a Catholic perspective as well as daily devotionals and articles that will help you to grow in holiness and live a life consistent with the teachings of the Church.

In 2013, Sophia Institute launched Sophia Institute for Teachers to renew and rebuild Catholic culture through service to Catholic education. With the goal of nurturing the spiritual, moral, and cultural life of souls, and an abiding respect for the role and work of teachers, we strive to provide materials and programs that are at once enlightening to the mind and ennobling to the heart; faithful and complete, as well as useful and practical.

Sophia Institute gratefully recognizes the Solidarity Association for preserving and encouraging the growth of our apostolate over the course of many years. Without their generous and timely support, this book would not be in your hands.

www.SophiaInstitute.com
www.CatholicExchange.com
www.CrisisMagazine.com
www.SophiaInstituteforTeachers.org

Sophia Institute Press® is a registered trademark of Sophia Institute.
Sophia Institute is a tax-exempt institution as defined by the
Internal Revenue Code, Section 501(c)(3). Tax I.D. 22-2548708.